MR. PRESIDENT,
HOW LONG
MUST WE WAIT?

ALSO BY TINA CASSIDY

Birth: The Surprising History of How We Are Born

Jackie After O: One Remarkable Year When Jacqueline Kennedy Onassis Defied Expectations and Rediscovered Her Dreams

MR. PRESIDENT, HOW LONG MUST WE WAIT?

ALICE PAUL, WOODROW WILSON,
and
THE FIGHT FOR THE RIGHT TO VOTE

TINA CASSIDY

37INK
—
ATRIA

NEW YORK   LONDON   TORONTO   SYDNEY   NEW DELHI

37INK

ATRIA

An Imprint of Simon & Schuster, Inc.
1230 Avenue of the Americas
New York, NY 10020

First 37 INK/Atria Books hardcover edition March 2019

37INK **/ ATRIA** BOOKS and colophon are trademarks of Simon & Schuster, Inc.

For information about special discounts for bulk purchases, please contact Simon & Schuster Special Sales at 1-866-506-1949 or business@simonandschuster.com.

The Simon & Schuster Speakers Bureau can bring authors to your live event. For more information, or to book an event, contact the Simon & Schuster Speakers Bureau at 1-866-248-3049 or visit our website at www.simonspeakers.com.

Interior design by Kyoko Watanabe

Manufactured in the United States of America

10 9 8 7 6 5 4 3 2 1

Library of Congress Cataloging-in-Publication Data has been applied for.

ISBN 978-1-5011-7776-7
ISBN 978-1-5011-7778-1 (ebook)

For my mother, Gloria Cassidy

If there is no struggle, there is no progress. Those who profess to favor freedom, and yet depreciate agitation, are men who want crops without plowing up the ground. They want rain without thunder and lightning. They want the ocean without the awful roar of its many waters. This struggle may be a moral one; or it may be a physical one; or it may be both moral and physical; but it must be a struggle. Power concedes nothing without a demand. It never did and it never will.

—*Frederick Douglass*

Contents

Preface

In the summer of 2016, at the height of the presidential election, I was vacationing with my family and using the quiet early mornings to write. As I watched the sunrise and sipped my coffee, I couldn't resist sneaking a peek at the news. For weeks, the headlines had been shocking: hacked campaign emails; growing angst over economic, racial, and gender inequality; animosity toward immigrants; and the rise of new protest movements, including Black Lives Matter. Our democracy seemed to be challenged and provoked, functioning and fracturing all at once. After digesting several disheartening articles, I scanned the trending hashtags on Twitter. There, I stumbled upon #WomensEqualityDay, commemorating the adoption of the 19th Amendment on August 26, 1920, which gave all American women the right to vote.

I was surprised to be freshly discovering Women's Equality Day, created in 1973 by New York congresswoman Bella Abzug, who famously said, "This woman's place is in the House—the House of Representatives." I realized, to my chagrin, that my knowledge of the suffrage movement trailed off somewhere around Susan B. Anthony's death in 1906. I had never heard the details of how the 19th Amendment came to pass, but the rough outlines of the story piqued my interest. There was a clear protagonist: a quirky young Quaker from New Jersey named Alice Paul, who had the vision, strategy, persistence, and personal dedication to demand nothing short of equal suffrage. And there was a clear foil: a moralistic president, Woodrow Wilson, who claimed to be a Progressive Democrat but offered only regression on gender and racial issues.

While there are several biographies of Paul and dozens of Wilson, I found that these books typically posed the pair on parallel tracks—each figure focused on their own goals—and never on the obvious collision course for which they were destined. As we approach the centennial of the adoption of the 19th Amendment, it's imperative that more of us know who Paul was and what she was able to accomplish in the face of relentless adversity. Equally, it is paramount that we consider Wilson from his many angles, flattering and unflattering alike.

The mystery of why Paul was forgotten while Wilson was perpetually deemed a hero occupied my thoughts as I dug through layers upon layers of information: historical newsprint and photographs, presidential papers, personal and professional correspondence, and physical artifacts. I sat in Paul's childhood bedroom, went to the White House and the Capitol Building, and walked the paths of history in Washington.

What surprised me most about my findings was how much I seemed to be looking not at the past, but at our present. The issues at the heart of American democracy remain the same today as they did a century ago. We fight the enemy abroad and battle each other at home. We hold sacred ideals but struggle to meet them ourselves. We forget that progress can be slow and sometimes indirect. But most of all, we fail to remember that it takes just one person—however imperfect—who is utterly committed to change, to make it happen.

WASHINGTON, D.C., FEBRUARY 24, 2018

MR. PRESIDENT,
HOW LONG
MUST WE WAIT?

CHAPTER ONE

A Quaker from New Jersey

Alice Paul. Published in 1918.

November 20, 1907. Birmingham, England. Alice Paul finished dinner with classmates at Woodbrooke, an imposing limestone Georgian estate set in the countryside at almost exactly the center of England. Quakers, like Paul, traveled here from around the world to study social justice and other progressive pursuits. As the servants began clearing the long dining table, Paul excused herself and hastened upstairs to her corner room—a shared space with two large windows and a fireplace as its only source of heat—to prepare for the night.

The fur coat she had begged her mother to ship from the closet in the family farmhouse in Moorestown, New Jersey, in early October

1

had not yet arrived. A perceived extravagance, the fur was a practical staple for the daughter of William Paul, who was a wealthy banker, but contrasted starkly with Paul's student wardrobe, which reflected her necessary thrift as well as a lack of focus on fashion. Her plain clothes were so threadbare that she would fashion a ragged silk dress into a top, as she had just done, rather than throw it away. She bundled up as warmly as she could and did not fuss with jewelry or makeup on her deep-set blue eyes. She grabbed her ticket for the event and walked out into the dark and damp.

Gathering up her long, heavy skirt, she mounted a rented bike and began the familiar four-mile pedal into town. It was uncommon for a woman to ride a bike, but Paul was athletic—a basketball and hockey player—and had been encouraged by her parents since childhood to participate in sports, which girls seldom did. As Quakers, the Pauls believed that all people were equal in the eyes of God, regardless of gender or race; that boys and girls should be given the same opportunities; and that they all had a responsibility to stand up for equality. They believed in justice and fairness and practiced these concepts in their daily lives.

Paul rode boldly through the fog to Town Hall in Birmingham. Her chestnut hair—parted in the middle and loosely pinned in a bun—was swept back in wild strands as she sped toward the industrial city. She was journeying to see two "suffragettes," the term for militant activists working for women's right to vote.

It was nearly 8 p.m. when Paul parked her bike and made her way through the Town Hall's arched entry. Hundreds of people were inside. Many were male students from the University of Birmingham where Paul was taking classes, in addition to her twelve courses at Woodbrooke. She was the first and only woman enrolled in the university's Department of Commerce. She was fearless around them; unabashed, she strove for what she wanted.

Paul had come to listen to a mother-daughter team talk about their Votes for Women campaign. The men at Town Hall, however, had a different agenda, conspiring to undermine these rising leaders of England's suffrage movement. The pair, a widow named Emmeline Pankhurst and her daughter Christabel, had been making headlines for their tactics:

spitting at the police, interrupting the speeches of politicians by shouting "Votes for Women!" and handing out leaflets on street corners. The men inside Town Hall, like most of their peers, thought granting women the right to vote was outrageous. They believed women belonged at home, their minds uncorrupted by politics, and that these Pankhurst women—ringleaders who were whipping up pro-suffrage sentiment all over Britain—needed to be silenced.

Paul surveyed the room in search of a seat. A crush of students thronged the main floor and the upper galleries overlooking the stage. An organist played in an effort to settle the audience into their seats, however, the music instead stirred the men into action. They began to shake rattles, ring bells, and blow whistles and toy trumpets. This auditory battle between organist and crowd escalated for several minutes until it became so rowdy that four policemen intervened. The Bobbies' presence only triggered sarcastic cheers.

"Stop!" the police inspector shouted.

"Speeeeeech," the men shouted back at him.

Unfazed by the chaos, Christabel Pankhurst stepped onto the stage with striking poise. She seemed effortlessly confident; nothing like the newspapers' recent reports of an uncouth woman verbally attacking members of Parliament. When Christabel smiled at the surrounding mob, her face was illuminated. Paul could not help but consider her own smile, which revealed dimples and two slightly protruding front teeth. She noted how polished and attractive the twenty-seven-year-old Christabel, just four years her senior, appeared in comparison. The men, however, were not so softened by her affect. They roared at the suffragette for several minutes, waving their hats, sticks, and handkerchiefs provocatively as she patiently endured.

"Ladies and gentlemen!" Christabel projected over the din. "The students of Birmingham gave us on the occasion of our last visit so kind a welcome that I am not surprised to find their enthusiasm for women's suffrage is still unabated."

Despite her straining, Paul could not make out Christabel's words and was horrified by the rude antics of the audience. As a child growing up in New Jersey, Paul had attended suffrage meetings with her mother,

Tacie Paul, and other Quakers, including men, where everyone agreed unanimously on the issue. She also belonged to a suffrage society, the Moorestown League. Quakers were taught to listen respectfully to others. The intense discord with which Paul was now confronted was both a shock and a thrill.

"Tit for tat," the students chanted.

"There seem to be one or two of you in the gallery who are not quite out of the nursery and brought your toys with you," Christabel said. Such acerbic wit would have served her well had she pursued her dream of becoming a lawyer. Unfortunately, the English bar did not accept women, leading Christabel to choose a different path: joining her mother and sisters, Sylvia and Adela, to fight for voting rights.

"We have come to explain our tactics," Christabel asserted, trying again to pierce the pandemonium.

The crowd hushed briefly before someone hurled a dead mouse into the air, causing the hall to erupt in hysteria as the rodent was squeamishly caught and tossed like a hot potato. Christabel called her mother to the stage to take her place. Emmeline obliged as a woman in the audience rose to her feet in defense of the suffragettes, chastising the men: "Don't interrupt!"

"We have just come from a meeting with dockworkers and fishermen," Emmeline proclaimed, increasing the volume. They listened. "Are the educated young men of Birmingham afraid of what we have to say?"

A student, wearing glasses and a hat, sounded a bugle. The young woman seated beside him immediately plucked his hat from his head and pelted him with it. In a final act of defiance, he launched the bugle toward the stage as a steward and three policemen descended upon him.

Emmeline engaged with the struggle in a diplomatic effort to defuse the situation, reaching to shake the student's hand and assuring him that he could stay if he promised to stop.

"Now, as I was saying . . ."

The crowd again interrupted, expressing their objection with rattles and horns, bursting into a rendition of the national anthem, "God Save the King," as forty more officers flooded into the hall.

Paul remained transfixed by Emmeline Pankhurst.

"I'm prepared to stay here all night," Emmeline announced, with her arms outstretched to the audience. "If your mothers were here tonight they must blush to think they have borne such creatures."

The men, standing on their seats and assaulting their instruments in jarring unison, launched into "Auld Lang Syne." Emmeline folded her arms and held her ground for a full hour, determined to be heard. "We've played by the constitutional rules for forty years!" she shouted. For Emmeline, a little time on this stage, waiting for the crowd to behave, was only a drop of dedication in an ocean of effort.

■ ■ ■

British women had been fighting for voting rights for decades. Historically, only men who owned significant amounts of land could vote. By 1868, the government had extended the right to all male heads of household, defined as a working man with at least one child to support. But on both sides of the Atlantic, women were still struggling to make progress.

In America, Elizabeth Cady Stanton had organized the first women's rights convention, held in Seneca Falls, New York, in 1848. Her friend and fellow Quaker suffragist Susan B. Anthony became a household name when, in protest, she attempted to vote in 1872 and was arrested for doing so. The U.S. Constitution did not explicitly grant voting rights to anyone. Instead, it allowed those who could already vote the ability to give or withhold those same rights from anyone else. Those in the pioneering American West were among the first willing to let women cast ballots: Wyoming in 1869 and Utah in 1870, before either was a state; Colorado in 1893; and Idaho in 1896. Internationally, things were more advanced. New Zealand and Australia, for example, allowed women to vote as of 1893 and 1902, respectively. America, despite the efforts of women's suffrage advocates across the nation, was trailing far behind the progress of other countries on the issue. In fact, Paul's mother had worked for suffrage and even brought a young Alice to the Pennsylvania state suffrage convention in 1900.

■ ■ ■

Now it was 1907. After years of dwindling momentum in England and the United States, the Pankhursts were committed to rallying new women to the cause. That night in Birmingham, they couldn't have known how lucky they were to have the quiet American in their midst. Inspired and disturbed, Paul was riveted, absorbing every moment—until her senses were suddenly overwhelmed by the offensive odor of rotten eggs. Someone had released a hydrogen-sulfide stink bomb, creating an atmosphere so foul that the room emptied within seconds. Emmeline left the stage. The organist struck the keys once more, as if leading a church recessional. Paul climbed back on her bicycle and returned to Woodbrooke. She could feel the electricity in her body. It was unlike anything she had felt before.

Later that night, back in her dormitory, Paul felt a profound sense of change. Her environment seemed smaller, beyond the physical sense. Paul recognized that while some of her fellow scholars had enrolled at Woodbrooke in sincere pursuit of knowledge and social education, other students—like her American roommate—were seeking frivolity. Activities on the estate included tennis and afternoon tea, a ritual enjoyed outside on a sweeping lawn so picturesque it was featured on the postcards available to be sent back home.

Paul, a fast talker and faster thinker, had little interest in her roommate's vacant expressions and intellectual idleness—or any idleness at all. At age sixteen, Paul had been elected high school valedictorian at a Quaker school in Moorestown, near the gentleman's farm on which she was raised. Later, at Swarthmore College, she had majored in biology; not because she wanted to, but because she felt an obligation to strengthen her understanding of the subject about which she knew least. After graduation, she had completed a yearlong fellowship at a settlement house in lower Manhattan. There, Paul helped people from eastern and central Europe—mostly Jews and Italians—assimilate to American life at this historic peak of immigration, with 1.3 million people entering the United States as legal residents. She had also helped to form a labor union while she earned another degree, this one in social work, from the New York School of Philanthropy.

Paul believed it was her purpose in life to help others and assumed that the best way to achieve this was through social work. But she became disillusioned with this conviction when confronted with the prevailing struggles of citizens all around her, her efforts making little difference. In search of solutions to the injustices she witnessed, Paul returned to school. She was interested in attending Princeton, but the university did not accept women—or black men. The school's president, Woodrow Wilson, presided over this exclusion. Instead, she attended the University of Pennsylvania, where she earned a master's degree in sociology; one of the only women to do so. Her thesis was called "Toward Equality."

Despite earning three degrees in three years—1905, 1906, and 1907—her diplomas were not enough to quench Paul's thirst for learning. Her intellectual appetite led her to England and Woodbrooke and inspired a heavy course load, including German, Islam, sociology, and economics. During her stay, Paul realized that she still had much to learn about life beyond academia. As the school year drew to a close, she felt a reluctance to return home, as though her experience was not yet complete. Seeking a new challenge, Paul's instinct was validated when she witnessed a Quaker named Lucy Gardner deliver a lecture at Woodbrooke. Gardner was the leader of the London district Charity Organisation Society, which coordinated social services for the poor. Intrigued by what she had heard, Paul spoke with Gardner, who offered Paul a job as her assistant at the end of the academic year.

Paul seized the opportunity and moved into a settlement house in Hoxton, a poor section in East London, living among those she helped. Every moment of every day was infused with some kind of harsh reality: parents burying their children, men and women desperately searching for jobs, people lacking education and opportunity. But, fearless in the face of adversity, Paul proved a natural for the position. She was a formidable taskmaster, assessing three of her aides as incompetent, and a brilliant organizer, who was able to work on little food or rest without complaint. Not long after Paul arrived in Hoxton, a member of the settlement staff—a suffragist—informed her of two upcoming Votes for Women rallies. More than curious, she chose to attend both.

Paul rode the underground to the first of the two big protests. She emerged at Embankment Station to find herself buffeted by a moody wind and thousands of like-minded people swirling outside on a mid-June day, all of them joining a massive march in support of votes for women. Seeking direction, her eyes fell on an event steward sporting the National Union of Women's Suffrage Societies' (NUWSS) red and white colors, which stood out against the gray sky. The leader of the NUWSS, Millicent Garrett Fawcett, was a popular figure, known for refuting the many ridiculous reasons why women should not be permitted to vote. The arguments against suffrage included: that men alone already sufficiently represented women with their best interests in mind; that women were too easily influenced by men, and therefore, their vote would only echo that of the men; that women were so obstinate they might vote differently from their family, creating discord; that domestic life should have one leader, a structure that would be destroyed if women voted; and finally, that women were intellectually inferior to men.

The NUWSS was the more mainstream of the two key suffrage groups in the United Kingdom. The other was the Pankhursts' Women's Social and Political Union (WSPU), whose members distinguished themselves from ordinary suffragists by calling themselves suffragettes. Fawcett often openly criticized the WSPU's tactics—friction the press exploited.

The event steward guided Paul to the marching section for the American participants, where she merged with the lineup behind Dr. Anna Howard Shaw. Shaw was president of the National American Woman Suffrage Association (NAWSA), the foremost women's enfranchisement group in the United States. Although British-born, Shaw had immigrated to America as a child and grew up in the deep woods of Michigan. These rural formative years instilled physical stamina and fortitude, enabling her to become a physician and America's first female

Methodist minister. Now, silver-haired and sixty-one, Shaw's vigor endured as she took to the global stage, fighting for women's rights. Paul was fast on her heels.

Paul fell into step behind Shaw and followed her as one of the thirteen thousand marching to a ticketed rally at Royal Albert Hall. Awestruck and exhilarated, Paul absorbed the colorful scene around her as they progressed. The women were dressed in capes and academic robes. Some carried signs acknowledging professional sections of midwives, teachers, and nurses. Others held vivid velvet, silk, and embroidered banners, expressing artists' depictions of Joan of Arc, Queen Elizabeth, and other historically heroic women. When the parade reached its destination, the women settled inside the hall and Fawcett took center stage.

"This magnificent demonstration filled our hearts with hopefulness and courage and seems to bring us within measurable distance of our final triumph! Our cause is the greatest in the world. I appeal to all of you—dedicate your life to its success."

When Fawcett concluded, she invited Shaw to speak. The bold American was blunter in her delivery. "It's impossible to be just to men," she said, "so long as men are incapable of being just to women."

Despite Shaw's sharp remarks, the next day's papers noted how well behaved the NUWSS members were, compared with those at past Pankhurst events. "The speeches made in the Albert Hall at the end of the long walk were distinguished for their dignity and reserve," the *Times of London* wrote, "and were in marked contrast to the childish and vexatious methods adopted by the more excitable advocates of the same cause." A week later, Paul had the opportunity to judge for herself the contrast between these two rival suffrage groups.

Paul rode the tube yet again to Embankment Station, this time for the WSPU's first large-scale public event, which organizers christened "Suffrage Sunday." She exited the underground and was met by a warm summer day, bright blue skies, and a massive number of women—much more than the previous week's march.

In place of the usual long black skirts, most of the women wore white dresses. Broad straw hats, parasols, and belts were decorated with purple, white, and green ribbons; these were the WSPU's colors, representing freedom, purity, and hope. Others wore "Votes for Women" sashes.

Marching bands, megaphones, and bugles led the demonstration, while writers, artists, cotton spinners, factory workers, slum dwellers, and upper-class women followed on foot, by car, by carriage, or aboard special trains that brought them close to the demonstration area. Spectators flanked the streets, smiling and excitedly waving handkerchiefs. Some hung from their windows to watch the activity below. In Trafalgar Square, George Bernard Shaw, the famous playwright, stood on the curb, watching his wife, Charlotte Frances Payne-Townshend, go by.

Paul joined a section with Christabel Pankhurst and Emmeline Pethick-Lawrence, the WSPU's treasurer. The front line carried an eight-by-ten-foot banner that read REBELLION TO TYRANTS IS OBEDIENCE TO GOD. The French contingent banner simply said LA SOLIDARITÉ DES FEMMES.

Resolute, they pressed on toward Hyde Park, a former royal hunting ground near Buckingham Palace. Women from all walks of life filed through every gate, over the Serpentine Bridge, and onto the lush lawn, where spring had bloomed. Nearly half a million people assembled against the cherry-blossomed backdrop, united in the name of progress.

Twenty temporary platforms spread out across the park supported passionate suffrage speakers as crowds clustered tightly around them. The Pankhurst stage drew the most attention, with attendees straining to catch a glimpse of Emmeline and Christabel. Men, some curious and some hostile, heckled the suffragettes and began shoving to get closer, causing a near panic. Verbal and physical altercations erupted.

"Why not try to be gentlemen in the presence of ladies?" one woman yelled.

"Do you think we're going to be governed by women? If they want to be men, why don't they be men? Let 'em go work on a ship," a young man responded. "Let 'em go home and mind the baby!"

It continued like this for hours. At 5 p.m., after eighty speeches, the sound of bugles signaled the end of the program and the creation of a resolution that would be sent to Prime Minister Herbert Asquith the following day, demanding that, if taxed, women should have a say in how the government spent their money.

"Votes for Women!" the crowd cheered. "Votes for Women! Votes for Women!"

The chant rung in Paul's ears long into that night and throughout the rest of the summer.

When fall came around, Paul began classes at the London School of Economics, as well as a new job at the Peel Institute, a charity with strong Quaker roots. She moved into a shoddy apartment, a two-room attic space with the rustling sounds of rodents and no running water. But she could barely afford even these meager accommodations. The family wealth back home was there, but her widowed mother was increasingly parsimonious, and had much to manage with the family farm and Paul's three siblings, William, Helen, and Parry, all younger.

There were very few women at the London School of Economics, so when Paul spotted Rachel Barrett on campus she naturally introduced herself. Barrett told Paul she was a WSPU organizer and asked her if she would sell *Votes for Women*—the group's newspaper—with her. Fully aware that helping might provoke the anger of strangers, Paul agreed. Standing on the street, waving the suffrage paper, people pelted Paul with rotten food and stones. On another day, a cab driver swerved toward her, forcing her to the ground. Even women cursed her. But she persevered. As word spread through the WSPU ranks that Paul was something special, she received another assignment—public speaking on the street, at tube stations, and inside trains. Throughout the winter months, day after day, Paul would literally stand on a soap box on the streets of London, appealing to the public on behalf of the suffrage cause. In the midst of this excitement, Paul realized that she had neglected to answer her mother's letters for some time. She hurried a note home, explaining her extracurricular activities: "I have joined the 'suffragettes'—the militant party," she wrote.

———

With the school year almost at an end, Paul's future was undecided. After nearly two years abroad, not only was she homesick, but her mother missed her terribly and yearned for her return. Paul booked her passage on a transatlantic ship and began counting down the days until her departure the following month.

CHAPTER TWO

Password: Kitchen

Alice Paul was looking forward to returning home to her family in New Jersey. In the midst of packing and saying good-byes, a life-changing letter arrived. She opened it right away and pored over the words, her eyes fastening to an important request: Would she organize with Mrs. Pankhurst and go on a "deputation" to see the prime minister, a confrontation that would probably put her in danger of being arrested and imprisoned? "So you must not accept this invitation," the letter said, "unless you are willing to do this."

Paul sat down to digest, deliberate, and ultimately compose her response. With great care, she sealed the envelope and carried it to the nearest post office. When she reached its doors, Paul suddenly panicked and paced the building to calm her nerves until she possessed the courage to enter and mail her acceptance letter, committing to spend the summer working for the Women's Social and Political Union (WSPU).

Her first assignment was on June 29. Paul took extra care in dressing for the occasion: she stuffed raw cotton under her clothes to serve as protective padding from rough police handling and went to London's Caxton Hall for a rally. On the stage, Christabel stated that, because Prime Minister Asquith had been ignoring their pleas, they should leave right then to storm Parliament Square and personally present him with their demands. With Paul following, Emmeline Pankhurst led the march to the House of Commons and tangled with police upon arrival.

As they arrested her, she implored the suffragettes behind her to push past security. Women in the rear buttressed those in the front, like a rugby scrum. When it was Paul's turn to follow suit, she was grabbed by police, so aggressively that the buttons of her coat popped, spilling her padding. Witnesses laughed and cheered as police hauled her away.

Paul had never been arrested before. Inside the Canon Row Police Station, police kept her in the billiards room where she sat on a pool table and processed this alien experience, noting every detail and stripe of humanity: drunks, thieves, and disorderlies, as well as dozens of women—suffragettes—with their clothes torn apart. One woman in particular stood out, a redhead wearing an American flag pin on the lapel of her suit. Paul introduced herself to the woman. Her name was Lucy Burns, a Catholic from Brooklyn, also the daughter of a banker. Burns was six years Paul's senior and had come to Europe to study for two years at the University of Berlin—after Vassar and Yale—before signing up with the suffragettes in Britain. The two women talked for hours, until a man they had never met before approached and sat down beside them. He said he would bail them out . . . on one condition.

Lucy Burns. Published in 1913.

"I am leaving this money, but I need you to be there for your court date [in July]," he said. The man was Frederick Pethick-Lawrence, the wealthy husband of suffragette Emmeline Pethick-Lawrence. (Frederick was progressive enough to merge his last name with his wife's when they married.) His role in the cause involved regularly supplying bail for arrested suffragettes.

"You know," Paul told him, "I have a return ticket for America on the boat, which is before the time that I have to be there."

"The only thing you can do I guess is to cancel your return ticket because by order of the court you have to appear at this time."

Paul promised she would.

Released by the police at around 1 a.m., Burns and Paul were exhausted but emboldened. So committed were they to the cause that, in the month between their arrest and their delayed court appearance, both women accepted additional assignments targeting cabinet ministers. Their next directive: to confront a rising politician, Winston Churchill.

As a new husband and father and president of the Board of Trade, Winston Churchill was many things, including a person who did not believe that women should have the right to vote, a stance that, when combined with his political ascendance, made him a prime target for the suffragettes. He was scheduled to give a talk in Norwich about England's economy. Paul and Burns arrived four days in advance to generate a less than enthusiastic greeting. They scrawled with chalk on sidewalks, hung signs, knocked on doors, and invited everyone they encountered to attend their protest during Churchill's speech. Their efforts were effective. Despite heavy security in the form of locked doors, iron gates, and a police force to protect him from the encroaching mob outside, when Churchill took the stage, he could barely hear himself speak. The distracting din caused him to falter, providing an opportunity for a suffrage sympathizer to heckle him.

"Why tax voteless women?" one man challenged, as others joined the chorus in support of suffrage. As tensions mounted outside the hall, the audience inside grew restless. Police began arresting and hauling off to jail the protesters who were crowding the entrance, including Paul. This time, however, police chose not to prosecute the suffragettes, believing that doing so would only give them what they wanted—more attention.

Such arrests became so commonplace that the Pankhursts needed to develop new tactics to maintain front-page headlines and boost morale among their ranks. They devised a plan to hold a mass ceremony in the streets of London, publicly honoring suffragettes, including Burns and

Paul, who had been imprisoned. They gave each woman a symbolic gift—lapel pins shaped like prison doors—and publicized the event so that people could witness, firsthand, the women who were willing to make such sacrifices. Many in attendance were shameless gawkers, crowding around the stage as if beholding a circus act. Some were there for more genuine reasons. Mohandas Gandhi, who as the leader of the Indian independence movement was developing a philosophy of passive resistance, took in the scene, noting there was "much to learn" from the suffragettes because their willingness to be imprisoned or die made them a "soul force."

Paul and Burns wore their pins proudly, like badges of honor, status symbols within an ever-expanding movement. But they did not rest on their laurels. The very next day, on July 30, they joined eleven other suffragettes in storming the doors of a hall where Chancellor of the Exchequer David Lloyd George was speaking, in Limehouse, a borough on the northern banks of the Thames. The punishment for this brash offense was swift and harsh: two weeks in Holloway Gaol (pronounced *jail*). During this period of imprisonment, Paul's courage and resourcefulness escalated. In her first act of protest, she refused all food, taking only water. While fasting is always difficult and dangerous, Paul had a lifelong capacity to subsist on very little sustenance and she committed quickly to the hunger strike. Her next rebellion involved rejecting the prison clothes, electing instead to remain naked. These severe methods of self-deprivation led to Paul's early release, on day four, by which time she was so weak that they had to carry her out on a litter.

Three arrests and one hunger strike in the span of a month took a toll on Paul, but it also elevated her status within the suffragette ranks. In September, Emmeline Pankhurst asked Paul and Burns to travel with her to Scotland to create momentum within the movement there. Elated by the invitation, they also were delighted to learn a female chauffeur—in a green Austin with white wheels and a purple stripe along its body—would drive them there.

"This was something absolutely unheard of. Nobody had ever *seen* a woman chauffeur," Paul later explained. "It was unusual for a woman to drive a car but to have a woman chauffeur—! So she was quite a picture on her expedition. Only Mrs. Pankhurst, Lucy Burns and myself, and this woman chauffeur. Then we would stop at meetings along the way; great meetings had been arranged for Mrs. Pankhurst, and she would make one of her great speeches to enormous crowds; and then we would go on to the next stopping place where she would make another speech."

On September 12, they were resolved to harass Churchill again, in Dundee's Great Hall. For breaking windows, Paul and Burns were arrested yet again. Like other women across the United Kingdom who continued to be thrown in jail and go on hunger strikes—some were even being violently force-fed—the two refused food. They grew frail quickly because this was their second hunger strike in two weeks. Released after four days, they were sent to recuperate at the estate of Miss MacGregor, a suffrage supporter.

"When we got there," Paul said later, "we were far out in the country, and Lucy Burns and I thought we would go out for a walk, and Miss MacGregor was very much embarrassed. She said, 'You know, no lady goes out without having a hat and a coat and gloves and so on. I wouldn't want anybody to go out from my house without being properly gowned.' So we gradually learned all the right customs [laughing] and conformed to them, I guess all right."

The stay in the Scottish countryside, a break from the harrowing rigors of protesting, served its purpose. Feeling a little bit restored, the women returned to London for their next assignment—their most significant yet.

It was a frosty dawn on November 9, 1909. Paul dressed in a faded uniform, one she had borrowed to disguise herself as a cleaning lady, and set out into the streets of downtown London. She was accompanied by her friend, Amelia Brown, a middle-aged nurse, also incognito, carrying a bucket and brushes. The two women made their way to the imposing front door of Guildhall, a medieval stone municipal building in the City of London.

At about 8 a.m., the women gained entry by providing a password—"kitchen"—and persuading the guards on duty that they were workers, assigned to prepare the hall for the Lord Mayor's Banquet. An annual event since 1502, dignitaries and journalists traveled from far and wide to hear the prime minister give a notable speech on world affairs. Inside the great hall, Paul and Brown found a massive room with soaring, arched ceilings and five-foot-thick walls. There were two Gothic stained-glass windows looming on either end, portraying previous lord mayors. The colored glass filtered morning light onto the statues and banners that lined the sides of the hall. Paul and Brown disappeared inside and managed to remain hidden until late in the day, crouching under benches or skulking in dark corners to stay out of sight, pretending to be lost should anyone become aware of their presence. As the space began to fill with flowers, pretty linens, and candles, a warm glow radiated throughout. Elaborate chandeliers twinkled overhead as the women ascended the staircase to an enclosed gallery, where they discreetly waited for Burns to arrive.

As Paul and Brown remained concealed, Burns strode into Guildhall, dressed in a beautiful evening gown, arm in arm with Labour Party MP Arthur Henderson—an iron union labor organizer and advocate for women's voting rights. Security had tightened, in part due to the suffragettes' daring, and required verification of all invitations. Henderson produced his ticket and explained that he had left the other behind. The guard referenced the guest list as Burns cast her eyes over the crowd, scanning for the target. At last, she spied Churchill, entering the banquet hall with his wife, Clementine.

"How can you dine here while women are starving in prison?" she shouted at Churchill, referring to women across England—from Manchester to Bristol—who were hunger striking behind bars. She waved a tiny banner in his face.

Churchill froze. His wife, who had been out of the public eye recuperating after childbirth, was horrified. Guards quickly escorted Henderson and Burns off the premises. But the incident put politicians on notice that they could not avoid the protests, not on this night, despite security.

It was 9 p.m., and the hidden women readied the next ambush. The guests settled into their seats and a quiet descended as the lord mayor rose to toast to the health of King Edward, Queen Victoria's oldest son, on his sixty-eighth birthday. In the stillness of that solemn moment, Brown and Paul shattered an unadorned pane of the stained-glass window with their shoes; showering shards all over the floor below and onto a statue of the Duke of Wellington.

The women leaned through the broken pane and yelled "Votes for Women! Votes for Women!" So enormous was the hall that it almost swallowed their cries, but all eyes looked toward the origin of the shattered glass. The band began to play to distract the guests from the mayhem as security dashed upstairs. Some well-dressed dignitaries joined the pursuit and an intensive search began, leading the hunters all the way through the dirty wooden rafters and onto the tiled roof in a misguided effort to find the women. Though the women were eventually apprehended in the gallery, Paul and Brown continued to bellow "Votes for Women!" as police dragged them out of Guildhall. The women had stashed feeding tubes in their clothes; shocking little props intended to be waved in Asquith's face to embarrass him publicly about the horrific forced feedings being inflicted upon the suffragettes. But police dragged them out of Guildhall too quickly for them to do so. Paul and Brown arrived at the jail and went through the now-routine process of posting bail. The next day, in front of a judge, Brown strayed from the plan and pled guilty. Paul did not.

"I should like to explain that we feel we have broken no moral law whatsoever in doing this," Paul said. "We feel that it is incumbent on every woman to rebel against [the] state of political subjection in which we are placed."

The magistrate interrupted Paul's statement. "Hysterical creatures!" he called them.

"You said you would allow us to give an explanation," Paul said.

"You don't seem to have any plea or justification for your conduct."

"I should only be too delighted to give it."

Without letting her finish, the magistrate offered them a choice: a fine of five pounds and damages of two pounds ten pence, or a month of hard labor back in Holloway. They chose the latter.

After a summer and fall of marches, demonstrations, and constant suffragette confrontations with the authorities, the pressure built and the government struggled with its response. Paul had been arrested six times in the last six months and gone on two hunger strikes. She was becoming a minor celebrity and a major oddity, an American sacrificing so much of her youth, time, and health to fight alongside British women for voting rights.

When Paul was sentenced to another prison term, her subsequent punishment was much more severe. Press flocked to the hearing and the *New York Times* sent a reporter to interview Paul's mother, Tacie, on her farmhouse porch. The paper splashed the story across the front page the next day, saying Mrs. Paul "was much agitated when she heard of her daughter's predicament." Friends and family asked the American Embassy if a diplomat could help but were told the office could not interfere with English justice.

In prison, Paul lay shivering on her bed, weak from refusing food for several days and cold from rejecting the mandatory prison clothes, yet again. But the guards were not going to release her this time. Instead, they wrapped her in blankets and took her to another cell. There, the largest female guard entered and sat across Paul's knees and pinned her shoulders to the cot. Two others sat on either side of Paul and held her arms. They wrapped a towel around her throat as a doctor came up from behind and forced her head back while shoving a tube up her nostril.

Through this tube, about six feet long and as thick as a finger, they pumped a mixture of eggs and milk down her throat. Sometimes the tube ended up in her mouth and she would bite a hole in it before they pried her jaw open with an instrument. After the first time this happened, she thrashed around and broke a jug so they tied her down with sheets. She refused to give in.

Each time the ordeal ended, she trembled, cried, bled from her nose, and lay drenched in sweat. This happened twice a day for nearly three weeks, causing physical damage that would only become apparent later and plague her for the rest of her life. Her only respite came during those times when she was too ill to even be touched, therefore escaping force feeding. When her thirty-day sentence ended, two of the female wardens helped her into a cab and took her to the home of a friend to recover. There, Paul gained her strength back, slowly, with the goal of traveling home as soon as possible.

Paul was still recovering from the prison ordeal when she arrived at the dock in Liverpool on January 6, 1910. Although she told no one but her mother that she was going home, there was a crowd and some media standing near the *Haverford*, wanting to hear from this suffragette one last time before she left for America. She was so weak, however, she could barely stand to talk before embarking.

Her passage across the Atlantic was stormy, made even more trying because of her fragile health. She seemed far from the robust, energetic young woman who ventured into Europe three years earlier. But the transformation was more than physical. Paul had become a global sensation and an even more confident woman.

When the ship arrived in Philadelphia at dusk, four days late, on January 20, Paul was dressed in a high lace collar over her brown tailored suit and a beaver tricorn hat. She looked sharp, making a statement as the last person to walk down the gangplank. Her mother and her fifteen-year-old brother Parry spotted her, surprised by how frail and thin she was. Paul was thrilled to see them, and hugged her mother tightly for a long time. Then she looked at Parry.

"You've grown so much!" she said to him. He told her she sounded different, with a twinge of an English accent.

Several reporters interrupted the reunion, asking questions as Paul waited for her luggage. She answered patiently and removed her glasses to pose for pictures. Reporters found that the reality of Paul clashed with the fantastical character they had envisioned. As one wrote, "There is nothing about Miss Paul's appearance that would lead one to suppose that she could possibly raise disturbance enough" to be imprisoned. They pressed her for details about the force feeding. She told them all about it and equated it with "vivisection." They also wanted to know if she was going to continue as a militant in America.

"The women here," she told them, "will not have to pursue militant methods to gain equal franchise with men. Their position is far in advance of the English woman. And if they really want the vote they can get it unless—unless the big corporations and the political bosses oppose them."

When the interviews concluded, Paul retreated from the crowd and disappeared into the dark with her family helping her along. It was not long before she craved another challenge.

The following September, she entered the doctoral program at the University of Pennsylvania, where she was a star drawing admirers into her orbit. One of those admirers was graduate assistant William Parker. Parker was from upstate New York and the same age as Paul. But while he took an interest in this famous suffragist, she mostly just took an interest in her thesis on "The Legal Position of Women in Pennsylvania," a paper that analyzed the statutes, court decisions, and constitutional provisions that led to marginalization. Paul, always earnest and straightforward, was not the type to play hard to get, or to be easily distracted, no matter how hard Parker tried. Eventually, he left the university, rejecting a job offer in academia, to become a bond salesman in New York. There, he tried to entice her with his prospects for success.

"As I believe I forecasted," he wrote Paul in September of 1912, "I am about to make a million. . . .[C]aptured body and soul by Wall St. which is somewhat different from what we in our bucolic fields imagined it. . . . I have a little nest under the roof of #1 University Place overlooking Wash. Square which delighteth me much. Let me know when you come over, and we have dinner [sic] at a little Hungarian place I know. But don't hasten to leave your resting place." And then, before completing the letter, Parker dangled one last offer in front of Paul. "You know I am going to make a salon, and you are going to light it up and be amused and warmed by the glow of all the good spirits." He also told her to build up her strength and "eat like a bear. No one is looking. You have a tremendous constitution, and if you only don't break yourself to pieces, you will conquer the world. Ah, *mon amie*."

Whether Paul visited him in New York is unknown, but their paths would cross again, in Washington, D.C.

CHAPTER THREE

A Southern Boy

On November 6, 1860, Thomas Woodrow Wilson, just a month shy of his fourth birthday, was standing outside his family's large brick Colonial in Augusta, Georgia—they had recently moved there from Virginia, where he was born—when he saw a man running down the street.

"Abraham Lincoln has been elected!" the man shouted. "There's going to be a war!"

The boy—"Tommy" to his family—was too young to understand the South's obsession with Lincoln, or the president-elect's aggressively anti-slavery Republican Party, but he understood the urgency of this stranger's declaration and hurried inside to see his father. Joseph Ruggles Wilson, a Presbyterian minister and Democrat, found himself surrounded by his inquiring family: his wife, Jessie, an English immigrant; his daughters, Marion and Annie; and his perplexed young son. They huddled close to him, listening intently, as the household servants worked silently around them.

Their questions could have ranged from the seemingly simple: *Why does Lincoln's election mean there will be a war? Who would fight and why? Why did the North think slavery was wrong?* To the more sophisticated: *How were plantations supposed to function without slaves? How would the economy thrive without cotton plantations? Why was the North interfering with two hundred and fifty years of southern tradition? Wouldn't slaves be worse off without their masters?*

Slavery was a constant feature of Tommy's southern childhood. His own home was tended to by freed blacks—provided by the church—and slaves. Tommy's uncle owned a plantation in Mississippi. Georgia was the birthplace of the cotton gin and Eli Whitney's revolutionary machine enabled one person to clean seeds from one thousand pounds of cotton in a day, versus five pounds by hand. This invention encouraged large-scale plantations, requiring armies of workers—slaves in this case—to pick the cotton. With one million residents living in Georgia in 1860, almost 50 percent of its population were slaves.

Reverend Wilson gathered his thoughts. As his loved ones looked to him for answers, he turned to the Bible for unequivocal moral guidance. And he found it.

In early January 1861, eight weeks after Lincoln's election, Augustans filled the pews of the First Presbyterian Church and watched with interest as Reverend Wilson stepped up to the pulpit. The son of immigrants from the north of Ireland and a graduate of the Princeton Theological Seminary (then called the College of New Jersey), he was respected by the congregation and they were eager to hear his perspective on these changing times. The reverend's face was thin and angular, his high cheekbones conjuring an impression of sternness. His greasy hair was side-parted and fell in salt-and-pepper layers; long enough for him to tuck behind his large ears—a feature his son inherited. Tommy sat in the audience with his mother and sisters. In a balcony above, segregated slaves were seated, permitted by Reverend Wilson to attend the church.

A respectful silence came over the congregation as Reverend Wilson began his sermon. Titled "Mutual Relation of Masters and Slaves as Taught in the Bible," it was a message intended as much for blacks as it was for whites. He opened with a passage from Ephesians: "Servants, be obedient to them that are your masters according to the flesh, with fear and trembling, in singleness of your heart, as unto Christ. . . . And, ye masters, do the same things unto them, forbearing threatening, knowing that your Master also is in Heaven; neither is there respect of persons with him."

Reverend Wilson continued for some time, building his misguided argument for why and how the Bible condones slavery. He added:

> I am sure that you will bear with me while I take another step in this great argument, and show how completely the Bible brings human slavery underneath the sanction of divine authority, upon other and stronger grounds. . . . There must be such inequalities in society; . . . God has evidently made one to serve another. . . . Surely the Bible is clear enough upon this point to satisfy the most sensitive conscience. . . . [Slavery is] directly sanctioned by both the utterance and silence of Scripture.

Deeply religious, Tommy lapped up his father's words, believing not only that God condoned slavery, but that God condoned inequality. Neither Tommy nor any of his fellow congregants had a reason to mistrust Reverend Wilson's preaching. He was expressing the very sentiments they were hungry to hear and determined to justify. Nodding vigorously, they agreed that Georgia had the right to do whatever it deemed lawful—even if that meant seceding from the Union, as South Carolina had done two weeks earlier. The worshippers left the church buzzing. So pleased were they with Reverend Wilson's sermon, they requested to publish his wisdom in the form of a booklet, something that could be widely distributed. He granted them permission.

The anger of the Deep South was rapidly intensifying. Just three days after Reverend Wilson delivered his popular sermon, Mississippi seceded, followed the next day by Florida and, the day after that, by Alabama. A week after Alabama's secession, Georgia pulled out of the Union, sending ripples of anxiety through the Wilson household. Louisiana and Texas were next to secede.

These Confederate states wasted no time organizing themselves and, on April 12, 1861, rebels attacked the poorly supplied U.S. Army forces stationed at Fort Sumter near Charleston, South Carolina. After two days of gunfire, the U.S. Army surrendered. President Lincoln called for seventy-five thousand volunteers to quell the "insurrection." But he and most everyone else knew the Civil War had begun.

Although Augusta was not a battlefield, the war took its toll on Tommy's hometown and deeply affected his daily life. Two thousand men from the community marched off to fight. Those remaining scrambled to build the primary powder works for the Confederacy. The facility—a series of mills a mile and a half long—was constructed in just seven months and supplied three and a half tons of gunpowder per day. The city also provided food for the Confederate Army. It wasn't long before thousands of refugees, fleeing from ravaged cities across the South, began crowding into Augusta, straining the city's supply of food and shelter. Even the upper-middle-class Wilsons were low on provisions. They ate cowpea soup for supper, night after night, as the war crept closer.

In late September of 1863, a bloody battle raged in Chickamauga, 260 miles north of Augusta. For three dreadful days, thousands of soldiers engaged in brutal combat, with men slain on both sides. The field was littered with the consequences of war: thirty-four thousand casualties; half of them Confederates. In the aftermath, the small Augusta hospital was quickly overwhelmed, so Reverend Wilson cleared his church to accommodate the injured and built a stockade out back for the captured Union soldiers. Tommy witnessed the tragedy firsthand, as a sanctuary became an infirmary with blood-drenched cots holding broken men replacing pews. The boy was pierced by the hollowed eyes of weary prisoners, their blue uniforms in tatters. Upsetting as these scenes were, Tommy was even more frightened when his father left soon after, to serve as a chaplain in the field. The thin boy began suffering from stomachaches and sometimes cried in church when he was moved by hymns, such as "'Twas on That Dark, That Doleful Night." He was relieved when his father returned, unharmed, a few months later.

In September of 1864, Union general William Tecumseh Sherman captured Atlanta in the northwestern part of Georgia, and began burning a 285-mile path between it and Savannah, all the way to the Atlantic Ocean. Augusta lay just outside Sherman's apparent route of destruction but, given the city's role supplying gunpowder to the Confederacy, the residents took no chances in preparing to defend themselves. They brought all of their stored cotton to the main road, piled it as a peace offering, and held their collective breath until Sherman bypassed Augusta. But eight months later, in May of 1865, the city suffered a final humiliation. After a massive manhunt, Union forces found Jefferson Davis, president of the Confederacy, near Irwinville in southern Georgia. They captured Davis, who was sick and draped in a shawl his wife had given him for comfort, and paraded him through the streets of Augusta. Tommy stood with everyone else, dumbstruck, as the end of the Civil War unfolded before their very eyes.

The War Between the States had bracketed Tommy's childhood and affected him profoundly. At nine years old, he had yet to attend school and his family lived under martial law, imposed by the Union Army. With the South in shambles, few cities or towns had mandatory schooling. Augusta was no exception. Reverend Wilson had been informally teaching Tommy at home and read to him every night. But the boy struggled to learn how to read; modern scholars believe he likely had a learning disorder, such as dyslexia. Outside of the home, Tommy spent his time playing sports. He organized a group called the Lightfoot Baseball Club, which met in the barn loft behind his house. He was the team's second baseman and the group's president, writing the bylaws and requiring members to follow the rules of parliamentary procedure during meetings.

It may seem odd for a child of his age to even know that parliamentary procedures existed, but Tommy had a precocious interest in government and politics. And, after four years of civil war, Americans from the North and South were focused on how the executive, legislative, and legal branches should function, as well as how the Constitution should be interpreted and whether it needed more amending.

■ ■ ■

The U.S. Constitution's first ten amendments, known as the Bill of Rights, were ratified on the same day in 1791 to ensure more individual freedoms and limit government power. These amendments include freedom of the press, religion, and speech; the right to bear arms; protection against unreasonable search and seizure; the right to a speedy and fair trial; and, as the 10th Amendment states: "The powers not delegated to the United States by the Constitution, nor prohibited by it to the states, are reserved to the states respectively, or to the people."

The 11th Amendment, ratified in 1795, gave states legal immunity from foreign courts. And the 12th Amendment, revising the Electoral College process, passed in 1804. There had been no constitutional amendments since that legislative spate—not one in all of Reverend Wilson's lifetime. But in a three-year burst of activity immediately after the Civil War, three major amendments were ratified in quick succession, the results of cooperative efforts to revise America's guidebook for how to be a nation.

The 13th Amendment, adopted in 1865, abolished slavery. While this change to the U.S. Constitution radically transformed the South and the childhood that Tommy knew, two more amendments ratified during his teenage years dramatically changed the United States. The 14th Amendment in 1868 granted citizenship to African Americans and equal protection under the law, but that was not all. The 14th Amendment also specifically excluded woman suffrage by inserting the word "male" in a section about voting.

Suffragists would spend decades trying to get the reference to men deleted from the text. In 1870, the 15th Amendment allowed African American *men* to vote, stating that they could not be denied suffrage "on account of race, color, or previous condition of servitude." But southern states did not want this amendment and did what they could to sabotage its success, including implementing poll taxes, literacy tests, and other means to effectively block black men from voting. The amendment sparked further social tension, causing a schism between civil rights activists. For years, suffrage pioneers like Elizabeth Cady Stanton and Susan B. Anthony had linked the abolition of slavery and voting rights, understanding that denying basic rights to anyone was wrong. But when females were excluded from the 15th Amendment, they were outraged. In particular, many white women, including Anthony, believed they had become political inferiors to a race whose freedom they helped champion. This issue propelled them toward their own agenda; a singular focus, ahead of all others. They did not believe there was

enough room in the nation's collective conscience, nor enough philan-
thropic donations, to support both racial and women's rights. And they
saw these issues as separate.

■ ■ ■

Having witnessed so much political turmoil throughout his early childhood, Tommy's interest in government was deeply rooted, intensifying
as college approached. In 1875, after one year of classes at Davidson
College in North Carolina, he applied to Princeton and was accepted.
A serious student on the all-white, all-male campus, he assigned himself
extra reading, and was secretary of the Football Association, president
of the Baseball Association, and managing editor of *The Princetonian*.
He also organized a public affairs discussion group for students and was
elected speaker of the American Whig Society—one of the oldest col-
legiate debate and political unions in America—by his peers. Evidence
that his political ideals were already forming, in his diary from 1876,
he wrote, among other things: "Universal suffrage is at the foundation
of every evil in this country."

CHAPTER FOUR

From Princeton to Public Office

After graduating from Princeton, Tommy Wilson dropped what had become to him an unsuitable nickname and enrolled as Woodrow Wilson at the University of Virginia in 1879 to study law. With that degree in hand, he moved to Atlanta to practice law, but found the work uninteresting. His personal life fared better: he met a woman in church named Ellen Louise Axson, whose father was also a Presbyterian minister. When graduate school took him to Johns Hopkins University to study political science and history, they exchanged romantic letters. Not all of Wilson's notes were of the love variety; some expressed views that he would hold throughout his career. In one letter to Axson, he described attending the Association for the Advancement of Women in Baltimore's women's congress. "Barring the chilled, scandalized feeling that always overcomes me when I see and hear women speak in public," he wrote, "I derived a good deal of whimsical delight . . . from the proceedings."

His 1885 doctoral dissertation, "Congressional Government," examined how the federal system had evolved from its original intent. Congress, he wrote, had become more powerful in influencing nominations, confirmations, and appropriations and in supervising executive agencies and the treaty process. He believed the intent of the electoral system—to have trustworthy, nonpartisan men elect the president—had been corrupted by party conventions that pushed votes to preselected candidates. He also complained that the balance of power had tilted away from the states and toward the federal government. The only recourse of the states to arrest the growth of congressional power, he said, was the Supreme Court. The dissertation was so well received that Houghton Mifflin published it, establishing Wilson as a premier political scientist. He dedicated the book to his father, "the patient guide of his youth."

As praise for Wilson's work spread through the academic world like wildfire, the leaders of a new college named Bryn Mawr, just outside Philadelphia, invited Wilson to be the school's first professor of history. Bryn Mawr had been the dying wish of the Quaker physician Joseph W. Taylor. Taylor wanted to establish a college "for the advanced education of females." There were few colleges in America for women. But there were none that offered both undergraduate and graduate degrees, until Bryn Mawr. Wilson, still finishing his studies at Johns Hopkins, was unsure whether to accept the position. He wrote to Ellen—his intended wife—asking for her advice. Ellen was dubious.

"Do you think there *is* much reputation to be made in a girls school?" Ellen wrote back to Wilson. "Can you be content to serve in that sort of institution?"

"The question of higher education of women is certain to be settled in the affirmative, in this country at least, whether my sympathy be enlisted or not," he replied.

He told Ellen that, although he would prefer to teach men, there were several benefits to the Bryn Mawr offer. The light course load associated with the position would leave Wilson time to invest in his own academic aspirations; the college campus was located in the northeast, a region notorious for cultivating curious, studious minds, so Wilson believed his work and interests would be better appreciated in this ambitious environment than they had been in the South; and he could finally devote time to the textbook on government that he had long wanted to write. He had convinced himself to accept. Ellen, who was studying art in New York City, informed Wilson that she would leave her creative path, marry him, and join him on campus.

"As compared with the privilege of loving and serving you and the blessedness of being loved by you, the praise and admiration of all the world and generations yet unborn would be lighter than vanity," she wrote to him. "If now I held such greatness in my hand I should toss it away without a second thought that the hand might be free to clasp in yours."

Wilson seemed oblivious to Ellen's sacrifices, believing it was in fact his dreams that were on hold. "I do feel a very real regret that I have been shut out from my heart's first—primary—ambition and purpose, which was to take an active, if possible a leading, part in public life, and strike out for myself, if I had the ability, a statesman's career," he told her. "That is my heart's—or, rather, my mind's—deepest secret, little lady."

Bryn Mawr's campus was still under construction when the Wilsons stepped off the train in Pennsylvania in the autumn of 1885. Just two student buildings stood—Taylor and Merion halls—imposing stone structures, modeled in the Jacobean Gothic style of the distinguished men's colleges at Oxford and Cambridge. These halls would soon overlook a common green, designed by the famous landscape architect Frederick Law Olmsted, and house the first class of forty-two women.

After the Wilsons settled into one of three small faculty houses, they attended the inauguration ceremony in Taylor Hall. Wilson, seated on stage, listened to an address by Bryn Mawr's president James E. Rhoads. "All discussion of the question whether women ought to share equally with men facilities for mental culture in its highest forms is obsolete," Rhoads said. Wilson's own beliefs were in such opposition that, as he and his wife listened, they came to the mutual conclusion that Bryn Mawr would be their home only briefly. It would prove a purposeful period; Ellen was already pregnant, and her husband was using his lecture research as fuel to develop his textbook project: an extensive survey of how government functioned, spanning decades, continents, and civilizations. For one section of the book, he would explore the various suffrage laws in the United States, noting that women could vote in some elections. For example, in Connecticut and Massachusetts, women who could read could cast ballots in local and school elections. He immersed himself so deeply in his manuscript that it soon became evident to his students that he was not engaged with his teaching role or with acclimating to Bryn Mawr. One woman said his lectures came off as auditions. A dean and professor at Northwestern University, who was a graduate fellow and peer, found Wilson patronizing. Another, the daughter of abolitionists from Massachusetts, stated it was uncomfortable meeting "a Southerner who had no special sympathy for Negroes as human beings."

When Ellen returned south in June of 1886 to give birth to a daughter, Margaret, while her husband finished up the semester, he wrote to her, expressing his frustrations: "I'm tired of carrying female Fellows on my shoulders. When I think of you, my little wife, I love this 'College for Women,' because you are a woman; but when I think only of myself, I hate the place very cordially." Despite his antagonism, Wilson retained his teaching position as his family expanded. The couple's second daughter, Jessie, was born in 1887.

After three years at Bryn Mawr, in 1888, Wilson welcomed an offer to become chair of history and political economy at Wesleyan University in Middletown, Connecticut, a school with only a small number of female students. During his two-year tenure, he coached the football team to a championship win, reconstituted a debating society for students called the Wesleyan House of Commons, and he and Ellen added another daughter, Eleanor, to their family. While at Wesleyan, Wilson completed his textbook *The State*. In that book, he denigrated socialism and the "modern industrial organization." On the final full page of his work, he wrote: "In politics, nothing radically novel may safely be attempted. No result of value can ever be reached in politics except through slow and gradual development, the careful adaptations and nice modifications of growth. Nothing may be done by leaps. More than that, each people, each nation, must live upon the lines of its own experience."

The book expanded Wilson's reputation as a scholar, and in the fall of 1890, Princeton University presented him with an offer: to be a professor of law and political economy. It was his dream job. He accepted without hesitation and thrust himself into his new role. In a burst of creative energy, he developed a strong pre-law curriculum and, over the course of the next decade, wrote four books, including *Division and Reunion*. In it, he defended slavery and the treatment of slaves, and at times seemed to be referencing his personal experience. "But the voting population of the southern States was in a sense the most political in the world—the least likely to follow blindly," he wrote. In a chapter called "A Century under the Constitution," he discussed how, by 1889, the country had sewn itself back together, prospering, thanks to electricity and steam, and creating unimaginable individual fortunes for finance, steel, and railroad robber barons. "The growth of wealth throughout the country was unprecedented, marvelous," Wilson noted. "New troubles came, hot conflicts between capital and labor; but the new troubles bred new thinkers, and the intellectual life of the nation was but the more deeply stirred. . . . The century closed with a sense of preparation, a new seriousness, and a new hope." For Wilson—and indeed, America—these ideas were formative ones. The power of big business at the turn of the twentieth century had created hostility among the middle and working classes. Pious intellectuals such as Wilson were developing new concepts that could alter the balance of power, favoring regular people rather than millionaires. Wilson knew that populist policies such as these, central to the Progressive Era, might not only lead to radical change in the nation's economy, but establish a platform from which he could run for elected office.

On a brisk October day in 1902, twelve years after he arrived, trustees named the ambitious professor Princeton University's thirteenth president. The campus was alive with excitement. Vibrant banners billowed from turrets and towers above and the orange and black of the Princeton coat of arms was proudly on display as the school bells pealed. Draped in his academic robe, Wilson was supported by a procession of 1,500 people, including former president of the United States Grover Cleveland and author Mark Twain. The attendees were neither all-male nor all-white. Wilson had invited three female representatives of women's colleges (Wellesley, Mount Holyoke, and Radcliffe), as well as the prominent African American Booker T. Washington, founder of the Tuskegee Normal and Industrial Institute in Alabama. Wilson felt his beliefs aligned with Washington's, with both men agreeing that race relations could gradually improve, though progress could not be forced.

The procession concluded inside Alexander Hall, filled to capacity with spillover outside, as a band played Felix Mendelssohn's march from *Athalie*. Wilson rose to speak and was met with waves of booming cheers. He emphasized that education would have to evolve in order to keep up with the world, then ended on a philosophical note.

> I have studied the history of America. I have seen her grow great in the paths of liberty and of progress by following after great ideals. Every concrete thing that she has done has seemed to rise out of some abstract principle, some vision of the mind. Her greatest victories have been victories of peace and of humanity.

After the speech, Wilson and his guests attended lunch. Washington, believed to be the only black guest at the inauguration, was not invited to join in the meal. He was also segregated from staying with Princeton faculty members on campus and checked into a room at a black boarding house in town.

Wilson's baby steps at inclusiveness sent a confusing message. Was he a progressive? Politically, he was casting himself as one, so much so that in 1909 an African American asked Wilson if he could apply to Princeton. But to Wilson, admitting a black man would be a step too far. "It is altogether inadvisable," he wrote back, "for a colored man to enter Princeton."

As the university's president, Wilson resided at Prospect House, which was only thirty-five miles from where Paul lay recuperating from her time in England. During his eight years as president of Princeton, Wilson gazed beyond the enormous, winter-bare elms, to the iron fence he had installed on the property perimeter—a preventative measure intended to deter unruly students from traipsing across his acres of lawn and trampling the garden that his wife had so thoughtfully redesigned. The garden adorned the stone Italianate mansion, which had views of the southern edge of the Ivy league campus and boasted twenty rooms, high ceilings, a four-story tower, and a porte cochere. This place had shaped him as an undergraduate; it later supported him as a prolific law professor. Princeton was a pivotal component of his foundation and he was intentional about the changes he had brought to the campus since his presidency commenced. There were the physical ones, such as the construction of a lake, a gymnasium, McCosh Hall, Palmer Laboratory, Guyot Hall, and four dormitories: Seventy-Nine, Patton, Campbell, and Holder. And then there were his invisible transformations: revamping Princeton's curriculum, organizing general studies for freshman and sophomores, and concentrating their focus around a major in the last two years, a novel idea he believed would produce more well-rounded graduates. He tightened admission standards, even for well-connected applicants; replaced a fundamentalist biblical instructor with a scholar; ended conservative Presbyterian control over the board of trustees, making the university non-sectarian; and even appointed the first Roman Catholic and Jewish professors to the faculty. In response to growing class sizes—an issue at premier schools nationwide—and in an effort to engage students more in their coursework, Wilson introduced a new preceptor teaching system, hiring forty-five assistant professors to meet regularly with students outside of the monologues of large lectures. In these groups of three to six students, they would discuss reading material, and preceptors would help individuals choose what classes to take, generally serving as undergraduate counselors. By one measure, the program was a success; the number of books borrowed from the library rose sharply. These were significant innovations for not just the campus, but for higher education in general.

At fifty-four years of age, however, although handsome, lean, and tall, Wilson was feeling the pressure of time and struggling with the constraints of governing within such a conservative place, which was home to the privileged few. In fact, Princeton was sarcastically referred to by some as "one of America's finest country clubs." In some ways, it was—bucolically set, still the domain of white men, with neither female nor black students allowed. The only African Americans on campus were those in service jobs, such as the waiters at the Alligators Eating Club, where Wilson had been a member as an undergraduate.

Eating clubs had developed in response to the fact that the school neither allowed fraternities nor provided dining services.

But now, as Wilson saw it, the clubs had become snobby cloisters, excluding those from lower classes, or anyone who was not a white Anglo-Saxon Protestant. In effect, they were daily reminders of the vast income inequality of the Gilded Age, the defining decades of Wilson's early adulthood. He wanted to replace the eating clubs with "quadrangles," random mixes of upperclassmen and sophomores who lived and ate together. While the trustees initially approved Wilson's quadrangle plan, alumni and powerful donors—mostly from New York and Philadelphia—vehemently opposed his proposal. The backlash caused contributions to the endowment to fall and the board withdrew their approval.

The stress of this defeat sent Wilson reeling. He wrote a letter to his daughter Jessie, saying "it is most humiliating; and I have not yet seen my way to the next step I should take." But even stringing these sen-

Wilson (middle row, third from right), at the Alligators Eating Club at Princeton, circa 1879.

tences together was a challenge. Wilson noticed that his right arm was painful and numb. It wasn't the first time that stress seemed to trigger this strange malady. But on this occasion, it was so bad, he could hardly hold a pen. He tried to ignore the problem.

Wilson retreated from the eating club battle only to face a new controversy. He wanted a campus that was not divided by status. But the dean of the graduate school, Andrew West, wanted the program housed in a remote location so his students would not be distracted by those "unruly" undergrads. Wilson insisted that the graduate college be located at the center of campus, preferably near Prospect House, so that all students would have a natural opportunity to interact, broadening their academic and social understanding. These opposing views divided the university, alumni, donors, and the board of trustees.

The graduate school battle had touched on a national issue about society's stratification, coming into conflict with Wilson's own progressive ideals. It seemed as if the rest of the country understood better than he that while building new dormitories or changing the curriculum was challenging, it was nothing like trying to evolve cultural norms involving status and power. His campus efforts had now become national news. On one cold morning, Wilson put on his trademark pince-nez glasses to read the *New York Times.* His gray eyes scanned the headlines and landed on an editorial titled: "Princeton."

> The nation is aroused against special privilege. . . . The question at Princeton is not simply of locating a new building for the Graduate College. [It's about] . . . fostering mutually exclusive social cliques, stolid groups of wealth and fashion, devoted to non-essentials and the smatterings of culture. All the college Presidents have cried out against this stultifying influence, and none more earnestly than President Woodrow Wilson of Princeton.

Wilson may have been pleased by the *Times'* endorsement, but shortly after it was published, a Princeton alumnus passed away, bequeathing millions of dollars to build West's vision for a graduate school and dooming Wilson's plan.

"The game is up," Wilson said. "We've beaten the living, but we can't fight the dead."

Although he tried to apply new ideas to student life, radically transforming one of America's oldest colleges both physically and academically, Wilson was exhausted by academia's recalcitrance, having been defeated any time he tried to alter the power structure on campus. He'd had enough of it, even joking that he was considering leaving Princeton for a role that was less political: public office.

With so much to think about, Wilson arranged for some time away from the university with his family. They booked a trip to an artists' colony in Old Lyme, Connecticut, called the Florence Griswold House, a magnet for American impressionists, where Ellen could paint. Within days of their arrival, Wilson discovered his path forward. He found Ellen and the girls in their quarters and he rested on a steamer trunk to deliver the news: two New Jersey party bosses had tracked him down and requested that he accept the nomination for governor of their state. New Jersey politics were especially dirty, sullied with kickbacks and patronage jobs. The Democratic Party needed someone who could run on an anti-corruption platform at a time when voters were demanding more reform, not just in government but in all aspects of society. They told him the role "will inevitably lead to the Presidency." The Wilson women knew how long he had dreamed of becoming a government leader, with the autonomy to practice his academic ideas about how the American system of democracy should function. They gave him their support and he accepted the nomination without hesitation.

Despite his upbringing, his voluminous writings documenting his narrow views about states' rights, and the devotion of so much of his life to a staid institution, Wilson decided to run for governor as a progressive Democrat. Perhaps he truly considered himself an agent of change given his achievements at Princeton. However, a more cynical observer could maintain that Wilson knew there was no other way he would ever be elected to a major office, a dream he'd held his whole life.

Regardless, his political strategy proved successful when, in November 1910, voters elected Wilson governor of New Jersey by a wide margin. Given his extensive knowledge of government and politics, Wilson accomplished some major reforms within his first few months in office. He worked with the legislature to pass a law that required candidates to file financial statements, limited campaign expenditures, and outlawed corporate contributions to political campaigns. He pushed through a worker's compensation act to help families of those killed or injured on the job, and then he signed a law regulating utility rates. He held daily press conferences while the legislature was in session, something no other governor had done before in that state. And he campaigned against a U.S. Senate bid by James Smith Jr., New Jersey's longtime political boss who had helped elect Wilson governor. Smith served as a Democratic senator in Congress from 1893 to 1899. During that term, Smith had fought to raise the tariff on sugar while secretly buying up stock in sugar companies. Wilson did not believe Smith deserved another term in the Senate, and his voice helped defeat him.

With these stunning populist wins as fodder for a speaking circuit, Wilson toured America, effectively campaigning for president of the United States without yet declaring his candidacy for the 1912 election. During a speech in Indiana, he revealed a far more progressive conclusion about government than he ever would have printed in one of his own textbooks, saying he did "not find the problems of 1911 solved in the Declaration of Independence." He affirmed that the world had changed since the days of Thomas Jefferson, and today, America grappled with corporate greed and social stratification. "Monopoly, private control, the authority of privilege, [and] the concealed mastery of a few men, cunning enough to rule without showing their power . . . law in our day must come to the assistance of the individual." No one was more aware than Wilson that these newly adopted and expressly working-class views were in direct conflict with his earlier writings and opinions about government and immigration. He was so concerned about being exposed as a fraud that he asked his publisher if he could amend certain anti-immigrant sections of volume five of his *History of the American People*, published in 1902, in which he wrote about "the multitudes of men of the meaner sort out of Hungary and Poland, men out of the ranks where there was neither skill nor energy nor any initiative of quick intelligence."

On June 25, 1912, twenty thousand Democrats crammed into the sweltering Fifth Regiment Armory in Maryland for their national convention to choose a presidential candidate from a long list of prospects. In addition to Wilson, the other men included the governors of Massachusetts, North Dakota, Connecticut, Indiana, and Ohio and Speaker of the House Champ Clark, the front-runner from Missouri. Delegates voted repeatedly, but no tallies showed Wilson in the lead. Yet Wilson's supporters refused to let him lose to lesser men. As Wilson waited for news at Sea Girt, the governor's mansion by the Jersey shore, over the course of six days, his backers orchestrated behind-the-scenes deals while a circus-like atmosphere developed outside the venue, with food vendors and growing crowds. Finally, after the forty-sixth ballot, they called Wilson with the good news: he had received a total of 990 votes, enough to earn him the win. Stunned, Wilson rushed into the house to find Ellen and share his success. When he did this, an aide leapt outside onto the porch, waving his arms to coax a brass band—discreetly on standby—from the bushes to perform "Hail to the Chief."

While Wilson's Democratic nomination for president of the United States was hard fought, the final leg of the 1912 campaign was no less chaotic. He ran on the platform of The New Freedom, which included a vision for limited government but also lowering tariffs, busting monopolies, and reforming the banking system—economic reforms that would benefit regular people.

President William Howard Taft, a Republican, was running for reelection despite having lost the confidence of party leaders such as Theodore Roosevelt. Roosevelt, who had already served as president from 1901 to 1909 and had helped Taft win the White House, challenged Taft for the nomination because he now thought he was too conservative. When Roosevelt did not succeed at the GOP convention, he launched a third party, the Progressives, and set out on the campaign trail. Roosevelt was in favor of woman suffrage; Wilson and Taft were not.

A few weeks before the national election, Roosevelt was in Milwaukee when a mentally ill man shot him in the chest, precisely where his fifty-page stump speech was folded over twice in his pocket along with a metal case for his glasses; the bulk saved his life. When reporters later asked Roosevelt how he was feeling, he said he was as fit as a "Bull Moose," a term the press used as a synonym for the Progressive Party campaign.

In the end, the Republicans were too badly fractured and Wilson walked away with nearly 60 percent of the vote.

CHAPTER FIVE

The Suffrage Procession

T he Wilsons finished their final breakfast at the dining table in the governor's large Tudor house at 25 Cleveland Lane in Princeton. It was March 3, 1913, moving day. Woodrow Wilson made sure that his new scarf pin, decorated with the presidential seal, was safely tucked somewhere on his person. He was superstitious, always had been, and wanted a talisman to wear during his inauguration and as long as he remained in office, just as he had done in his previous roles, wearing a Princeton coat of arms and the seal of the State of New Jersey. Ready to bid the campus farewell, the family gathered out front. The group included the president-elect; Ellen; their three daughters, Margaret, Jessie, and Eleanor; Wilson's brother-in-law Stockton Axson; two Secret Service agents; and three servants. They stood in front of several hundred undergraduates who had gathered to sing them off with their university song, "Old Nassau," complete with hat-tipping hand gestures during the chorus. Wilson sang along, his emotions making his voice tremble through the words:

> *Tune every harp and every voice,*
> *Bid every care withdraw;*
> *Let all with one accord rejoice,*
> *In praise of old Nassau.*

In praise of old Nassau, my boys,
Hurrah! hurrah! hurrah!
Her sons will give while they shall live,
Three cheers for old Nassau.

Afterward, the family posed for photographs. Wilson looked especially polished because he had made the decision to remove a prominent
mole from the middle of his forehead—a cosmetic adjustment widely
noted in the press coverage of the dashing new president. The family
and its entourage piled into a parade of cars, but Wilson and his wife
decided to walk a mile to Princeton Station, making a slight detour
past their old house at Library Lane to see it one last time. When they
arrived at the station, there were many well-wishers gathered, waving
and cheering. They shook as many hands as time would allow before
boarding a reserved Pullman car. The eight other attached train cars
were packed with reporters and students. Wilson held on to the Pullman's exterior rail, his overcoat open to the winds, as the town paid
homage with Princeton's Tiger roar.

"Great cheering," Wilson said, as a few tears slid down his cheeks. "I
wish that I could give as good a cheer in response."

He raised his silk top hat to say good-bye.

The conductor signaled departure with a wave of his arm and the
train pulled away, as the remaining crowd began to sing:

Here's to you, Woodrow Wilson;
Here's to you, my jovial son.
And we'll drink before we part the sacred company;
We'll drink before we part.
Here's to you, Woodrow Wilson.

Inside the car, Wilson was crowded by newspaper correspondents,
commenting on his dandy hat and quizzing him about his potential
cabinet. The president-elect deflected these questions. The train slowed
as it passed through Trenton, where Wilson caught a glimpse of his
former gubernatorial stenographer tearfully waving to him from the

platform. He waved back through the window. The train soon arrived at its first stop, Philadelphia, where Wilson's sister Annie boarded with her daughter, her sixteen-month-old granddaughter, and the baby's nanny.

As his train continued south toward Washington's Union Station, the U.S. Capitol was preparing not just for Wilson's inauguration as the twenty-eighth president (and first Democrat to move into the White House in twenty years), but for another event, unlike anything the city had ever seen before: a massive suffrage procession, timed to coincide with Wilson's arrival, expected at 3:45 p.m. The platforms and public areas were crowded with those arriving on "Suffragette Specials" from cities near and far; thousands of women, dressed in white and colorful capes, planned to participate in the protest.

Wilson was aware the suffragists were planning a large demonstration. The papers had been reporting on it for months. But he had no idea what to expect. As New Jersey receded behind him to the clacking soundtrack of the train, the one thing he was certain of was that he was about to fulfill a dream and bear a great responsibility by becoming president of the United States.

■ ■ ■

In Washington, the morning was clear and frosty, about twenty-seven degrees with a forecast of rising temperatures. Despite the cold start, the plans that Alice Paul and UK associate Lucy Burns had set in motion three months earlier were coming to fruition. The two women had joined the National American Woman Suffrage Association (NAWSA, commonly called "The National" or the "National American"), the organization that Susan B. Anthony oversaw until she died in 1906. Now led by Anna Howard Shaw, NAWSA's strategy focused on changing the law at the state level as opposed to the federal level because it assumed a federal amendment would be impossible to achieve. Paul and Burns were more optimistic. As new, high-profile members of NAWSA renowned for their suffrage work in England, the women had a reputation. Some NAWSA members respected them for it, while others did not want to be associated with their militant ideas and actions. The two women asked Shaw if they could try a more aggressive strategy to lobby for a federal amendment; they wanted to form a committee dedicated to the cause within the organization.

Burns was especially convincing; it was one of her talents. She was a sophisticated public speaker, no doubt influenced by her life experiences: growing up in an Irish household in Brooklyn; attending upper-crust schools such as Vassar, Yale, and Oxford; living abroad; studying at the University of Berlin; and traveling with the Pankhursts throughout England and Scotland. As a friend described her, "Miss Burns is in appearance the very symbol of woman in revolt . . . appealing, persuading—she could move the most resistant person. Her talent as an orator is of the kind that makes for instant intimacy with her audience. Her emotional quality is so powerful that her intellectual capacity, which is quite as great, is not always at once perceived."

The first major act that Paul and Burns had pitched was an enormous protest, bigger and more beautiful than anything the country had ever seen, and deliberately timed to coincide with Wilson's inauguration. Shaw, certainly aware of the women's work in Britain, was skeptical. But after listening to their idea, she agreed to what they all euphemistically referred to as a "procession."

With only three months between the inception of their bold idea and its execution on the day before Wilson's inauguration, in January 1913, Paul and Burns established the Congressional Committee headquarters in a storefront at 1420 F Street in Washington. It was in close proximity to both the White House and the Quaker boarding house in which the two women had adjoining rooms.

The headquarters was composed of three small rooms—one of them Paul's office—and a central space, their base of operations, with the capacity to seat around 130 people. This main room was lit by large windows overlooking the city sidewalk, where pedestrians often paused to gawk at the activity inside. As the space was not well heated, Paul wore her hat and coat indoors during these winter months, working elbow to elbow with busy volunteers. The suffrage signage that framed the storefront windows had drawn the curiosity of so many in recent weeks that Paul had stationed greeters near the door to welcome guests and put them to work.

The first headquarters of NAWSA's Congressional Committee in Washington, D.C., at 1420 F Street.

On the morning of the procession, Paul and Burns rose early, as usual, and hastened over to headquarters. From there, Paul set out to check on preparations and walk the route in reverse. Up and down the avenue, she saw patriotic decorations of red, white, and blue competing with the "gaudy violet, white and green of the suffrage advocates clamoring for recognition," as one skeptical newspaper described the scene. Spectators wanting front-row seats to watch the women's parade had begun filling up the grandstands. This bold exercise had not been cheap; the costumes, floats, and flags cost an intimidating $14,000. NAWSA had refused to help fund an event that filled them with such doubt. "It will have no direct bearing on suffrage itself," Shaw wrote Paul. In the absence of this financial support, an undeterred Paul launched an aggressive fundraising campaign to cover the bills. She struck a profit-sharing deal with the inaugural grandstand contractor, who was selling tickets ranging from two to five dollars. And she was happy to see so many people buying not just seats but her printed program, a colorful twenty-page handout that explained the reason for the march:

We ask that the newly elected Congress and Administration shall hasten to do their part in removing this ancient sex discrimination. We ask that this be done immediately upon the convening of Congress. There is no other issue facing the new Congress and the new Administration comparable to this in importance.

We march today to give evidence to the world of our determination that this simple act of justice shall be done. We march that the world may realize that, save in [suffrage] states, the newly elected President has been chosen by only one half of the people. We march in a spirit of protest against the present political organization of society, from which women are excluded.

As she progressed past the route's storefronts, Paul noticed jewelers had cleared their wares to make floor space for indoor viewing; a place to witness history was more precious than diamonds on this day. Boarding houses facing the path of the procession were selling rooms for $50 per day, about $1,200 in today's economy, with a four-day minimum.

Paul soaked up the scene. Vendors of every kind were peddling food, mementos, and bold ideas. The smell of coffee and hot dogs wafted temptation through the streets and "lusty-lunged women," as the press had dubbed them, gave impromptu suffrage speeches on street corners. Girls sold Votes for Women pamphlets and papers. Others hawked fifteen-cent bouquets of violets. Those preferring to capitalize on the inaugural excitement offered replicas of Wilson's blackboard pointer.

As Paul neared the starting point, the din escalated with the clip-clop of police horses and shouting spectators. "Votes for Women!" a suffragist yelled. "Tell your troubles to Woodrow," a man retorted. Soldiers and sailors sarcastically cheered as suffragists walked to the staging area and then laughed behind their backs. The visual elements also engaged in competition: ladies carrying "Votes for Women" pennants versus males with "Votes for Men" signs—or raunchier versions; one featured miniature "trousers patched where patches usually are, with two brilliant yellow spots on which appeared 'Votes for Women.'"

In an effort to contain the crowds, the sewer department employees had hung five miles of rope tied to white posts to cordon the length of Pennsylvania Avenue. It stretched from the procession starting point—the Peace Monument in front of the U.S. Capitol—all the way to the conclusion at the mall behind the White House. However, no ropes could contain the growing tension in the city, now bloated with a record half a million visitors, a combustible mix of suffragists, their supporters and detractors, agitators, the curious in search of entertainment, and Wilson voters who mostly fell into the latter two categories. People ignored the boundaries and engulfed the streets. Paul began to worry. Police Chief Richard Sylvester had called in reinforcements from other cities and hired female detectives to bait any men looking for prostitutes. Yet even this collaborative force could not keep the mob behind the ropes.

Paul reached the Peace Monument and joined the gathering parade vanguard. Although the procession would not begin until three in the afternoon, they had scheduled this assembly for noon to allow the necessary time to organize the elaborate, deliberate flow of seven sections, each with color-coded costumes, full of symbolism and allegory, representing various time periods, issues, and constituencies. Throughout the planning, Paul had stressed that the event needed to exude dignity and poise to counteract the cultural assumption that it was unladylike for women to be out walking on their own. She wanted the procession to show strength and intelligence, to remind the audience how hard women work, not just at home, but in factories, schools, and on farms.

The inclusion of all races was another priority. Paul had specifically invited black women to participate and she encouraged volunteers to do the same. But when word spread throughout the organizers that many African American women planned to join the procession, some white suffragists expressed concern. "We ought to be intelligent enough to avoid a race war," one volunteer, Mary Beard, wrote to Paul. "This is a perfect nightmare to me." Beard was worried that with so many southerners attending the inauguration, an integrated march could provoke violence. Even many planning to march—northerners and southerners alike—did not want black women walking beside them. Paul considered these factors and changed course, explaining her views to the editor of *Woman's Journal*.

"I am a Northern woman and have never lived in the South," she wrote. "Moreover, I belong to a Quaker family which has always taken a stand for the rights of the negro and all of the traditions of my family and the influence of my home are such as to make me predisposed to side with, and not against, the negro in any question of racial difference. I hope, therefore, that I am viewing this present question with an unbiased mind." Paul went on to explain in her note that black women would be scattered among the northern and Quaker groups in the parade. The goal, she reminded the editor, was to win voting rights so that all women would benefit. Now that it was the day of the parade, Paul surveyed the crowd and hoped everything would go smoothly.

A tall brunette with a star-tipped tiara on her head swung her leg over a white horse named Gray Dawn and took her position as the symbolic figure of the procession. She was a striking sight, wearing white kid boots and a pale blue cloak adorned with a cross on the back. Paul had chosen the woman, twenty-seven-year-old Inez Milholland, as the parade herald and placed her not just in the saddle but on the program cover for a reason. More than just a pretty face, she was a true suffragist. The wealthy daughter of the inventor of a pneumatic tube system, Milholland had grown up in the United States and London, where she was influenced by the Pankhursts' activity. She attended Vassar, organizing suffrage meetings on campus, and, after completing her studies there, Harvard, Yale, and Cambridge all denied her law school admission because she was a woman. She earned her law degree from New York University and opened a legal practice devoted to women and striking laborers. Paul understood that Milholland's beauty could counter public perception that the suffrage movement lacked femininity, youth, and respectability.

Milholland was thrilled that Paul had asked her to participate in the procession and wrote to Burns that her role should suggest "the free woman of the future, crowned with the star of hope, armed with the cross of mercy, circled with the blue mantle of freedom, breasted with

Inez Milholland prepares to lead the suffrage parade.

the torch of knowledge and carrying the trumpet which is to herald the
dawn of a new day of heroic endeavor of womanhood."

She looked as statuesque as the neoclassical figures on the Peace
Monument, with its marble depiction of Grief weeping on the shoulder
of History, holding a tablet inscribed, "They died that their country
might live."

Half an hour later than planned, Grand Marshal Jane Burleson
gave the signal from on top of her horse and the procession of about
eight thousand women began to march. Two police cars carved a clear
path ahead of the front line. Milholland blew her horn and trotted
her horse slowly as the crowd, bustling with agitated men, closed in
behind her.

The first section of the parade featured the officers of NAWSA.
There was Margaret Foley, carrying a large "Votes for Women" flag;
Mary Frances Farquhar, carrying an American flag; and a float trimmed
with a special banner, making its debut: WE DEMAND AN AMENDMENT
TO THE UNITED STATES CONSTITUTION ENFRANCHISING WOMEN OF THIS
COUNTRY.

The suffrage procession.

The procession moved with reasonable ease and order for a couple of blocks. At Fourth Street, a Massachusetts National Guard regiment provided some assistance in clearing the way. By Sixth Street, the police were so overwhelmed and the street so suffocated, marchers could only push forward in pairs. A group of female college students locked arms to form a crowd-breaking plow. Burleson could barely move her horse forward. Behind her, Milholland was suffering the same struggle but was able to encourage Gray Dawn to plod along. The police were ineffective; their chief was at Union Station, waiting for Wilson to arrive from New Jersey.

The next section of the parade featured women in traditional dress, representing countries with full suffrage: Norway, Finland, New Zealand, and Australia. Then came countries with partial women's suffrage: Sweden, Denmark, Iceland, Great Britain, Austria-Hungary, and Belgium. WOMEN OF THE WORLD UNITE, their banner read.

A series of floats followed. One depicted the first women's rights convention in Seneca Falls in 1840. Another cluster of floats staged vignettes, demonstrating how women contributed to society on the farm, in the

WOMEN REPRESENTING FOREIGN COUNTRIES SUFFRAGETTE'S PARADE MARCH 3 -1913 -WASHINGTON-D-C

The foreign country section.

home, in the military, education, law, medicine, labor, and government, but were not treated with respect. The college section featured one thousand females in their academic robes—Paul among them, too humble to march up front with NAWSA leadership—holding banners for Swarthmore, Bryn Mawr, Vassar, Wellesley, Smith, Goucher, George Washington, Radcliffe, Michigan, and Cornell. Howard, a historically black college founded after the Civil War, was also represented, with a contingent of nearly forty women of color. Most of them were members of the Delta Sigma Theta sorority, founded the previous month for the purpose of joining the march.

Women of color also mixed within the labor section, portraying massive wage inequality. THE TOLL OF WOMEN HELPS TO MAKE THE NATION RICH, one banner emphasized. A float carried dirty, disheveled women and children bending over sewing machines. There was a section for state delegations, including a place for the senators and representatives from the nine suffrage states, though only a few attended. Those who were there included Senator Miles Poindexter of Washington, Senator John Shafroth of Colorado, and Representative Victor Murdock of Kansas, all with their female secretaries.

The college section of the suffrage parade.

Paul deliberately arranged the thirty-nine non-suffrage states be-hind this group in alphabetical order, beginning with Alabama and ending with Wisconsin. In the middle of this lineup was the Illinois contingent, a group of sixty-five that included Ida B. Wells, a prom-inent African American journalist who, years before, had exposed the widespread horror of lynching and had sued the railroad successfully for not letting her sit in the women's car. She had also helped found the National Association for the Advancement of Colored People in 1909. While the march was a shocking and radical act, the likes of which had never occurred in America, racially integrating the procession was even more so, and it almost did not happen. Earlier in the day, when the Illinois women lined up for a practice drill, their leader, Grace Wilbur Trout, saw Wells and questioned whether she should be there. Her racist comment shocked the group, sending a buzz through the crowd; some were so embarrassed they were speechless.

Trout explained herself by saying "many of the eastern and southern women have greatly resented the fact that there are to be colored women in the delegations. Some have even gone so far as to say they will not march if negro women are allowed to take part." She blamed the decision on the leader of the National, as well as on Alice Paul. Trout looked around for approval and found some. But another suffragist, Virginia Brooks, came to the defense of Wells.

"We have come here to march for equal rights," Brooks said, adding that "if the women of other states lack moral courage, we should show that we are not afraid of public opinion."

Wells was deeply hurt by Trout's remarks and let slip two large tears, which she wiped from beneath her veil.

Alice Paul in her march costume, an academic robe adorned with the prison door pin, known as the "Holloway Brooch," which the Pankhursts gave her.

"If the Illinois women do not take a stand now in this great democratic parade then the colored women are lost," Wells said before storming off. At some point after the procession began, Wells jumped back into the Illinois delegation to march in her rightful place, while black women also marched with the Delaware, New York, West Virginia, and Michigan sections. There was one group, however, that was segregated in the back. When word spread that Mary Church Terrell, a prominent African American, would lead a strong showing of the National Association of Colored Women and that southerners threated a boycott, the men's section offered to march between these black and white groups.

The procession forced its way forward—the twenty-five-piece Missouri Ladies Military Band, the "Petticoat Cavalry," close behind them—charging toward those trying to impede progress. Another woman on a horse struck a man with her riding crop after he shouted a "scurrilous remark" at her. The closing section of the parade carried its identifying banner: NATIONAL MEN'S LEAGUE FOR EQUAL SUFFRAGE. They, too, were harassed. "Henpecko," the crowd shouted at the men who were marching. "Where are your skirts?"

CHAPTER SIX

Where Are All the People?

As soon as Inez Milholland rode into view on her steed, the women standing at the top of the broad steps of the U.S. Treasury Building took it as their cue to begin their performance. With "The Star-Spangled Banner" as their background music, they emerged from behind towering granite columns dressed as allegorical feminine symbols, lead by the commanding figure of Columbia, the female embodiment of America, adorned in national colors. Columbia, Justice, Charity, Liberty, Peace, and Hope, dressed in purple and scarlet robes and scarves, danced for the crowd.

By now, the procession participants below on Pennsylvania Avenue had to lean in, fighting their way into a headwind of humanity that had clustered densely at the foot of the Treasury. Alice Paul began to panic about the chaos. She, Lucy Burns, and committee chairs Glenna Tinnin and Patricia Street jumped into cars to more easily monitor the mayhem, inching their way up to the front. Street stood on a running board with a megaphone asking police for help and begging people to "stand aside." When a man spit on a marcher, Street pled with a policeman to protect the assaulted woman.

"There would be nothing like this happening if you stayed home," the officer told her.

Paul left the car to personally push people behind the ropes. All around her, men cursed, shoved, pushed, slapped, hooted, and jeered

The Treasury Tableau.

at the marchers while the police barely lifted a finger to intervene.

Women were separated from their assigned places in the procession lineup. Some marchers burst into tears, some fainted, fell, or were trampled. One woman told her neighbors to use their hat pins in self-defense. In refreshing contrast, some Boy Scouts intervened to protect women near the back. But the ordeal was too much for some. Helen Keller, the deaf-blind political activist who was part of the procession and scheduled to address the participants later in the day, left the event early. This was a failure so upsetting to Paul that she later offered to personally reimburse Keller for the trip.

Keller was not the only important person impeded from watching from a safe place. Vice President–elect Thomas Marshall and his wife, Lois, unable to penetrate the surging crowd, could not reach their grandstand seats from which they'd intended to watch the procession. And First Lady Nellie Taft, despite having successfully settled into the grandstand with other White House guests before the rush, was so offended by the lewdness of some men in front that she left before the procession reached her vantage point.

The police chief, still waiting at Union Station for President-elect

The mob closes in on the suffrage parade, March 3, 1913.

Woodrow Wilson to arrive, got word that men were attacking the suffragists and finally called in the U.S. Cavalry.

Just as the Cavalry activated, Wilson's train chugged into Union Station. As he stepped from the railcar onto the platform, about five hundred students from Princeton held their hats across their hearts and formed two silent lines, creating an aisle to lead the president-elect into the quiet station. A special inaugural welcoming committee, comprised of men in high hats from the military, Congress, and several churches, was also there to greet them.

President Taft had sent touring cars and chauffeurs to drive the Wilsons to the Shoreham Hotel under a two-motorcycle escort. As the group walked from the station to the cars, Princeton men wearing orange-and-black pins lined the way and gave the college cry. Wilson smiled back, lifted his hat, and helped his wife into the car. His daughters piled into another vehicle. Around them was a "small but vociferous" group of supporters who "made up in noise what they lacked in numbers," according to the next day's *New York Times* report.

The cars took a roundabout route to get to the hotel, down an eerily deserted, unadorned Massachusetts Avenue, to H Street and then Fifteenth Street, avoiding the suffragists. Few people even noticed the motorcade.

"Where are all the people?" Wilson asked as he peered out the car window.

"On the Avenue, watching the suffrage parade."

By now, it was about 4:30 in the afternoon and the Cavalry was beginning to advance. They arrived just as the procession leaders neared the Treasury. Those in the viewing stands erupted in cheers as the Cavalry formed two lines to charge the crowd and push them toward the sidewalks. The horses reared up and whipped around. Some mounted police swung clubs. The people retreated—but success was spotty and temporary.

Milholland, shouting and waving her free hand, helped the others on horseback to force the crowd back further still. Police then used cars to try to stave off the flow of humanity, but it was like plugging a dike with one finger while leaks sprung out of reach. The thinnest of passageways opened down the middle of Pennsylvania Avenue and the procession trickled through. The marchers did not lash out, but many began to quit when the mob turned vicious, dragging women out of the lineup, assaulting emergency medics, tearing badges from police, and even fighting with each other. An ambulance, a car, and a horse-drawn carriage struggled to make their way through. Emergency workers responded to more than fifty calls, ranging from women who were overcome with exhaustion to those who were seriously injured. Over the course of six hours, about one hundred people were injured—none fatally. The police made no arrests.

The procession was designed to be a dignified and educational call for women's voting rights, but had devolved into an unmanageable, enormous, frightening, frustrating, and, at times, violent event—the largest of its kind in American history.

The crowds at the suffrage parade were so unruly that ambulances could not pass.

Approximately two thousand suffragists completed the procession, just a quarter of those who began it. Exhausted, they made their way to a pre-planned rally at Memorial Continental Hall, just two blocks from the White House with a view of the Washington Monument. The new white-stone building, its portico consisting of thirteen columns—one for each of the original colonies—was constructed as the headquarters of the Daughters of the American Revolution. The multilevel auditorium was a grand space with box seats, crowned with American eagles, their wings outstretched. Weary suffragists sank into every available seat until the building was at capacity and many marchers had to be turned away.

The gathering was originally intended to be a celebration of the day and its participants; it was meant to acknowledge and inspire. Instead, speakers focused on the police's failure to maintain order, stoking the burning outrage in order to generate more sympathy for their cause. Paul, perpetually reverential to the movement's elders, retreated into the background while others took to the stage.

"I was never so proud in my life," Anna Howard Shaw told the audience. "I never was so thankful to be one of your members and I never was so ashamed at our national capital as I am tonight. A faltering suffragist will never falter again after the exhibition today of the methods to which the anti-suffragists will stoop. If anything was needed to prove that the women need the ballot, the occurrences of today and the treatment received by us in the Capital of the nation would be ample. . . . Come what may, nothing shall deter us until we can compel the Congress to protect us as it will protect the men tomorrow. We were told we must not vote because women across the sea are unable to control themselves," she said, referring to the British suffragettes. "We are told American men do not treat women as Englishmen treat their women. But men are men the world over and their domination differs only in degree. In closing, I want to say that we will come down to Washington on next inauguration day and be protected as American citizens should be. Ten more states will impress the party in power more than any bill of rights."

The hall erupted in "three cheers for the women!"

Before leaving, National American Woman Suffrage Association (NAWSA) leadership agreed on a plan to fan the outrage over crowd interference. Shaw issued a statement to the press, charging not only the police but the "whole official government" in Washington with making a determined effort to mar the success of the parade because they were annoyed it interfered with Wilson's inaugural. Their plan worked.

■ ■ ■

The next morning, on Inauguration Day, Wilson woke up in Washington's Shoreham Hotel and scanned the papers, which were blaring headlines sympathetic to the suffragists. The *Chicago Tribune* summed it up well: "Hoodlums vs. Gentlewomen." The *New-York Tribune* said the lack of crowd control was a "disgrace to the Capitol" and called for an investigation. The press also praised the procession. The *Washington Star* called Pennsylvania Avenue a "battlefield captured by Amazons." Kept away by meetings and social obligations, Wilson had missed the entire affair.

Now it was time for him to head to the White House to meet with

President Taft. Ellen felt unwell and stayed behind to rest until she was needed at his inaugural address. Princeton students wearing orange sashes lined the route as Wilson rode in an open carriage pulled by two horses. Later it was still overcast when the president-elect arrived at the Capitol, put his hand on Ellen's Bible, took the oath of office, and then stood at a podium in front of a hundred thousand people to deliver his speech.

"There can be no equality or opportunity, the first essential of justice in the body politic, if men and women and children be not shielded in their lives, their very vitality, from the consequences of great industrial and social processes which they cannot alter, control, or singly cope with," he told America. "Society must see to it that it does not itself crush or weaken or damage its own constituent parts. . . . Sanitary laws, pure food laws, and laws determining conditions of labor which individuals are powerless to determine for themselves are intimate parts of the very business of justice and legal efficiency."

While he spoke on topics that appealed to the masses, suffragists passed out handbills urging people to complain to their elected officials about the lack of security during the procession. The pressure worked; Congress immediately called for an investigation.

By March 6, a Senate subcommittee began interviewing witnesses, including Paul, and grilled Police Chief Sylvester for two days. Although the inquiry found that the police acted with "more or less indifference," there was insufficient evidence to blame any individual. Sylvester was exonerated, which only stoked the suffragists' outrage. The outcome produced so many protest meetings, petitions, and resolutions around the country that *Woman's Journal* said it was impossible to count them all.

Where the authorities failed, Paul succeeded. Her procession pleased Shaw because it successfully drove more women to the cause, as measured in NAWSA membership. Yet Shaw wasn't entirely content because she felt threatened by this young activist and the influence Paul could have within the suffrage movement, as well as in the public domain. More emboldened than ever, Paul was becoming a powerful force. Just how powerful, Wilson and Shaw were about to discover.

CHAPTER SEVEN

In the Oval Office

Nearly two weeks after the suffrage procession, Alice Paul and her work remained front-page news. But Paul knew that generating sympathy for her cause was not enough; she needed to capitalize on it. And so she scheduled a face-to-face meeting with President Woodrow Wilson.

Paul carefully curated a group of women from National American Woman Suffrage Association (NAWSA) to go with her, choosing each suffragist for her particular political muscle. There was Anna Kelton Wiley of Washington, D.C., president of the Housekeepers' Alliance, which had a strong membership; Ida Husted Harper, a pioneering journalist and biographer of Susan B. Anthony; Genevieve Stone, the wife of Illinois Democratic congressman Claude Stone; and Mary Bartlett Dixon of Baltimore, a cousin of another Democratic congressman, A. Mitchell Palmer of Pennsylvania, who was one of Wilson's most trusted lieutenants in the House.

The women met at the F Street suffrage headquarters and formed their own tiny procession down Pennsylvania Avenue toward the White House. Suffragists had never taken their cause directly to the Oval Office. Nervous but unyielding when they arrived at 1600 Pennsylvania Avenue, they entered through the front gates without any fuss. In fact, in his first days as president, Wilson had established an unprecedented and literal open-door policy in the executive branch, allowing the press and the public to observe officials at work in their White House offices.

The idea was a bold effort to make the government more accessible and transparent, a practice he'd brought with him from New Jersey. Two days before this meeting with Paul, Wilson had invited 125 journalists into his office for the first-ever White House press briefing.

The women were shown to the Oval Office. It was an all-green room with vibrant green sea grass walls, a rug of the same color, and coordinating drapes with eagle valances. The room had a fireplace with candelabras at one end and the presidential desk at the other. The women took their seats, which had already been arranged—five chairs in a row, with one in front, like a classroom—and gathered their thoughts as they waited for the president to arrive and fill the empty spot. Paul had much to reflect on. After all, Wilson had been governor of her home state, but she had not had the right to vote for him when he was running for that office. And now, as her president he had even more power over the thing she wanted most: suffrage.

The atmosphere was tense as the president strolled into the Oval Office and took his seat. Wilson could sense their unease.

"Don't be nervous," he said.

Paul introduced herself and her colleagues and, always forthright, immediately got to the point.

"Suffrage is the paramount issue of the day," she told him. "When you speak to Congress at the opening of the special session, we'd like you to consider talking about an amendment to the Federal Constitution giving women equal suffrage with men throughout the United States." One-ninth of the House of Representatives were chosen in part by the several million women in the nine states that had granted women the right to vote.

Wiley picked up the conversation from Paul.

"Mothers need the vote in order to control the future of their children," she said. Wiley explained that women were behind many humanitarian reforms that he supported, including the Pure Food and Drug Act of 1906, a hallmark of the Progressive Era that banned misbranded, poisonous, or deleterious foods, drugs, medicines, and liquors.

Wilson listened politely as Wiley ceded to Stone, who spoke for the women of the West, the region that pioneered voting rights for women.

She talked about how challenging it can be to pass suffrage at the state level—but that those states that had were reaping benefits, attracting women to sparsely populated areas, rewarding politically those in power who gave women the vote, or even helping to fill juries. Those states that didn't pass suffrage would struggle.

The women then turned to Husted, who cracked open Wilson's just-published book *The New Freedom*, a collection of his presidential campaign speeches from the previous year. She read his words out loud: "I don't want a smug lot of experts to sit down behind closed doors in Washington and play Providence to me. I will not live under trustees if I can help it. If any part of our people want to be wards, if they want to have guardians put over them, if they want to be children patronized by the government, I am sorry for them, because it will sap the manhood of America."

Their words washed over Wilson, who sat stiffly. Husted explained to him that Susan B. Anthony had asked President Theodore Roosevelt to recognize the suffrage cause in vain, and that women had asked the same of the following president, William Howard Taft. Couldn't he do better than the two Republicans who had preceded him?

As her question hung in the air, Dixon found her opening in the conversation. She said she wanted to speak for the women of the South. "The Republicans," she said, "have the credit for giving the negro the vote. The Democrats now find themselves confronted with an opportunity to enfranchise women. This would give the Democrats as much right to claim to be the party of all the people."

Wilson listened politely, but he refused their plea.

"So many subjects are pressing for a place in my message to Congress," he told them coldly. He mentioned currency and tariff reform as the two that were most important to him.

The women were angered by his quick dismissal but not surprised by such a predictable response. Paul, never one to hold back her thoughts, took up the debate.

"But Mr. President, do you not understand that the administration has no right to legislate for currency, tariff and any other reform without first getting the consent of women?"

Wilson was taken aback by Paul's assertiveness and immediately adjusted himself to work harder at placating the women in front of him.

"I can't promise that I can comply with your request, but I will admit I am considering your cause," he said, giving her the tiniest opening for hope. "You must not think I am against you if I don't ask Congress to take up woman suffrage."

He also explained that as someone from the South who believed in states' rights and all of its traditions, he felt states should decide on their own by referendum. As he spoke, Paul reeled inside. She imagined another generation of women wasting their efforts on attempts to pass state referendums, which would rely on *male* voters for approval. It was humiliating. Why was it up to the men to decide if women could vote?

Paul believed that she had given him her best arguments, but knew that the ten-minute meeting hadn't changed his opinion at all. The only way she could force him or Congress to act on a federal amendment was by converting public opinion. She and the other women stood, thanked Wilson, and said good-bye. They walked back down Pennsylvania Av-

Woodrow Wilson in the Oval Office.

enue to NAWSA's Congressional Committee (CC) headquarters and descended the stairs into the main room. Reporters were there waiting for them with notebooks and pens, ready for interviews.

A week later, Paul had heard nothing from the president—no news about whether the amendment would be on his agenda. She decided to visit him again. This time, she brought with her some women from the College Equal Suffrage League, led by Elsie Hill, to the Oval Office. Hill was a Vassar graduate, thirty years old, and the daughter of Connecticut Republican congressman Ebenezer Hill. She was Paul's friend and had helped plan the suffrage procession, so she was a reliable colleague. The women came into the Oval Office and made the same argument about the importance of the amendment and why Wilson should address it with Congress. And once again, the president told the suffragists that the House and Senate would be occupied with tariff and currency instead. The women left the Oval Office no less willing to push the cause.

With time running out before the president's scheduled address on April 8, Paul waited only three more days before sending a third deputation, the largest yet, to see Wilson. The group of nine was led by Dr. Cora Smith King of Seattle, Washington, a state where women could vote. King was now living in D.C. and was a member of the National Council of Women Voters. Inside the Oval Office, King told the president that her group represented two million voting women who favored a suffrage amendment. Although she did not say so, the underlying political message was obvious: at some point, voting women could turn against the party that was impeding women's progress. King and her colleagues pleaded with Wilson to recommend a federal amendment in his address. But the president's answer was the same: tariff and currency were the main topics on his list.

If she did not know before, Paul was now certain it would take more than a few meetings with Wilson to change his mind. She and the rest of the CC regrouped at headquarters and quickly mapped out a broad political strategy. The main idea was to apply pressure from every possible angle. In addition to continuing to confront Wilson directly, they urged suffragists nationwide to write letters to Congress and the president, asking them to endorse a federal amendment. These letters began pouring in right away. Next, while the Senate already had a Woman Suffrage Committee, the House did not. So Paul and her colleagues worked quickly with the Progressive caucus to establish a suffrage committee before the 63rd Congress assembled. While the Progressives endorsed the idea, the rest of the Democrats, mirroring the president's stance, ignored the plan and refused to cooperate. It was time to pressure Capitol Hill more visibly.

At dawn, on April 7, 1913, it seemed as if all of Washington was springing to life. The cherry blossoms, a gift of friendship from Japan the previous year, were putting on a big show, opening their pink buds and dropping petal confetti along the banks of the Potomac. Over at the Quaker boarding house, Paul, who at this point was barely sleeping given all the organizing work she had to do, popped out of bed and dressed quickly. She pinned up her hair, put on a white dress, and pulled on a hat before heading over to the Columbia Theater on F Street. There, inside the 1,200-seat playhouse, Paul greeted women streaming in from all over America and directed them to take their seats.

Although the last month had been busy dealing with the aftermath of the suffrage procession, three deputations to see President Wilson, and the letter-writing campaign to Congress, Paul and her core team of helpers inside NAWSA had organized yet another complex and symbolic event that was about to begin: a march from the theater to the steps of the U.S. Capitol Building. There were no floats or allegories as part of this procession, but Paul's thoughtful touch was evident. When the speeches by Paul and other prominent suffragists concluded inside the theater, 531 women—two from every state and one from each congressional district—walked out carrying small envelopes with a copy of a petition for her representative in Congress.

Led by a couple of marching bands, the women wore white under their spring jackets and carried flags, yellow ones for suffrage or the symbols of their home state. Spectators lined the street, but this time, the crowds were polite and the police stationed at regular intervals had

Suffragists arrive single-file at the U.S. Capitol.

no trouble keeping the route clear. There was one point of friction, however. The police tried to confine the women to one side of Pennsylvania Avenue so that cars could pass, but the suffragists insisted on marching down the center, blocking traffic.

As the suffragists arrived at the foot of Capitol Hill, the police halted the bands and required the women to walk in a narrow column up one of the paths through the grounds until they met Senator Harry Lane of Oregon, who was waiting to greet them outside. Lane was part of a prominent Democratic family—his grandfather had run for vice president on the ticket that lost to Abraham Lincoln. But the senator was far more progressive than his relatives. As a medical doctor in Portland, Lane often served the poor for free. As mayor of that city, he swore in one of the first female police officers in America. He was a champion of Native Americans and a strong supporter of women's voting rights. Paul was glad to have him on her side.

After his brief remarks supporting suffrage, Lane, his face deeply creased with smile lines, led the women into the rotunda. There, they shook the hands of nine other senators and some representatives—all from suffrage states—as they placed their petitions in a box and walked to the House and Senate galleries. Inside the chambers, they sat down to watch not just the presentation of their petitions but something even more important. On the Senate floor, George Chamberlain, another Oregon Democrat, filed a formal resolution proposing a constitutional amendment giving women the right to vote. In the House, Representative Franklin Mondell, a Wyoming Republican, did the same. The Senate referred this resolution to the Woman Suffrage Committee, and the House to the Judiciary Committee.

Initially named the Chamberlain-Mondell Amendment, the language was the same as what Susan B. Anthony had drafted for its first introduction to Congress in 1878 by Senator Aaron Sargent of California. The text, just two sentences long, was simple, clear, and potent.

Section 1. The right of citizens of the United States to vote shall not be denied or abridged by any State on account of sex.

Section 2. Congress shall have power by appropriate legislation to enforce the provisions of this article.

And so it was that in less than four months of relentless work, a committee of five women, including Paul as chairwoman, had set one of the key agenda items for the nation. Now they had to wait and see how Wilson would respond the following afternoon in his speech to Congress.

■ ■ ■

The next day, Wilson woke to newspaper coverage blaring the news about the federal suffrage amendment. If this bothered him, he did not admit it when he sat down to write a letter to Mary Hulbert Peck. Peck had become a confidante, and probably more than that, since he first met her five years earlier on a winter vacation to Bermuda without his wife, who had sent him alone for a break from the stresses of Princeton.

Peck, an American who spent her winters on the island, was charming, intriguing, and in a loveless marriage. Her flirtation with Wilson at a dinner party during that trip evolved over time and became a lasting relationship, most likely a romantic one, based on the more than two hundred letters they wrote to each other at important moments in their lives, as well as his furtive visits to her home in New York when he was in the city. On the day of his first address to Congress, he took time to write her:

> I am very glad indeed to have this opportunity to address the two Houses directly and verify for myself the impression that the President of the United States is a person, not a mere department of the Government hailing Congress from some isolated island of jealous power, sending messages, not speaking naturally and with his own voice—that he is a human being trying to cooperate with other human beings in a common service.

Wilson's first address to Congress, April 8, 1913.

At 1 p.m. on April 8, 1913, the first session of the 63rd Congress opened. U.S. senators and representatives assembled in the House chamber, while other spectators jammed every seat. Some women, mostly wives and daughters of elected officials, added splashes of colorful dress to the galleries. The first lady was there with her three daughters, occupying seats in an upper front row, known as the "President's Pew." Around the Wilson women were a cousin, the governor of Missouri, and cabinet members. They assembled not just to hear what Wilson had to say but to witness the breaking of a custom. For the first time in 112 years, a president was delivering a message to Congress—not in writing but in person.

Wilson's decision to address Congress was groundbreaking, just like some of the progressive ideas he was about to propose. But there was always a limit to what he would do. For one thing, Wilson did not want people to think he was being imperious. He arrived at the House chamber alone, trailed by only one Secret Service agent, James Sloan, who had driven him there from the White House. Wilson's cabinet made their own way to the Capitol. Well-heeled people without invitations crowded the doors, trying to glimpse him at the podium.

He wore a black coat, light trousers, and a gray-striped cravat, entering from the rear left of the rostrum. He shook the Speaker's hand and stepped up to the podium. A giant American flag and a clock loomed behind him. Those in the chamber stood to applaud. Wilson bowed. Congress quieted as the president pulled from his coat his address, written on small slips of paper with wide spaces between the lines. In his speech, he called for tariff reform to reduce the cost of imports, benefiting American manufacturers who relied on raw materials and making everything from sweaters to groceries cheaper for consumers. To Wilson, greater economic opportunity and less government intervention were progressive.

Mr. Speaker, Mr. [Senate] President, Gentlemen of the Congress . . .
I have called the Congress together in extraordinary session because . . . the business interests of the country may not be kept too long in suspense as to what the fiscal changes are to be to which they

will be required to adjust themselves. It is clear to the whole country that the tariff duties must be altered. . . . It is plain what those principles must be. We must abolish everything that bears even the semblance of privilege or of any kind of artificial advantage. . . . I thank you for your courtesy.

When he was done ten minutes later, Congress applauded again. Wilson tucked the papers inside his jacket, bowed, and left through the same door he had arrived by. There was no mention of suffrage in his address. Indeed, the press coverage the next day said nothing of the fact that women had been pleading with him to include a mention of it.

■ ■ ■

Wilson's tariff address to Congress was all the proof that Paul needed. The president had no intentions of taking up suffrage. It was also clear to her that lobbying Congress would consume even more time and effort than her committee had been giving it—which was a lot. In order to really pressure the House and Senate, she believed NAWSA needed a large, well-funded entity solely focused on pushing legislation on Capitol Hill. She knew the federal amendment was a sensitive subject inside NAWSA, whose base was still committed to the state-by-state strategy. Clearly, the movement was at a crossroads.

Paul studied NAWSA's bylaws, which had specific rules on how to form an official group within the organization. Such a group needed three hundred members, all of whom had to pay dues to the National American. Paul and other members of the CC's idea was to find women living in the Washington area who were not already affiliated with the National American and had no state campaign to work on. These new members would be part of a brand-new group within NAWSA called the Congressional Union (CU), and their focus would be pushing for an amendment on Capitol Hill.

Paul and Burns went to Shaw's home and broached the idea. Shaw approved of their strategy to form this new branch—at least for now. But she told them they would have to cover all of their own expenses while still paying dues to the National American. Paul agreed to the deal. She installed herself as the chairwoman of the CU and Burns as her number two. They adopted the colors of purple, white, and gold, a variation on the British suffrage flag. They set their intention on securing a hearing before the Senate Woman Suffrage Committee and began organizing suffrage demonstrations nationwide throughout the summer.

CU members were not the only ones busy in Washington that spring. Congress was figuring out its agenda and how it fit in with the president's; the two seemed fairly aligned. The House of Representatives, which, like the Senate, was controlled by Democrats, quickly passed tariff reform by a vote of 281–139 on May 8. Known as the Underwood Act, it slashed duties on woolens, for example, from 56 to 18.5 percent. The act also introduced a federal income tax: 1 percent of earnings on the rich.

Many assumed the Senate would also focus on tariffs. Instead, they took up suffrage and gave it the first favorable majority report on the topic in twenty-three years. Across America, it was as if long-dormant desert seeds, given just a bit of water, were blooming. Suffrage support was sprouting in many new places. Before the month was over, the women of Illinois won the right to vote for president, progress at the state level even if it was not full voting rights. Sensing some momentum in their favor, Paul's CU sent a delegation to meet with the House Rules Committee to ask Chairman Robert Lee Henry to release the amendment from its graveyard. The group included the author Helen Gardener and the wives of several elected officials, including Senator John Shafroth of Colorado and representatives John E. Raker of California, Claude Stone of Illinois, and Edward Taylor of Colorado. But the chairman rebuffed them.

"We couldn't possibly take up the amendment under the current program this session," Chairman Henry told them. "But we would be glad to hear the suffragists between the first week of December and the Christmas holidays." Gardener reminded him that in the 1916 election four million women would be voting, and would remember this. It was time to implement the next phase of the CU's plan.

CHAPTER EIGHT

The Siege of the Senate

In Boston, in mid-July of 1913, a group of suffragists the press teasingly called "Company No. 2 of the Votes for Women Army" gathered outside the headquarters of the Political Equality League in Back Bay. The car they had arrived in, decorated with green banners, served as the backdrop for a large rally, the starting point for a signature campaign. Their next stops were the State House and then City Hall, where they collected letters of support from the governor and mayor. They headed south to Quincy, then Weymouth, Middleborough, and Plymouth, where hundreds of people gave them a loud welcome. The group collected more signatures and sold more "Votes for Women" buttons before moving on to bigger crowds in the mill towns of New Bedford and Fall River, speaking to overworked and underpaid factory workers, essential supporters of the cause. These activists mustered more than four thousand signatures from seamstresses, shoemakers, and other trades in Massachusetts. Then they moved on to Providence, Rhode Island, before driving up to Maine, New Hampshire, Vermont, and, ultimately, New York, where the petitioners boarded a train toward Washington.

These women were part of a larger "auto brigade" campaign Paul had set in motion to collect signatures across the country throughout the summer. The idea was to have the women drive the petitions to Washington in a parade of cars, creating a spectacle of liberation. Organizing this event was challenging for Paul and the participants. The long stunt generated so much publicity that it created an avalanche of interest—good and bad. Women were signing up to participate and there were so many letters flooding the mailbox at CU headquarters that Paul had to learn how to type because she did not have enough help to manage the correspondence.

The success of the campaign also brought out the opposition. In New Jersey, while suffragists collected signatures at the shore, the state chapter of the National Association Opposed to Woman Suffrage—a group comprised mostly of women—planned a huge counterdemonstration. The local branch of this group had been in existence less than a year and had a membership of six thousand, a considerable number. Clearly it was not just men concerned about ceding some of their political power who were standing in the way of equal suffrage. There were women, too, who felt voting rights could erode their standing in the home, which was the only real place where they had power.

The suffragists, always finding nonviolent ways to protest, interrupted the opposition's planning by throwing a huge bouquet of flowers into the auditorium where they were meeting. An attached sarcastic note read: "We desire to express our gratitude for the kind work which you are doing on our behalf. And beg for a continuation of your favors." It was signed "the Liquor Interests, the Child Labor Interests, the White Slave Interests, and Other Vice Interests." The bouquet was not the only way suffragists expressed their outrage leading up to the counterdemonstration. They also scrawled notes on the steps of the homes of their key opponents. The tactic had echoes of the sidewalk chalking that Paul and Burns had done in Edinburgh to promote their activity. On one New Jersey stoop, a suffragist wrote: "Here lives the president of the women traitors." On another: "To hell with the antis! Votes for Women! Hurrah for Mrs. Pankhurst." Emmeline Pankhurst had become infamous in the United States. The newspapers reported on her suffragette work and she'd stoked interest further by traveling to America to raise funds and give speeches. Her next trip to the United States was expected to happen in a few months, in the fall of 1913.

At the end of July, the auto brigades rolled into Hyattsville, Maryland, just outside Washington, D.C., to organize their cars for the final leg of the rally. They arrived just as a blustery storm blew in, overturning cars, uprooting trees, and transforming the roads into mud pits. Even nature was challenging the will of the suffragists, but they could not be stopped. The next morning, the weather cleared and sixty cars decked out in fluttering flags and pennants took off for the Capitol carrying hundreds of petitioners. Paul and other members of the Congressional Union (CU) were in the lead car, followed by members of the Senate Woman Suffrage Committee, and then the National American Woman Suffrage Association (NAWSA) leadership. They traveled the messy road to Washington feeling pleased with their success. Not only had these women collected front-page headlines across America, they had also secured more than two hundred thousand signatures.

Police Chief Sylvester met them at the district line with a strong force mounted on horses and bicycles and escorted the women to their destination. The CU had made arrangements for the women to park

The Congressional Union's auto brigade arriving on Capitol Hill.

directly in front of the Capitol Building. And after shutting down the automobiles, they moved in clusters up the limestone steps into the Senate wing in what one reporter called a "cloud of femininity [that shattered] . . . the dignified hush of the imposing marble room just off the Senate chamber." For nearly an hour, women representing their states handed over bundles of petitions tied up in yellow ribbons. The women flocked to the gallery, and then, for the first time in twenty-six years, thanks to the publicity generated by the CU and its constant lobbying, the chamber struck up a floor debate on suffrage. They watched as Senator Robert Owen, a progressive Democrat from Oklahoma, stood to speak. "The reasons for this request on the part of the country are overwhelming and unanswerable, and the time has come when they must be considered with dignity, with unbiased mind, free from prejudice or passion, in the interest of the welfare of the human race . . . the question can no longer be ignored," he said.

Not everyone agreed, however. Senator Reed Smoot, a Utah Republican, was the first voice to speak in opposition. After presenting the stack of petitions from his state, he told his colleagues not to reward the behavior of these women seeking constitutional change. "Suffrage should be given, not to the Pankhursts and the militant radicals among our women," he said, "but to those who follow in womanly footsteps of the American pioneers of suffrage . . . Susan B. Anthony and others."

Over the course of two hours, twenty-two senators spoke in favor of the amendment and three spoke against it. And then, just as the debate was leaning heavily in favor of suffrage—and likely because it was—one senator suggested that suffrage be set aside for another day in order to leave time for tariff debate. With that, a day of activism that the press dubbed the "siege of the Senate" ended without a vote on the amendment itself. Nor was there a final vote on tariff reform. That would happen more than a month later, in September, delivering Woodrow Wilson his first major presidential triumph.

In the midst of all the summer campaigning, Paul accomplished the remarkable: she launched a weekly newspaper called *The Suffragist*. The tabloid, sometimes with more than twenty pages of copy, contained news updates, editorials, profiles of activists, photographs, and pointed cartoons on the cover. She saw the newspaper as an important tool, one that would not only educate and inspire, but also help fund the movement through subscriptions. She asked Rheta Childe Dorr, a well-known journalist in New York City, if she would move to Washington and be its editor, an unsalaried position. Dorr was interested but had to earn a living and delayed as she continued other work. Paul, desperate to have the paper printed in time for NAWSA's annual convention in December to spotlight the CU's congressional efforts, told Dorr she could keep writing for other outlets if she accepted the job immediately. Dorr agreed.

The paper made its debut on November 15, with little time to spare before the convention assembled. On the front page, Paul wrote that the suffrage amendment neared success and that women should stand "shoulder to shoulder behind the amendment. . . . There is no other issue comparable to the importance [of] the elementary question of self-government for the women of America." Among the other editorials in that edition was a column by Lucy Burns. Always direct, she argued that "one thing we may be sure of, until we ask for instant action, no one else will ask for it."

The paper was not the only way the CU was intensifying its work in the fall. Just two days after *The Suffragist* launched, Paul picked up the phone and called the White House executive office. She was growing impatient because a group of

Rheta Childe Dorr, the first editor of The Suffragist.

seventy-three women from Wilson's state of New Jersey had been try-ing fruitlessly to see the president with the help of their congressman, Democrat Walter McCoy. They had arrived over the weekend and there was still no response from the administration, a courtesy anyone would have expected at that time.

"As it's impossible to find out what hour would suit the convenience of the President to meet with the delegation, they will come and wait there until he is ready to receive them or would definitely refuse to do so," she told the clerk who answered.

"It would be impossible to see the President without an appoint-ment," he said. "Such a thing has never been done."

After Paul hung up, Representative McCoy called her and told her that he, too, had had no luck.

"The delegation is going anyway," she said.

"That's a terrible idea," he said. "You need to do this through official channels."

"The delegation has already started," she said.

Suffragists from New Jersey assemble at CU's headquarters
before walking to the White House to see Wilson.

The women were already on their seven-minute walk from the F Street headquarters, down Fifteenth Street, past the Treasury Department, and up Pennsylvania Avenue to the White House grounds. Two guards in uniform stood at the gate. They saluted and moved aside to let the women in, standing two by two as they entered the executive office unchallenged. An attendant greeted them and asked the group to wait while he showed just two of them in to see the president. They walked into the Oval Office, where Wilson, probably feeling as if he was out of excuses, listened as they asked him to support the amendment.

"I am pleased, indeed, to greet you and your adherents here," Wilson said. "And I will say to you that I was talking only yesterday with several members of Congress in regard to the Suffrage Committee in the House. The subject is one in which I am deeply interested, and you may rest assured that I will give it my earnest attention."

The women left feeling the smallest of victories, moving the president from "suffrage is not on my agenda" to a place where it could be. Such subtle shifts showed the glacial pace of progress during Alice Paul's first year—a year of firsts—in Washington. From the suffrage procession, to the Oval Office deputations, to the movement on Capitol Hill in favor of a suffrage amendment for the first time in more than two decades, it seemed as if this revitalized movement was gelling, except in one area. The more success the CU found, the more resistance from NAWSA's leadership.

Burns, in particular, drew Shaw's outrage. On the same day the New Jersey women were at the White House, Burns was nearby chalking the sidewalk to advertise a suffrage meeting. When an officer told her that writing on the ground was illegal, she stopped and said she did not know that was the case. Later, the police issued a warrant for her arrest. The incident was front-page news. Shaw was irate. She believed the warrant was evidence of the increasing militancy of the CU, and she did not want to be associated with it.

"You may think we are all a set of old fogies, and perhaps we are," Shaw wrote to Burns. "But I, for one, thank heaven that I am as much of an old fogy as I am, for I think there are certain laws of order which should be followed by everybody. It requires a good deal more courage to work steadily and steadfastly for forty or fifty years to gain an end than it does to do an impulsive, rash thing and lose it." Burns tried to smooth things over, writing back to say that she had paid her fine and insisting that neither she nor Paul were militant. But the damage was done.

CHAPTER NINE

A House Divided

Alice Paul stood facing the Masonic Temple, a brick and stone building with tiny windows in downtown Washington. From the outside, the structure looked like an impenetrable fortress rather than a welcoming place, but perhaps Paul's bleak perspective was the combined result of sleep deprivation, a raw head cold, and the Monday morning damp. It was day one of the forty-fifth annual convention of the National American Woman Suffrage Association (NAWSA), and Paul was slated to address a hall full of people. Now that her Congressional Union (CU) was operational in D.C., she had offered to help organize and host the event in order to keep the action within walking distance of the White House and Capitol Hill, just in case any attendees wanted to pay Woodrow Wilson a visit. NAWSA leadership agreed to let her oversee the convention on one condition: that she raise funds to cover the week's expenses, including their entertainment costs. Paul complied but assigned herself an additional challenge: the creation of a series of politically educational classes in Washington after the convention, designed to equip one thousand women with essential voter information, such as how to mark a ballot. That aspect was fully coordinated, scheduled, and ready to go.

The relentless work was taking a toll on Paul. Her exhaustion was compounded by the convention's curtain raiser the day before, a mass meeting presided over by Dr. Anna Howard Shaw, NAWSA's president.

Together they had celebrated the suffrage win in Illinois, marking the victory with a hotel reception that dragged into the night. The long day had worn on Paul, but was even harder on Shaw. Now in her ninth year as the leader of the National American, the sturdily built sixty-six-year-old, with her unmistakable shock of white hair tied back in a wispy bun, was nowhere to be found as Paul scanned the room. Also missing from the audience on this day was Carrie Chapman Catt, the previous president of NAWSA, who had been devoting her time to voting rights abroad. Catt, now back in the United States and focused on suffrage in New York, was considered one of the key leaders of the domestic movement. Everyone was waiting for her to arrive in Washington and participate in the convention.

The absence of these legendary suffrage figureheads granted Paul the unspoken authority to command the audience, and with it the freedom to confidently speak her mind. She stood center stage, against the backdrop of her choosing: a large square banner, more than six feet tall and nearly six feet wide, that had been carried in the suffrage procession nine months earlier. Its letters, cut from purple cloth and machine-stitched onto golden-yellow cotton, were bold in style and ver-biage, proclaiming: WE DEMAND AN AMENDMENT TO THE UNITED STATES CONSTITUTION ENFRANCHISING WOMEN. The audience before her was a riot of color, a welcome contrast to the gloom and gray outside. Purple and yellow flags from various suffrage societies hung on the walls, and hundreds of women in fancy hats decorated with black, white, and iridescent feathers sat in the audience.

Paul was bolstered by the sight of three familiar faces: her sister, Helen, serving as a convention delegate from New Jersey; Inez Mil-holland, the parade herald; and the dark-haired, finely dressed Alva Belmont, a key potential ally who was watching Paul carefully.

Paul calmed the crowd and made brief opening remarks. "Welcome everyone," she said. "We have assembled in Washington to ask the Democratic Party to enfranchise the women of America." She paused as cheers erupted. The audience understood how important Paul's de-ceptively simple statement was. The fact that she specifically called out Democrats, holding the party in power responsible for suffrage, was a controversial Pankhurst tactic. Many believed the movement should be nonpartisan, as it always had been. Indeed, Paul believed her suffrage work *was* nonpartisan; if Republicans controlled the government, she argued, she would hold them just as responsible. This was not about one party over another. It was about who was in charge.

"Victory is at hand," she continued. "I believe that the constitutional amendment will be agreed to within a very few years. In fact, the Congressional Union hoped to get it through at this session. I urge every delegate to give your Congressman, and any other elected official with whom you have influence, no peace until the amendment goes through."

As the audience applauded again, Paul called on Burns to speak. Since her arrest the previous month for chalking "Votes for Women" on sidewalks in Washington, Burns's celebrity was on the rise. The audience was spellbound by the redhead as she made her way to Paul's side. Although the two hurled themselves toward a shared, singular goal, these women were dissimilar in almost every way. While Paul was pale, thin, and businesslike, Burns was ruddy, solid, and belligerent, her fiery mane an expression of the burning passion at her core. And while Paul's language was direct and as unadorned as the inside of a Quaker meeting house, Burns was more engaging, and spoke in a way that was almost musical, her cadence reflective of her broad life experience. But these complementary differences in personality and approach were the recipe for the pair's unique balance.

The crowd grew silent as Burns began to speak.

"Rarely in the history of the country has a party been more powerful than the Democratic Party is today. It controls the Executive Office, the Senate and more than two-thirds of the members of the House of Representatives," Burns shouted.

It is in a position to give us effective and immediate help. We ask the Democrats to take action now. Those who hold power are responsible to the country for the use of it. They are responsible not only for what they do, but for what they do not do. Inaction establishes just as clear a record as does a policy of open hostility.

We have in our hands today not only the weapon of a just cause; we have the support of ten enfranchised states comprising one-fifth of the United States Senate, one-seventh of the House of Representatives, and one-sixth of the electoral vote. More than 3.6 million women have a vote in Presidential elections. It is unthinkable that a national government which represents women, and which appeals periodically for the suffrages of women, should ignore the issue of the right of all women to political freedom. We cannot wait until after the passage of scheduled Administration reforms. . . . Congress is free to take action on our question in the present session. We ask the Administration to support the woman suffrage amendment in Congress with its whole strength.

Her rhetorical call to arms emboldened the audience, jolting delegates toward a new state of impatience as 1913 came to a close, and set a tone of agitation for the week.

The next day, as Wilson delivered his first annual address to Congress—his second speech before the chambers since his inauguration—the attending suffragists felt hopeful about some of his leading phrases though, ultimately, all left disappointed. Wilson did, in fact, say that the time had come for greater social justice, and he vaguely acknowledged the need for a more equal democracy in America, but he recommended self-government for *Filipino men*, not women of the United States:

These are all matters of vital domestic concern, and besides them, outside the charmed circle of our own national life in which our affections command us, as well as our consciences, there stand out our obligations toward our territories over sea. Here we are trustees. Porto [*sic*] Rico, Hawaii, the Philippines, are ours, indeed, but not ours to do what we please with. Such territories, once regarded as mere possessions, are no longer to be selfishly exploited; they are part of the domain of public conscience and of serviceable and enlightened statesmanship. We must administer them for the people who live in them and with the same sense of responsibility to them as toward our own people in our domestic affairs . . . but in the Philippines we must go further. We must hold steadily in view their ultimate independence.

At an evening session later in the day, NAWSA delegates talked about little else. "President Wilson had the opportunity of speaking a word which might ultimately lead to the enfranchisement of a large part of the human family," a more rested Shaw told her members. "Even Lincoln, who by a word freed a race, had not this opportunity to release from the bonds one-half of [the] human family." Delegates enraptured by Shaw's strident remarks, which were more politically pointed than usual, quickly moved to adopt a resolution criticizing Wilson's address.

Shaw was no doubt furious with Wilson, but she was also aware that the National American's members were growing restless on several fronts. Among the items on the convention agenda were NAWSA's anemic funding, the lack of clarity around its organizational relationship with the CU—a rising subgroup—and its political strategy, and its annual election of its leadership, with nominations happening the next day. There was nothing close to agreement on any of these important matters.

The following afternoon, their anger over Wilson's speech spilled over when Ruth Hanna McCormick, the leader of the Illinois suffrage win, rallied the delegates to go to the White House and speak directly to the president. As the daughter of a Republican kingmaker from Ohio, and the wife of a U.S. senator from Chicago, she had the political power to challenge Wilson and encouraged NAWSA's membership to do the same. "I move that this convention wait upon the President in order to lay before him the importance of the suffrage question," McCormick said, "and urge him to make it an Administration measure, and send immediately to Congress the recommendation that it proceed with this measure before any other!"

"I second that motion!" several woman chimed, and the audience finally began to applaud.

Even though McCormick believed in the state-by-state approach, she knew she and other NAWSA leaders needed to be bolder because Paul's CU was pulling the organization to the left, more aggressive in its scope and purpose. The old guard faced a challenging balancing act as the movement's differences of opinion became more public.

As McCormick was speaking, in the back of the hall, ballot boxes were open for members to anonymously nominate whom they wanted to run the organization. Shaw's reelection was by no means guaranteed. For one thing, Alva Belmont, NAWSA's most important benefactor, was calling openly for Shaw's replacement. Her criticism of the National American was stunning, given that she funded the organization's press operation, the *Woman's Journal* and *Suffrage News*, and paid the $5,000 annual rent for its New York headquarters, occupying the seventeenth floor of 505 Fifth Avenue at Forty-Second Street. But the paper now had spunky competition from Paul's paper, *The Suffragist*, and NAWSA's office seemed about 225 miles north of where it should be, namely, in the District of Columbia.

On Thursday, having watched Shaw and now McCormick at the convention, Belmont saw the two factions growing further apart and she decided to stand, if not with Paul, at least with her vision. She rose from her seat and stated that she thought it was time to move NAWSA's headquarters to Washington, a symbolic but also logistically smart thing to do. Delegates tabled her motion because they were distracted by two other issues: the election results were in, showing Shaw reelected to another term as president; and Wilson declined to meet with the women, saying he was ill with a severe cold. All anyone could talk about was their next move with the president. What should their tactic be?

By Friday, the last day of the convention, the conflicts of the week were spiking inside Masonic Hall. Shaw, on the dais, and Catt, now in the front row, watched as Paul gave her required status update about the CU's work. Hers was a long list of accomplishments, beginning with a unanimously favorable Senate report on the suffrage amendment and the first Senate debate on suffrage in twenty-six years. In addition to opening the F Street headquarters, planning the largest protest march ever held in Washington, and organizing a series of deputations, pilgrimages, and fundraisers, Paul and her colleagues had put on the summer campaigns and the convention. They had established a press operation, including hiring a full-time public relations worker. *The*

Suffragist, one month old, already had 1,200 subscribers and was paying for itself with advertising. The group had disseminated 120,000 pieces of literature and created a Men's League, which had many congressmen as members. The CU, which she'd founded in April, already had one thousand members.

In addition, she said she had raised $27,377.99 in 1913 to cover the expenses of everything above. About $21,000 came from within Washington, with the next greatest amount from Philadelphia, Paul explained. While Paul did not directly compare her balance sheet with NAWSA's, which had raised $43,000 during the same time period, everyone in the hall knew what an outstanding achievement it was for the scrappy little group, and how comparatively paltry the National American's fundraising efforts were given their long history, substantial infrastructure, and a hundred thousand members. Not only that, but NAWSA had only raised ten dollars in 1912 for congressional work; their priority clearly was state work, not a federal amendment.

A suffragist from Boston named Margaret Foley was so impressed with Paul's report that she stood to lead a round of "Three cheers for Miss Alice Paul!" Hundreds of women rose to their feet.

"Hip, hip, hooray!"

"Hip, hip, hooray!"

"Hip, hip, hooray!"

As the delegates cheered for Paul, Catt remained in her seat, seething. Catt had been Susan B. Anthony's successor at NAWSA, leading the organization for four years until she stepped down to care for her sick husband, with Shaw assuming the leadership duties. A Midwestern-bred former teacher, Catt was now fifty-four years old, with a formidable presence, her white wavy hair parted severely in the middle and pulled back at the nape, and dark circles around her eyes. She had worked for women's rights not only in America, but all over the world. Now that she was back in the United States, Catt could see how Shaw was losing control over an obviously volatile situation, even though she had just been reelected president. She also felt it was her turn to be the rightful leader of the movement, a movement that should be focused on winning the next state—New York—and not wasting time on a federal amendment which she thought would never come. As she studied this waif from New Jersey being celebrated on stage, Catt assessed that Paul was the driving force behind "a dark conspiracy to capture the entire 'national' for the militant enterprise."

When the applause for Paul faded, Catt sprang to her feet. Heads turned and everyone froze so as not to miss a word. "I confess, I myself am a good deal razzle-dazzled by the situation," Catt said. "But the committee has done everything which the National ought to do? The question arises . . . to which society are we to owe loyalty. . . . May we have these questions answered in order that we may not criticize each other and not find fault but so we may get together on one unified program that is going to carry us to success."

Paul did not shrink from this confrontation.

She told the delegates that the women of Washington had done much to help the CU, but the congressional work absolutely needed support from women across America to continue to push for the federal amendment.

As Catt and Shaw exchanged meaningful glances, Paul was unapologetic. "You have raised something like $12,000 to carry on the office in New York," Paul said. "Nothing has been raised [by NAWSA] to carry through the federal amendment, which is, in my opinion the great work before us as a nation."

Not everyone was pleased with her response. NAWSA treasurer Katharine McCormick, a wealthy Bostonian, objected to the way Paul had handled the financial reports. "Not one penny of all this money has come into my national treasury," she said. "This is a situation that cannot be tolerated. That a committee—just a committee—should raise the money and keep the money."

Some of the women began whispering to each other, preparing to be witness to a fight. Jane Addams, a Chicago woman who had been a co-founder of the NAACP—which advocated for women's voting rights—stood in Paul's defense. Addams, just elected the first vice president of NAWSA, reminded delegates that the National American appointed Paul and Burns to the committee focused on a federal amendment and that the two women had agreed to raise their own operating funds because NAWSA demanded that they do so. "They honorably filled their pledge" and paid every one of their own bills, Addams told the crowd.

Emma Gillette, a lawyer and the CC's first treasurer, also defended Paul. "From the first penny that was raised until this procession was finished . . . phenomenal frugality was displayed, it seemed to me, by the people who were running this campaign."

Shaw issued the final word, exposing the bitter split to eager reporters, furiously scribbling down every utterance in their notebooks. "We, of course, had not the remotest idea in the world what this committee was going to do. . . . The national officers do not wish to be blamed for things which they have not done."

Paul was blindsided by this public rebuke. It was her first inkling that not only was she battling society's entrenched sexist views and President Wilson's recalcitrance, but she was fighting *women*, too—specifically the establishment of the suffrage movement. It was a devastating shock to her already compromised system to learn that not everyone appreciated her hard work. Some clearly felt threatened by what she had done, making her heart sink further. She had likely been too busy to notice these fractures before, but now it was all she could see. That night, she went home and collapsed into bed.

On Monday morning, Paul rallied to greet 150 women, including Shaw, outside the F Street headquarters. At noon, the women raised their colorful silk and satin banners and began marching to 1600 Pennsylvania Avenue. Now that the president was feeling better, he agreed to meet. It was the fifth and largest suffragist deputation to see Wilson yet. Once inside the White House, the women gathered in a meeting room and waited. Low shafts of winter light shone through the window and spot-lit Shaw. Paul stood right beside her.

Wilson sauntered in and uttered a pleasantry, "which he thought would please the 'ladies,'" one of the women recalled. "It did not provoke even a faint smile." Next, he explained why he could not promote suffrage to the House and Senate.

"I am merely the spokesman of my party," he said timidly. "I am not at liberty to urge upon Congress in messages, policies which have not had the organic consideration of those for whom I am spokesman. I am by my own principles shut out, in the language of the street, from 'starting anything.' I have to confine myself to those things which have been embodied as promises to the people at an election."

Shaw was having none of it. Her voice clear and resonant, she re-played all of the recent suffrage efforts in Congress and said legislation had been "buried in committee." She asked Wilson to send a message to the House and Senate encouraging them to enfranchise women, and for him to endorse the movement and create a suffrage committee in the White House.

"Mr. President, if you cannot speak for us and your party will not, who then, pray, is there to speak for us?"

"You seem very well able to speak for yourselves, ladies," he said with a broad smile. When no one returned even a smirk, Wilson flushed with embarrassment.

"We mean, Mr. President, who will speak for us with authority?" Shaw asked.

The president ignored her and turned to shake hands with the delegates. A few obliged him but many in the room, including Paul, walked out.

Shortly after the White House meeting, the NAWSA board called Paul and Burns to a meeting. Shaw and the board wanted to make it clear that they were in charge. They told Paul that she could remain as chair-man of the Congressional Committee (CC) if she pledged her "undi-vided loyalty" to the National American, not her own splinter group.

"Well," Paul said, "the Congressional Union's only purpose is to raise money and get members to finance the Congressional Committee's campaign. So we don't see any conflict at all. I don't think I can func-tion without *some* kind of a group to help us. I don't want to disown the group that I have created and has given us such enormous support." The board, not wanting Paul to run both organizations, asked Burns to lead the CC. When she refused out of loyalty to her friend, they appointed McCormick, the woman from Illinois, to replace Paul. In a small gesture of diplomacy, Paul agreed to be just a rank-and-file member of the CC and invited McCormick to be a member of the CU; this way, the older generation would know what the new guard was doing at all times.

But the détente would be short-lived. As soon as the suffrage classes concluded in mid-December, Paul packed her bags and boarded a train for Philadelphia, where she was to get some much-needed rest. She was escaping to the home of her suffragist friend, Dora Lewis, a married mother of three in her mid-fifties from a prominent Philadelphia family. Paul had instructed Burns to continue working without her. But her convalescence, like the truce, was cut short when a frantic letter from Burns arrived, explaining that two congressmen—Senator John Shafroth of Colorado and Representative Mitchell Palmer of Pennsylvania—were filing a federal suffrage amendment. On its face, this news may have seemed welcome. However, in a devious twist, McCormick had encouraged the legislation, which would compete with Paul's. Not only would that legislation split the vote, it would confuse the public about the need for two different amendments.

The Bristow-Mondell Amendment—formerly known as the Chamberlain-Mondell Amendment—that Paul had been promoting was drafted by Susan B. Anthony herself with clear and simple language stating that "the right of citizens of the United States to vote shall not be denied or abridged by the United States or any state on account of sex." The new amendment to be put forth by Shafroth and Palmer would require states to hold a referendum on women's suffrage whenever 8 percent of their (male) voters requested such a vote. Paul believed it was futile to give men the power to control whether women in their state could vote. How did this advance the cause?

Some on the CU's board felt so defeated by McCormick's move that they wanted to give up, shutter the organization, and allow the National American to take the lead on an amendment. But Paul and Burns had invested so much in the cause, and they were not willing to concede. Instead, in a final attempt at unity, they set up a meeting with the leadership of NAWSA early in the new year.

Paul, Burns, and two of their key supporters, Dora Lewis and Elizabeth Kent, the wife of wealthy California congressman William Kent, arrived at the National American's headquarters. The narrow office building was located on the corner, diagonally across from the New York Public Library, where two magnificent lion statues kept watch as the women walked by. Once inside on the seventeenth floor, they passed through the reception room, furnished with black carved oak furniture, and were brought to Shaw's office. The walls were decorated with fine portraits of other pioneering suffragists. But there was no feeling of sisterhood here. NAWSA's treasurer Katharine McCormick had turned her chair so her back faced those from the CU. She also refused to speak to them.

Paul asked the National American women why they were pushing for a new amendment, one that privileged the state-by-state approach over a federal one. Shaw claimed that NAWSA was unaware of the Sha-froth-Palmer bill, which was not yet public knowledge. Shaw also said it did not matter if she did know about that amendment from its inception because she believed McCormick was politically savvy enough to make such decisions on her own; if that meant a new version of the suffrage amendment so be it.

Paul knew the meeting would be challenging, but she did not expect it to begin so badly. She had held out hope until this moment that the relationship could be repaired, knowing the perils of competing efforts and fundraising. But if the National American wanted to keep the young militant working under the old banner, they did a poor job convincing her to do so at the meeting. If anything, they pushed her away. Paul quit NAWSA.

For Paul, having to start over at age twenty-nine felt more daunting than creating the CC or CU. She was emotionally and physically depleted. Outside on the sidewalk after the meeting, she allowed herself to recognize what everyone else could already see—that she was gaunt and worn out, her digestion still affected by the hunger strikes and prison stays in England. Her loved ones had been encouraging her to admit herself to a hospital to recover. She finally agreed.

Paul sat up in her bed at the Woman's Hospital of Philadelphia, a Quaker facility founded by a female doctor. The facility was also a rare training ground for women in medicine. The atmosphere was restorative. The staff encouraged Paul to stay in bed, eat, and sleep more. But Paul felt unable to switch off completely. There was so much to do. Her newly independent organization—the Congressional Union for Woman Suffrage (CUWS)—which she had founded after she broke off from NAWSA, no longer had a clear funding source. Despite her lack of funds, Paul requested a stenographer to sit by her bedside and began dictating letters as soon as she arrived. One note, sent to the CUWS's treasurer, Joy Webster, reflects Paul's discomfort at being removed from the action: "Will you not send me word as to our bank balance? I shall have to come back to Washington to see if you do not let me know—I am consumed with anxiety as to whether there is plenty of money on hand."

When Paul was not dictating letters, or reading those she received from the Washington office, or enjoying daily visits from her friend Dora Lewis, she was reading the newspapers. On March 1, about two weeks into her hospital stay, the *Philadelphia Inquirer* announced that the women of Paris had won the right to vote. Then, on the first anniversary of her suffrage procession, came the news that NAWSA had introduced the Shafroth-Palmer Amendment at a congressional hearing. The feud between the rival suffrage organizations was now visible for all to see.

Paul knew it was time for her to leave the hospital. After a three-week stay, she left for Lewis's home and stayed a week. Then, in early April, with the cherry blossoms blooming once again along the Potomac, Paul marched into the F Street headquarters feeling renewed. But not everyone was pleased to have Paul back in the office. Rheta Childe Dorr, disgruntled over Paul's incessant control—even from her sick bed—over *The Suffragist*'s coverage and staffing, quit; she had been on the job a mere six months. Paul did not miss a beat. She eliminated the role of business manager for the paper and appointed Lucy Burns as editor. Together, they launched a wildly successful campaign that would boost subscriptions by one thousand in just one month. In addition to taking on more work with the paper, Paul also began organizing mass demonstrations across the country, scheduled for May 2—May Day.

CHAPTER TEN

Dark Days

Just one month into Woodrow Wilson's new administration, the men of the cabinet were gathered around a table for a small, closed meeting. Albert Burleson, a wealthy Texan from a Confederate family, was the new U.S. postmaster general with an important matter to discuss.

"There are certain intolerable conditions in the Railway Mail Services," he said. "Whites not only had to work with blacks, but were forced to use the same drinking glasses, towels and washrooms. It would be to the advantage of both races to be separated in their work." He explained to everyone in the room that he intended to segregate the postal service gradually—so that "employing Negroes would not be objectionable"—and he hoped that all federal departments would follow his lead. Burleson also asked the president to reconsider appointing African Americans to mid-level clerical jobs.

If anyone in the room thought Burleson's idea was scandalous, they did not say so. Certainly not Navy Secretary Josephus Daniels. For years, Daniels had been editor of the Raleigh *News and Observer*, championing white supremacy in local elections and successfully editorializing for a state amendment that stripped most blacks of their right to vote, excluded them from juries, and subjected them to legal racial segregation.

Treasury Secretary William McAdoo also remained silent. As a leader in the Democratic National Committee, he had helped Wilson get elected by luring black male voters away from the party of Lincoln with promises of fair play and "a square deal." But on this day, he made no protest, perhaps because he was distracted; the fifty-year-old widower had a romantic interest in the president's youngest daughter, Eleanor, who was half his age.

After listening to the discussion, Wilson expressed that he did not want any friction in federal service posts. The implications of this statement provided Burleson with the nod he needed to proceed with his plan. There would be no public announcement about segregation. There would be no executive order. And there would be no notification to any federal employees about the change, not even the black workers who comprised about 5 percent of the government's workforce. The men agreed that this idea would be quietly implemented.

Burleson immediately had screens installed in post offices to hide African Americans from public view. In Washington—widely considered the center of black society—separate windows, manned by black clerks, were installed to service black people. Federal office bathrooms, lunchrooms, and offices became segregated, often leaving African Americans to toil in terrible conditions, whether it was a basement facility, or a poorly lit and badly ventilated nook. At the Post Office Department, blacks had no place to eat at all, while whites took their lunch to a comfortable dining room. Soon, the practice spread to other government departments, including the Census, Auditor of the Navy, and Bureau of Engraving and Printing, where black women who had dined with white women for nearly a decade were suddenly relegated to a separate table. Word of these new practices started to leak out, first reported by the black press and then, marginally, by outlets such as the *New York Times*.

Among those arguing against segregation was Wilson's close friend and loyal supporter Oswald Garrison Villard. Villard was editor of the liberal *New-York Evening Post*, grandson of abolitionist William Lloyd Garrison, and a white cofounder of the four-year-old NAACP, which had been pushing more aggressively to advance the rights of blacks at a time when progress was terribly slow. During the presidential campaign, Wilson told Villard he would consider creating a race commission to study the relationship between blacks and whites in America. Now Villard felt duped, questioning Wilson's real intentions, and told him so in an angry letter. In a response to Villard, the president took no responsibility for allowing segregation, saying it was due to "the initiative and suggestion of the heads of departments." But, tellingly, he also said he believed that segregation was in the interest of both races, because it made black workers "more safe in their possession of office and less likely to be discriminated against."

Villard was not the only one writing to Wilson in outrage. In addition to sending letters, angry Americans also sent petitions, some with twenty thousand signatures, urging an end to segregation. Wilson, showing a stubborn streak, refused to change course. As 1914 dawned, photographs were required as part of the civil service job application.

On May 7, 1914, the U.S. Marine Band, dapper in their red jackets, began to play love songs in the hallway outside the Blue Room of the White House. Their repertoire was much the same as the last wedding they had performed there, when the president's oldest daughter, Margaret, was married in an elaborate ceremony the previous fall. This wedding, uniting Eleanor and Treasury Secretary McAdoo, was much smaller, with fewer than a hundred guests. That was by design. The first lady had been feeling seriously ill for months, and Nell—as the Wilsons called their daughter—did not want to add to her mother's stress.

As guests took their seats, one of McAdoo's seven children from a previous marriage—twelve-year-old Sallie—led the bridal party down the stairs and toward the makeshift altar. Nell's two sisters, one in a light pink dress, the other in baby blue, each carried a shepherd's crook decorated with flowers. McAdoo and his best man, White House doctor Cary Travers Grayson, entered from the Red Room and waited. On cue, as the band began to play "Here Comes the Bride," Nell, in a gown made of draped ivory satin and trimmed in old point lace, dragged a three-foot train toward the dais. The platform, covered in silk that matched the walls, overlooked the sunny White House gardens. She took her place between two large cobalt blue vases—bursting with lilies—that the French government had sent as gifts years earlier. McAdoo gazed adoringly at his fiancée. The Presbyterian minister from Princeton waited for the room to quiet and then led the couple through the ceremony.

"I promise to be the loving, faithful, obedient wife of William McAdoo," Nell declared. They placed rings on each other's fingers and formed a receiving line in the Red Room, under Gilbert Stuart's portrait of George Washington. Nell cut the cake with a military sword. The first lady, wearing a cream lace dress, absorbed every detail, unaware that her brother Stockton Axson was watching her closely, concerned about her health. At one point, he asked Wilson how she was feeling.

"She is coming out of the woods," the president said.

When it was time for the newlyweds to leave, the Wilsons, who had been married for twenty-nine years, held hands in the doorway and kissed their daughter good-bye.

Wilson could feel his world shifting, and it wasn't a change for the better.

On June 28, 1914, a young Serb had waited for Archduke Franz Ferdinand and his wife, Sophie, to pull up alongside him in their open convertible on the streets of Sarajevo. The teenager seized his opportunity, aiming his gun, squeezing the trigger twice at point-blank range, and killing them both. The assassination of the heir-apparent to the Austro-Hungarian Empire was the catastrophic catalyst to a war over the future of Europe. The geopolitical structure of the globe was now in violent flux.

As mounting tensions spread throughout July, the president grew concerned about foreign affairs. He was also distracted by his wife's health, which was rapidly deteriorating. Dr. Cary Travers Grayson, perhaps not wanting to upset the president, had been downplaying the seriousness of her illness. But now that she could no longer get out of bed, he summoned other doctors to diagnose her condition. They deduced that she had Bright's disease; her kidneys were failing, and she would not recover. He carried the heavy news to Wilson's office.

"What am I to do?" Wilson cried. The president climbed the stairs to Ellen's room on the second floor of the White House and sat vigil by her bed as the world began to unravel.

Austria-Hungary declared war on Serbia on July 28. Days later, on August 1, Germany declared war on Russia and then on France two days later. Meanwhile, France, Russia, England, and its ally Japan were lining up against Germany. Inside the White House, the president felt helpless, unable to alleviate the suffering in Europe or in his own home.

Ellen slept most of the day on August 4. Wilson remained by her bed, holding on to her with one hand and writing messages with the other to the emperors of Germany and Austria-Hungary, the president of France, the king of England, and the czar of Russia, offering to broker peace. Britain had just declared war on Germany; Wilson had responded by issuing a formal proclamation of neutrality, forbidding any American citizen from fighting in the war on behalf of any nation. As Wilson was completing his dispatches, a doctor came in to check on Ellen and was alarmed by her condition. He advised Wilson to call the family to her side; the end was near. Wilson laid his pen to rest and openly wept.

Ellen, only fifty-four years old, held on for two more days. Moments before she died, she drew Dr. Grayson near: "Please take good care of Woodrow, Doctor." He promised her he would. At 5 p.m., in the presence of their family, Wilson folded her hands across her still chest, walked over to the window, and sobbed.

The next day, he wrote to Mary Hulbert Peck: "God has stricken me almost beyond what I can bear."

■ ■ ■

Alice Paul's recovery was as complete as it could be. With her sense of smell ruined and her interest in food, especially meat, diminished by the forced feedings in London, she remained thin and pale, even now, in late August. But she had recovered the spring in her step. The day she had been working toward for months had finally arrived.

The suffragists were awed as they made their way through the two-story entrance of Marble House, the opulent white-stone mansion on Bellevue Avenue in Newport, Rhode Island, that Alva Belmont had commissioned with her first husband, William Vanderbilt. The home was special for two reasons: Costing eleven million dollars when completed in 1892, this fifty-room "cottage" was the most expensive summer home in Newport. In addition, it was inspired by two buildings dedicated to women: the Petit Trianon at Versailles, for Madame de Pompadour; and the Parthenon, the Greek temple honoring Athena, the goddess of wisdom and war.

If there was one thing most people knew about Belmont, besides having both the personality and build of a bulldog, it was that she was a fearless and tireless advocate for women's rights. In 1895, after twenty years of marriage and three children, she divorced Vanderbilt, a railroad heir who struggled with fidelity. Her decision defied convention at the time. When her second husband died in 1908, Belmont began volunteering for progressive causes, using her great wealth to support women's rights. In 1909, she founded the Political Equality League to muster votes for suffrage-supporting New York State politicians and aided labor in the shirtwaist makers strike. She wrote articles for newspapers and donated significant amounts of money to suffrage causes in the United States and the United Kingdom, where she personally observed and was inspired by the Pankhursts' work. Opening her purse, and her home, for the cause centered Belmont in the movement.

The women were arriving at Marble House for a meeting of the Congressional Union for Woman Suffrage (CUWS), the group's first major assembly since splitting with the National American. For months, Paul had been developing a war chest; the membership of her splinter group and Belmont's offer to host helped her accomplish both more quickly. Newport in the summer was full of women who could write large checks and spend their time volunteering for a cause. The location also painted the CUWS in a more ladylike light after months of bad publicity about the dissension between the new and old branches of the suffrage movement. Even though Paul acknowledged that the elitist scene could make African American women and those representing labor feel unwelcome, she needed funding and fresh members desperately. So she accepted Belmont's offer to host.

As the women ambled curiously through the foyer, their eyes fell on the French doors at the back of Marble House framing a stunning scene. The large terrace was decorated with purple, white, and gold silk banners. Beyond that, acres of lawn stretched to a cliff's edge on the Atlantic Ocean; for now, the sea separated America from the horrors of war on the other side. In a far corner of the property was a newly constructed Chinese tea house, its green tile roofline resembling a dragon, mesmerizing against the bright blue sky. Tea was scheduled to be served there later in the day, in specially designed cups and saucers marked "Votes for Women."

But first, Paul and Lucy Burns had something more substantial to serve these guests in the twenty-two-carat Gold Room, where the walls and ceiling were covered in gilt. The invited press was there, waiting beneath a spectacular chandelier to hear what these organizers were going to do next. The women joined them, settling into their chairs to hear Burns explain the geography of the battlefield. She began with a survey of the politics. The Democratic Party, she said, was in total control of the federal government. President Wilson had been asked seven times to support the suffrage movement and seven times he refused. Meanwhile, Democratic leaders in the Senate had blocked the federal amendment by bringing it to a vote when they knew it would be defeated. And Henry, chairman of the House Rules Committee, which

Alva Belmont's china at Marble House.

had consistently blocked the measure, said he was doing so because it was in keeping with the policy of the Democrats. For these reasons, the midterm elections would be essential to the suffrage cause. That was because there was a newly ratified 17th Amendment, which held that voters—not their legislators—would elect U.S. senators directly for the first time. If suffragists used votes for women as an issue in the midterms, they might be able to elect more Republicans, and tip the balance in Congress. "It is up to all of you in the room to guide voters toward the GOP," Burns said. The election was only a couple of months away, and the CUWS should try to defeat the Democrats.

Her passionate presentation captivated the audience, which was peppered with potential defectors from the National American, still considering which organization to affiliate with. One of these waverers was Katharine Hepburn, of Connecticut. Hepburn, a Bryn Mawr graduate, was so dedicated to NAWSA that she had founded her state's branch for the National American. But over the last year, her engagement with the cause had intensified; she latched onto Paul's activities, including participating in a deputation to Wilson and hosting Emmeline Pankhurst when the British woman was in Hartford for a speaking engagement. Hepburn's very presence in the room was evidence that impatient NAWSA members could indeed be converted into more aggressive suffragists working with the CUWS. And as these converts listened to Burns's speech from their comfortable perches inside a gold-slathered room, they were feeling pleased with their choice. A handful of women delivered a standing ovation at the close of Burns's presentation.

With the crowd now sufficiently warmed up, it was Paul's turn to deliver their strategy for defeating Democrats at the polls. Before beginning, she intensified the drama of her pending revelation by asking the press to leave. When the last reporters had filtered out, the room fell to pin-drop silence, the air thick with anticipation.

"Please don't reveal this until the middle of September when the Congressional Union will be ready to put it into practical operation," Paul said. "We['re] determined to get the amendment through the 63rd Congress, or to make it very clear who had kept it from going through. . . . The point is first, who is our enemy, and then how shall that enemy be attacked?"

Paul had created a blacklist of eighteen key Democrats who were not moving suffrage forward and could be voted out by women casting ballots in their home states, sending a strong message to the national party that the movement was advancing beyond talk to direct mobilization with national political implications. Her plan to achieve this was ambitious and expensive. It involved sending two suffragists to each of the western states where women could vote. One of the women would organize the distribution of literature to every household while the other would speak at rallies in the largest cities. Across the rugged landscape they would go, to Wyoming, Colorado, Utah, Idaho, Washington, California, Oregon, Arizona, and Kansas. All of this would transpire while a batch of other states—North and South Dakota, Nebraska, Missouri, Ohio, and Nevada—had suffrage votes approaching in November. In Montana, which had passed woman suffrage in 1914, Jeannette Rankin would be on the ballot as the first woman to run for Congress.

"Now the time has come, we believe, when we can really go into national politics and use the nearly 4 million votes that we have to win the vote for the rest of us," Paul said. "We need no longer make our appeal simply to the men. The struggle in England has gotten down to a physical fight"—her mind could have flashed to Emmeline Pankhurst being carried away by the police outside Buckingham Palace just a few months prior. "Here our fight is simply a political one. The question is whether we are good enough politicians to take 4 million votes and organize them and use them so as to win the vote for the women who are still disenfranchised. We, of course, are a little body to undertake this. But we have to begin. We have not very much money. There are not many of us to go out against the real Democratic Party. Perhaps this time we won't be able to do so very much, though I know we can do a great deal, but if the party leaders see that some votes have been turned, they will know that we have at least realized this power that we possess and they will know that by 1916, we will have it organized. The mere announcement of the fact that the suffragists of the East have gone out to the West with this appeal will be enough to make every man in Congress sit up and take notice."

Sending women out by train across the Rocky Mountains was pioneering, not just for the terrain to be traversed. This would be the first time suffragists had ever involved themselves directly in a national election. The concept was shocking and betrayed nearly seven decades of America's polite suffrage legacy. But these women were ready for something new. Paul said she needed $15,000 to set up a field organization. She asked those in the room for their money. She asked them for their time. She asked them for their commitment to the cause. She asked them to go west.

The response was enthusiastic. The women opened their purses and donated $7,000. Burns, along with Rose Winslow, a former factory worker, agreed to open a headquarters in San Francisco. Pairs of women, including seasoned organizers such as Doris Stevens, lined up to take the rest of the states. Those who could afford to cover their own expenses did. Vida Milholland, Inez's sister, sold valuable jewelry to finance her trip. Paul sought sponsors for the others. Everyone was expected to raise funds along the way.

In mid-September, the western campaigners left from Washington's Union Station in a festooned railcar, each carrying a congressional directory, contacts, and pamphlets. Traveling together until Chicago, they wasted no time, using the train as a platform to sell issues of *The Suffragist*, raise money, and hold rallies. With less than two months before the midterm elections, every minute counted.

In Denver, the daughter of a former senator held a party with one hundred guests, mostly women, who listened closely to Stevens's appeal. One woman came up to Stevens after her talk and said: "I had no idea you women had been so rebuffed by my Party. I am convinced that my duty is to the women first, and my Party second." The campaigners took freight trains to tiny towns and, in one instance, even hijacked the attention of a group of people waiting for an auction to begin. The women spoke at libraries and in front of sheet metal unions. They canvassed stores, spoke with clerks, and ducked into factories. They swung by the offices of the *Kansas City Star* and spoke with the editor. At the Grand Canyon, they found twenty people to sell *The Suffragist* to.

It was exhausting and exhilarating. But was it successful? When the election ended, the CUWS took credit for defeating three candidates and for influencing the results in three other races; a small number, admittedly, but it was all that could be expected from an eight-week sprint, among neophytes spread thinly over half of the country. Nationwide, in the Senate, Democrats picked up four seats. But in the House, the party lost sixty votes, leaving them with only a thirty-four-vote majority, a shrinking margin that distressed Wilson greatly. Only two of the seven states voting on women's suffrage—Nevada and Montana—approved those measures during the midterm election. This lack of progress at the state level added even more urgency to Paul's push for a federal amendment. One way to bring more attention to her cause was to rename the Bristow-Mondell Amendment the Susan B. Anthony Amendment, which she did, giving it weight and underscoring the duration of the suffrage struggle in America. Publicity around the midterm efforts gave Paul more credibility. As her national stature grew, Wilson was confined to the White House, collapsing emotionally.

■ ■ ■

The results of the midterms, combined with the loss of his wife three months earlier, sent Wilson into a deep depression. He was picky about his food, now weighing just 176 pounds, and felt apathy toward the happenings out west, in Congress, and even in his own administration. He did not know what to do about Europe's disintegration, a distressing emergency, its impact on the United States further compounded by slowing exports that dragged down the fragile economy. Across the South, cotton was piling up with no place to go.

Out of concern for his health, Wilson's physician encouraged him to keep an almost daily routine of golf, as he had done since the beginning of his presidency. On many mornings, even in cold weather, the president would walk to the White House's covered carriage stop, climb into the black Pierce-Arrow that awaited him, and go play a round of golf. He played at Kirkside, in Chevy Chase Circle; the Washington

Country Club, across the Potomac in Virginia; or, occasionally, at the Town and Country. Wilson was a terrible golfer, once admitting to the press that he recorded a score of 146. He had poor peripheral vision in one eye from a small stroke years before, and the blind spots—both literal and proverbial, his critics would say—seemed to disrupt his focus in a mentally strenuous game. Now, with his wife's death still haunting him, Wilson needed a nudge to leave the White House more than ever. He was completely disengaged from his elected duties, wallowing in the tragedy of his personal life.

"My heart is in a whirl day and night," he wrote in a letter to Peck on November 8. "My own individual life has gone utterly to pieces, I do not care a fig for anything that affects me. I could laugh aloud to see the papers, and those for whom they write, assuming every day that a second term in 1916 is in my thoughts and that I want it! If they only knew my supreme indifference to that and to everything else that affects me personally, they would devote their foolish and futile brains to some other topic that they do not understand!"

Given his mind-set, Wilson was in no mood to receive visitors hospitably at the White House. But when African American activist William Monroe Trotter asked to see him, the president knew he needed to agree. He had to maintain a facade of sympathy, even if this would be an uncomfortable conversation. And so, just four days after the president's lament to Peck, Trotter arrived at the Oval Office with representatives from the National Equal Rights League, furious about segregation. They explained that black men had discovered their strength as a voting bloc, registered their outrage at the polls, and—like the suffragists—voted against every Democrat who had not opposed the separation of races in federal government. Wilson could feel the offense rising within him and abruptly halted Trotter's appeal.

"In the first place, let's leave politics out of it," Wilson said. "This is a human problem. . . . It takes the world generations to outlive all its prejudices." But the more Wilson spoke the more he revealed just how aligned he was with the federal policy on segregation. Wilson said the issue was one of "economic equality—whether the Negro can do the same things with equal efficiency."

Trotter shook his head. "Only two years ago you were heralded as perhaps the second Lincoln," Trotter said. "And now the Afro-American leaders who supported you are hounded as false leaders and traitors to the race. What a change segregation has wrought! You said that your colored fellow citizens could depend on you for everything which would assist in advancing the interest of their race in the United States. . . . Is there a 'new freedom' for white Americans and a 'new slavery' for your Afro-American fellow citizens?"

"Your tone, sir, offends me," Wilson said. "You are an American citizen as fully an American citizen as I am, but you are the only American citizen that has ever come into this office who has talked to me with a tone . . . of passion that was evident. Now, I want to say that if this association comes again, it must have another spokesman. You have spoiled the whole cause for which you came."

"I am sorry to hear that," Trotter said. "In an America that professed to be Christian—"

"I expect those who profess to be Christian to come to me in a Christian spirit."

Trotter continued to argue his case briefly before finally leading the delegation out to the street, where a scrum of reporters was waiting. The resulting coverage skewered Wilson, who seemed upset only about losing his temper, not about the substance of his argument. The issue of race continued to trail the president. As one Cleveland newspaper noted, "It was not what Trotter said to him that angered him, half as much as the fact that a 'Negro' had said it."

No matter how often Wilson said he had the best interests of African Americans in mind, his actions proved otherwise. Just a few months after the Trotter confrontation, Wilson's old friend and colleague from Johns Hopkins, Thomas Dixon Jr., had written a bestselling novel called *The Clansman*. It had been adapted into a film, known by its subtitle *The Birth of a Nation*. The movie, the most expensive yet to be made in America, featured white actors in blackface and heroically portrayed the Ku Klux Klan. It was premiering soon and Dixon, hoping for an endorsement by Wilson, whom he considered a fellow historian, asked the president if he could screen the film in the White House. Wilson said yes. On February 18, 1915, the president, his daughters, and his cabinet all gathered in the East Room to watch the ninety-minute movie, the first motion picture ever shown at 1600 Pennsylvania Avenue.

As word trickled out that Wilson had seen the film, outrage and calls for boycotting the production ensued. Trotter organized a rally in Boston, people debated censoring the film out of concerns that it could provoke riots, while others argued in favor of freedom of speech. Pickets erupted outside theaters across the country. In the South, the film served as a recruiting tool for a resurgent Ku Klux Klan. The president declined to speak directly about the movie. But he did have an aide release a statement saying he was "unaware of the character of the play before it was presented and has at no time expressed his approbation of it. Its exhibition at the White House was a courtesy extended to an old acquaintance."

Although Wilson tried to backpedal, his pattern of behavior was clear. The president was having an awful political season, all of his own doing. Wilson, previously careful and precise in his official duties, was clearly unmoored. Meanwhile, Dr. Grayson was watching him closely. Occasionally, Wilson refrained from golfing. On one cold, raw day in February, he and Dr. Grayson went for a drive around town in the Pierce-Arrow to get some fresh air. Not far from the White House, they passed a woman on foot, known to the doctor. He bowed to greet her.

"Who is that beautiful woman?" Wilson asked.

Happy to see a spark in the president, Dr. Grayson explained that she was Edith Bolling Galt, a forty-three-year-old widow. A bon vivant and independent spirit, Galt was the first woman to own and drive an electric car in Washington. She was also from Virginia, raised on a plantation with slaves, and had attended boarding school until the family's limited funds were diverted to her brothers. Galt, with black hair and blue eyes, had been married at twenty-four to a man who owned one of the premier jewelry stores in Washington. They had had one child, who'd died at three days old; Galt's husband, Norman, died five years later when she was thirty-five. Although she had no business experience, Galt had taken over his retail operation and was doing quite well for herself.

Wilson seemed intrigued enough to inspire Dr. Grayson to arrange a meeting. But because he did not believe the president would accept a direct introduction, he relied on Wilson's cousin and regular White House guest Helen Bones to serve as an intermediary. The two women became friends, and in March, Bones invited Galt for tea at the White House. The president dropped in on them when he returned from golf. They enjoyed chatting and, in the weeks ahead, afternoon tea progressed to chaperoned drives and White House dinners.

On May 4, less than two months after their first encounter, the president asked Galt to join him for a meal with his sister, niece, daughter, cousin, and doctor at the White House. It was a warm evening, and after they ate, Dr. Grayson went home while the rest of the group strolled to the south portico where coffee was served. The guests sauntered onto the lawn, leaving Wilson and Galt alone. Without wasting any time, Wilson pulled his chair close and looked directly into her eyes.

"I asked Margaret and Helen to give me an opportunity to tell you something tonight that I have already told them," Wilson said quietly. "I love you."

Galt was so surprised by how emotional he was, and by the fact that he even uttered those words, that she blurted out the first thing that came to mind.

"Oh, you can't love me, for you don't really know me; and it is less than a year since your wife died."

"Yes," he said. "I know you feel that; but, little girl, in this place time is not measured by weeks, or months, or years, but by deep human experiences; and since her death I have lived a lifetime of loneliness and heartache. I was afraid, knowing you, I would shock you; but I would be less than a gentleman if I continued to make opportunities to see you without telling you what I have told my daughters and Helen: that I want you to be my wife."

Galt was stunned and scared. She was concerned that the public would think she loved Wilson just because he was president. And she was insecure about her ability to be first lady, not knowing the first thing about it. She did find him charming and appreciated his candor, but after an hour's discussion, she told Wilson that if he required an immediate answer, it would have to be no.

"We're entitled to continue the friendship until I decide," she said, eager to preserve the option.

At 10 p.m., the president and Bones drove Galt home in silence. It was a short trip, just over a mile away, to Galt's small house in Dupont Circle, where she lived alone.

CHAPTER ELEVEN

Submarine Warfare

The *Lusitania* was six days into its journey from New York and about ten miles off the coast of Kinsale, Ireland, gliding through the sparkling ocean on a crisp spring day. Travelers were relieved at the sight of land, but such close proximity to the cliffs meant that the ocean liner was in a war zone. It was after lunch and, out on the deck, children skipped rope, adults lounged and read, others leaned on the rails, and a few noticed what looked like the tail of a fish cutting through the water on the starboard side, leaving a streak of froth in its wake.

"That isn't a torpedo, is it?" an American woman asked.

At 2:10 p.m. on May 7, 1915, 350 pounds of explosives blew a hole under the bridge of the ship, about ten feet below the waterline. From a distance, a German seaman raised the periscope of his U-boat and realized that not only had the torpedo landed a direct hit, it had struck the RMS *Lusitania* without warning. In just eighteen minutes, one of the largest, fastest vessels on the sea, a British ship the Germans believed was smuggling arms, had hit the seabed, taking down nearly 1,200 passengers and crew with it. One hundred and twenty-eight of them were American.

Wilson was just finishing lunch, about to golf, when he received the first bulletin about the sinking of the *Lusitania*. He was initially told there had been no loss of life, but he canceled his golf plans, anyway, opting to go for a reflective drive instead. When he returned to the

White House, updates by wire from the State Department provided more accurate reports of the horrific tragedy. The Royal Navy had been blockading German ships. In retaliation, German U-boats were attacking whatever they could find, even steamers carrying civilians.

The president was reeling. He was trying to stay out of the war, but the torpedoing of innocent Americans turned many neutral or noninterventionist Americans into hawks. And now Wilson, too, was rethinking his position, not just because of the shifting political reality, but also because it was his role as commander in chief to protect U.S. citizens. At a minimum, he knew the country needed to be prepared for the worst.

As he battled with the decision before him, Wilson was overwhelmed by how deeply lonely he felt; clearly he had more than the *Lusitania* on his mind. He feared that Galt was having second thoughts about their relationship and sat down to write her a letter. "My happiness absolutely depends upon your giving me your entire love," he wrote.

Upon signing the letter, he set romance aside and turned his attention to the crisis at hand, drafting a speech articulating his position on the war. Two days later, in Philadelphia, Wilson, at a naturalization ceremony for one thousand foreign-born citizens, presented his argument. He justified the reasons for maintaining neutrality as a nation, but also impressed that Americans should be prepared to fight.

> The example of America must be a special example. The example of America must be the example not merely of peace because it will not fight, but of peace because peace is the healing and elevating influence of the world and strife is not. There is such a thing as a man being too proud to fight. . . . There is such a thing as a nation being so right that it does not need to convince others by force that it is right.

For now, it appeared that the United States was staying out of any global conflict. The battles at home, however, were only intensifying.

Wilson was still hoping Galt would marry him, enticing her to accompany him on a boat trip from Washington to New York to inspect the

Atlantic fleet. They climbed aboard the *Mayflower*, a steamship that served as the presidential yacht, and sailed down the Potomac. The couple was joined for dinner by other family members and close aides. Wilson was quiet during the meal, and after the dishes were cleared, he and Galt retired to the deck alone, watching the silvery water.

"Let's lean on the rail instead of walking, as I want to talk to you," he said to Galt. "I am very much distressed over a letter I had late today from the Secretary of State [William Jennings Bryan] saying he cannot go on in the Department as he is a pacifist and cannot follow me in wishing to warn our own country and Germany that we may be forced to take up arms; therefore he feels it is his duty to resign."

Wilson paused and asked her what the public would think if Bryan resigned. Galt, who was opinionated and quick to offer her political advice, believed it would be a good thing because "many persons did not take Bryan seriously." She expressed her hope that Wilson would replace him with someone who commanded respect at home and abroad.

"What do you think of Robert Lansing?" he asked her.

"Isn't he only a clerk in the State Department?"

"He is a counselor of the Department, and he has a good schooling under old Mr. John W. Foster, his father-in-law, for whom I have great respect. I think he would steer Lansing and the combination would be of great help to me."

Galt was dubious about Lansing but refrained from expressing her skepticism, going to bed instead. The next day, the *Mayflower* hit rough water. Everyone on board became seasick, except for the president. He seemed impervious.

■ ■ ■

Throughout the first nine months of 1915, the suffrage booth at the Panama–Pacific International Exposition in San Francisco was thoughtfully decorated, displaying a portrait of Susan B. Anthony, hanging baskets of flower bouquets, a U.S. map revealing the suffrage vote of every member in the House, and a chart illustrating the present status of women's voting rights in each state. The venue was simple enough, but Alice Paul had slogged for a whole year to reach this point. After the western campaign, the Congressional Union for Woman Suffrage (CUWS) had been organizing every state at a grassroots level, culminating in a local convention to formulate a plan of attack for Congress, elect a chairwoman, and then send that person to a gathering of women voters here, at the expo, in September 1915.

The exposition, expecting some nineteen million visitors throughout the year, was laid out on the sprawling grounds of the Presidio and displayed a range of modern inventions and a vision for a progressive future. The expo included the first steam locomotive purchased by Southern Pacific railroad; a telephone line that connected the city with New York so people across the continent could hear the Pacific Ocean; a four hundred–foot Tower of Jewels, covered in cut-glass gems and lit up at night; and also, women who wanted to vote. At the CUWS's suffrage booth, visitors could meet real live suffragists, hear about the federal amendment, and sign a petition—on a large scroll—in favor of it.

In addition to the booth, Paul had planned a simultaneous suffrage convention for September; it would feature talks by prominent women, such as Alva Belmont, and an eight hundred–person luncheon. The next phase of her campaign involved finding volunteers to drive the petition cross-country to deliver it to the White House, giving speeches along the way. Two Swedish women, enamored with the cause, offered the use of a car they had just purchased with the intent of driving to Rhode Island. Paul was thrilled and asked Sara Bard Field—a thirty-three-year-old divorced mother, poet, and suffrage speaker from Oregon—if she wanted to accompany the Swedes.

"Do you realize service stations across the country are very scarce?" Field asked Paul. "And you have to have a great deal of mechanical knowledge in case the car has some accident?"

"Oh well, if that happens, I'm sure some good man will come along that'll help you," Paul said.

Despite the risk, Field consented and ten thousand people gathered to watch the three women leave. A huge chorus sang "The Woman's Hymn," a piece for which Field had written new lyrics:

We are women clad in new power
We march to set our sisters free

At midnight, as the fair lights powered off and a band began to play, Field climbed into the open-air car with her drivers, Ingeborg Kindstedt and Maria Kindberg. A great demand banner was attached along the side. The petition—believed to be the longest ever signed in one place: 18,333 feet long, with five hundred thousand names—was securely packed. They called the decorated car the "Suffrage Flier." They disappeared into the night and Paul caught a train back east.

In the days ahead, Field called from the road, submitting reports to Lucy Burns, who shaped them into stories for *The Suffragist*. Burns worked her writing magic, creating a serial adventure that was beloved by readers. To heighten suspense, the first-person account read as if Field was traveling solo: "I wake up at 6 a.m., jolt, bump, bounce and shake over one hundred miles of awful roads, land weary to the breaking point."

Suffrage envoy Sara Bard Field (left); her driver, Maria Kindberg (center); and machinist Ingeborg Kindstedt (right) during their cross-country journey to present suffrage petitions to Congress, September–December 1915.

It took three months for the women to cross the desert and the mountains; forge through rain, sleet, snow, and mud; break down and repair the car; and deliver the talks that Paul had scheduled. The venues ranged from a library in Kansas City, Kansas, to an automobile procession down New York's Fifth Avenue. While Field's progress was unavoidably and excruciatingly slow, the country she was traveling through was changing quickly.

As Field and Paul headed east in September, Wilson began signing a batch of legislation, including the Adamson Act, which created the eight-hour workday; the Wick's Bill, which prevented the sale of goods, produced with child labor, across state lines; and the Federal Employees' Compensation Act, providing benefits to civilian employees who were injured or disabled on the job—landmarks of the Progressive Era. Then, on October 6, the White House announced Wilson's engagement. In an accompanying statement, perhaps in an effort to quell public outrage (among females) that he was remarrying so soon after the death of his wife, the president said he would vote for women's suffrage in the state of New Jersey the following month.

More shocking news was just around the corner: in early November, under pressure from members, the NAWSA board withdrew the Shafroth-Palmer Amendment. Anna Howard Shaw admitted the amendment had not been "a wise measure" and acknowledged that people were losing faith in her leadership. Further, she announced she would cede control of the two million–member organization to Carrie Chapman Catt.

When Field arrived in Washington on December 6, met by a herald on a horse, it was as if the old America were welcoming a new version of itself. In a dramatic scene, Field ascended the Capitol stairs, trailing the four-mile petition behind her on huge spools. A band playing "La Marseillaise" and "Dixie" accompanied Field and three hundred others as they walked. Despite the spectacle—or perhaps because of it—no elected officials would meet with them. Rebuffed, the suffragists trekked to the White House.

Unlike the members of the House and Senate, Wilson begrudgingly agreed to receive a few of the suffragists in his office. Therein, Field

A procession of two thousand women, including those from western states with suffrage, march to the U.S. Capitol in December 1915.

engaged the president on the issue at hand and encouraged him to embrace the federal amendment, both personally and in his upcoming congressional address.

"We have seen that, like all great men, you have changed your mind on other questions," Field told him. "We have watched the change and development of your mind on [war] preparedness, and we honestly believe that circumstances have so altered that you may change your mind in this regard."

She then held up the scrolls, at last at their destination, and asked him to look at all of the signatures. He unfurled a section, smiled, and claimed that he had not expected to have to address the women.

"I hope it is true that I am not a man set stiffly beyond the possibility of learning," Wilson said, sounding humble and genuine. "I hope that I shall continue to be a learner as long as I live. I can only say to you this afternoon that nothing could be more impressive than the presentation of such a request in such numbers and backed by such influence as undoubtedly stands behind you. Unhappily it is too late for me to consider what is going into my message, because that went out to the newspapers about a week ago." Besides, he said, his message to Congress was focused on one thing: preparing for war. And although he did not disclose it, he was also busy preparing for his wedding.

■ ■ ■

December 18 was no ordinary day in Galt's town house. She wandered the lower floor, surveying its newly empty rooms. Decorators had removed every stick of furniture from the entry hall, dining room, and drawing room. The latter space featured a beautiful bay window—its best feature—in front of which Galt and Wilson would be married that evening. The ceremony was scheduled for 8:30 p.m. The groom arrived about half an hour in advance, alone except for his Secret Service detail, and waited with Galt in her upstairs sitting room until the White House usher tapped on the door: "Mr. President, it is 8:30." Galt smiled at Wilson. She was dressed strangely for a wedding, sheathed in a black velvet gown and carrying orchids. Together, they started down the stairs, where family, a few close friends, and "devoted old servitors of various households"—as the bride described the former slaves—gathered to witness the rite.

Her mother gave Galt's hand to Wilson and he placed a special ring on her finger; it was made from a large nugget of solid gold, given to him by the people of California as a gift. With the remaining gold, they had made an enameled scarf pin for the president in the shape of the official seal of the office; he added this to his collection, along with a signet ring.

After the exchange of vows and a bountiful buffet dinner with their guests, Wilson and Galt made their exit. The Secret Service had cordoned off a large section of the street so all was quiet as they climbed into the car and headed for the train station. It was midnight when they boarded a railcar, filled with congratulatory flowers. They nibbled on dainty sandwiches and fruit as they traveled the short distance to Alexandria, Virginia. There, they were guided into another White House limousine for the short trip to a hotel in Hot Springs, snow-coated from the ground to its highest mountain peaks. They stayed at the Homestead in a suite filled with chintz and warmed by a wood fire. Their rooms overlooked a golf course, where they played each morning. In the afternoons, they went for drives along old familiar roads they had both traveled as children. They had planned to stay three weeks. But on January 3, 1916, they received alarming news. A German U-boat, without warning, had torpedoed a British cruiser, killing 350 passengers off the coast of Crete. The Wilsons aborted their honeymoon and returned to Washington.

CHAPTER TWELVE

The Advancing Army

Woodrow Wilson quieted the audience at the Waldorf-Astoria in New York City. The 1,200 men seated in front of him and watching from balconies in their dark suits and stiff white collars were members of the Railway Business Association and this was their annual dinner. But the topic at hand wasn't the nation's trains. The Germans had marched through Luxembourg and Belgium, and in the month since the president's truncated honeymoon, they'd continued to advance. So had Wilson's thinking about the war. On this night, January 27, 1916, the president told the crowd that he still hoped for peace, but as the Germans threatened bloody attacks on France, the nation needed to be pragmatic and prepare for the worst; men needed to be ready to protect the Western Hemisphere and defend democracy and American values. Although he said that his thinking had evolved with the circumstances, the truth was that 1916 was a presidential election year and American sentiment had also become more pro-war since the *Lusitania* sank. That sentiment was intensifying with each German battle won. Wilson knew it was increasingly unpopular for him to be a pacifist and isolationist.

"We must see to it that a sufficient body of citizens is given the kind of training which will make them efficient now if called into the field in case of necessity," Wilson said. "What I am after, and what every American ought to insist upon, is a body of at least half a million trained citizens who will serve under conditions of danger as an immediately available national reserve." This reserve would be separate from the National Guard. He cautioned that the nation should put aside partisan differences not just "for the successful prosecution of the war," but also for the "successful prosecution of peace." The audience cheered.

While Wilson's public statements were stiffening, he continued to explore diplomatic options to end the war. On Valentine's Day, a couple of weeks after the president's preparedness speech, Wilson's chief European adviser Edward M. House attended a dinner at a private residence in London with several British government officials, including Prime Minister Herbert Asquith and British foreign secretary Sir Edward Grey. They talked for two hours, with House predicting that the Germans would attack the French at Verdun. After the servants left, at 10:30 p.m., the men discussed a peace plan. But the British were skeptical of Wilson's motives, understanding he was campaigning for reelection. Ultimately, there was no agreement.

Just days after the peace proposal evaporated, the German Fifth Army launched what would become one of the most epic battles of the war. For nine hours straight, they bombarded the French Second Army north of the historic city of Verdun, just as House had feared. Their goal was to bleed the French Army to death. At the same time, the Germans informed America that armed merchant ships would be treated in the same manner as cruisers: that is, they would be sunk. Initially, the Germans advanced past the bombed-out trenches to the east bank of the Meuse River but French reinforcements rushed in and pushed them back. Through the frozen winter and a muddy spring, the two sides ground each other down. Meanwhile, on the Eastern Front, the Russians obliged the French request to distract the Germans with a coordinated offense in Vilna and Lake Naroch. The Russians lost seventy thousand men, but overwhelmed the German Army, which still refused to give up the fight in Verdun. The Germans also kept pressure on the seas and torpedoed a passenger ferry, the *Sussex*, which was sailing under a French flag in the English Channel. At least fifty of the more than three hundred passengers died. While none of them were American, Wilson threatened to sever diplomatic ties with Germany over this latest U-boat attack.

The Germans were equally brutal on land. On a hot day in late June, 230 German guns propelled 110,000 phosgene gas grenades into the French encampment in Verdun. This lethal agent hung close to the ground, a yellow fog that smelled like fresh hay. The gas overwhelmed French masks and killed soldiers slowly over a couple of excruciating days, filling their lungs with fluid. One by one, their guns fell silent.

■ ■ ■

As the nation became consumed with news from the front lines of the war in Europe, Paul developed a new strategy to keep suffrage at the forefront of the nation's consciousness during this election year. In the early months of 1916, her plan involved coalescing all of the women voters in America into a force for change. In April, she created the National Woman's Party (NWP), an alternative to the Republican and Democratic parties. The NWP stood for one issue: passage of the Susan B. Anthony Amendment. It would have its maiden convention in early summer, coinciding with the combined convention for the GOP and Progressive parties, which were meeting jointly, as their ideals, candidates, and dislike for Wilson overlapped.

First, Paul needed to rally support for and attendance at the NWP convention. She sent twenty-three suffragists west to the voting states to generate interest in the organization. Lucy Burns, adventurous as ever, went to Seattle for an act of daring. Wearing a suffrage sash over her bomber jacket, Burns flew in a seaplane—which would take off and land on Puget Sound—and floated reams of NWP leaflets down from the sky. Her high-flying antics not only succeeded in distributing promotional material, they also served as a brilliant publicity stunt. Other activists jumped on a whistle-stop train, called "the Suffrage Special," to spread the news. Their combined tactics generated so much enthusiasm that one thousand members attended the NWP convention in early July in Chicago, Illinois.

The Congressional Union for Woman Suffrage (CUWS) sponsored the NWP convention, which unfolded at the Blackstone Hotel and its adjacent theater in Chicago; the venue was about a mile away from

Lucy Burns in a seaplane in Seattle, 1916.

the other conventions happening at the Coliseum and the Auditorium Building. The event began with pouring rain outside, thunderous applause inside, and a program that included Helen Keller, Inez Milholland, and speakers from several political parties.

One man who gave a speech was Wilson's friend Dudley Field Malone, a product of New York politics who had helped get the president elected. Malone, who had the same pillowy face as Winston Churchill, was a lawyer now working as the Collector of the Port of New York, an appointment from Wilson. He was also in favor of suffrage for women. But when Malone urged the NWP's members to be patient with Wilson, saying the president was doing his best to keep the country at peace and that "great men change their minds," the audience became so incensed they booed him off the stage. Harriot Stanton Blatch, in an effort to change the tone of the disgruntled audience, took his place on the stage and addressed the crowd.

"Mr. Malone tells us to be polite," Blatch said. "Good heavens we have been patient and polite. It was not until we began to respect ourselves—it was not until we felt in our very souls that democracy for women was as great as democracy for men—that things began to move!"

"Hear, hear!" the audience shouted. "Hear, hear!"

Blatch then pledged to deliver half a million votes against the Democrats, a bold idea that inspired Belmont—damp from the weather and dripping in diamonds—to stand.

"I'll raise $500,000 for the first Woman's Party campaign," she said. In an instant, the entire convention sprang to its feet, cheering.

As the speeches died down, Connecticut's CUWS leader Lillian Ascough took to the stage to thank Paul, not just for organizing the convention, but also for creating the NWP.

"She has been a tireless leader," Ascough said. "She has given her life to her work, and she has inspired in all of us not only enthusiasm and loyalty, but deep personal devotion." The attendees gave a rousing ovation. But Paul, always modest and busy, had disappeared.

After the final luncheon of the convention, the women marched in the drenching rain toward the Chicago Coliseum, where the Republican and Progressive conventions were about to begin. They mingled in the street with NAWSA members, who had come with the same intention. The unplanned, simultaneous arrival of members of both suffrage factions, made possible not by coordinated effort but by the presence of a shared goal—being seen and heard—offered a glimpse of what was achievable if they worked together. Inside the convention hall, the Progressives endorsed the federal amendment, the first political party to do so. The Republicans favored suffrage, but did not specify a change to the Constitution in their plank. However, the GOP's presidential nominee, Charles Evans Hughes, would support it.

With the NWP's success in Chicago, Paul quickly made her way to St. Louis, where the Democratic convention was getting under way. She was there to lobby delegates from the western states, but it quickly became clear to her that they were aligning with Wilson and his stance on suffrage. The president tried to pacify the suffragists, saying his party should recognize the cause, but, of course, he added, voting rights should be up to the states to decide. With suffrage dispatched as a minor topic, Wilson and many other Democrats focused their speeches on something women could stand behind: peace. But Paul knew advocating neutrality should not preclude granting suffrage; that was a false choice. The Democratic slogan was "He kept us out of war." NWP members added their own tag line: "He kept us out of suffrage."

In the political season, there was one more convention that drew attention. The National American hosted its mass meeting in Atlantic City. With the presidential election just over two months away, Carrie Chapman Catt took a gambit and invited Wilson to speak at her convention. Wilson surprised everyone by accepting and, in his speech, commended delegates for their persistence. He even predicated suffrage would win soon.

But, he said, winning "required moving masses. It is all very well to run ahead and beckon, but, after all, you have to wait for them to follow."

Anna Howard Shaw, the former leader of the organization—now seventy years old—rose from her seat in the audience. She, too, had grown impatient with his stalling and wanted to address him directly.

"We want suffrage to come in your administration!" she shouted. The crowd raved, joining her on her feet. Wilson smiled uncomfortably and retreated from the stage. But the drama did not leave with him. In a stunning turn of events, Catt announced to the NAWSA members that she would hire two hundred field workers to focus singularly on the passage of the Susan B. Anthony Amendment. She would need to increase her budget from $100,000 to a million dollars. State efforts, she explained, would now be secondary. Catt's announcement, clearly influenced by Paul's actions, altered the organization's decades-old focus on state-level voting. And while most of the National American's members were pleased to hear the news, there was one faction that wasn't: southern women.

Never idle, Paul believed it was essential to whip up one last campaign out West to weaken Wilson's chances of winning during the fall run-up to the election. It would be exhaustive and exhausting—a dash through dozens of cities in suffrage states in the short span of thirty-eight days.

A band of women thrust themselves into the task at hand, working hours that were so long, many of them became unwell. Inez Milholland, traveling with her sister Vida, suffered such a fate when she was struck down by tonsillitis about two weeks into the campaign. Inez, as feisty as ever, was now married to a man named Eugen Boissevain, whom she had proposed to. She had also survived a stint the previous year attempting to cover the Great War for the *New-York Tribune*, journeying from Rome to Bologna to Vicenza trying to reach the front lines in Italy before government officials censured her, she believed because she was a woman. But this trip out west for the NWP was more physically challenging for her than her time reporting from war-torn Europe. Paul, frantically organizing from an office in Chicago and churning out copy for *The Suffragist*, was drained, too, but refused to slow down; she did not understand why—even in the throes of illness—anyone would take a break. She did, however, try to reduce Milholland's schedule, slotting in other speakers so the star suffragist could rest. But even that was not enough to make the woman well. Milholland had already spoken in Wyoming, Idaho, Oregon, Washington, Montana, Utah, and Nevada. Sometimes her schedule would require that she would take a train at two in the morning to arrive at eight; and then a train at midnight, to arrive at five in the morning.

"She would come away from audiences and droop as a flower," a friend later wrote. "The hours between were hours of exhaustion and suffering. She would ride in the trains gazing from the windows, listless, almost lifeless, until one spoke; then again the sweet smile, the sudden interest, the quick sympathy. The courage of her was marvelous."

Milholland understood the power and influence she possessed, drawing crowds and changing minds; she showed Americans that feminists could be beautiful, smart, married women, not just homely spinsters. Cultivating this image was essential to the movement's success. If she could inspire mothers living in the mountains to sympathize with the cause, it could change the future of the nation. She carried that burden through the West and it was the only thing that kept her going, until the reality of her illness overwhelmed her. She reluctantly sent a telegram to Paul.

"Doctor insists upon two days rest to avoid complete collapse," Milholland wired.

Paul had heard similar complaints from everyone in the field and assumed Milholland would pull through. Vida confided in Paul: her sister was sick with an infected throat, and her heart was giving her trouble. She had been increasing the dosage of her medicine to no avail. At last, Paul realized the gravity of the situation. Despite negative headlines about Milholland's absence from venues where she was scheduled to be present, Paul advised her to skip Arizona and, in California, simply sit on stage and give a short talk.

In Los Angeles, Milholland pulled herself together to speak before a large audience, and did so briefly, responding to the president's directive to women to be patient. "How long must women wait for liberty?" Milholland begged of the audience. Not long after delivering this striking line, she suddenly collapsed and "lay stark upon the platform," as one journalist noted. Those around Milholland frantically tried to revive the suffragist before she was carried off stage. Although she regained consciousness, the Los Angeles talk was her last one. Milholland needed to go home. Blatch agreed to cover her appearances.

Meanwhile, Burns's flame was dwindling, too. In a letter from Montana, she confessed to Paul that she wanted to return to Brooklyn and leave the work to some married women for a change. Paul, whose journey had paralleled Burns's since their inaugural night in a London jail, could not relate at all to her friend's faltering commitment. Burns, at this point, was thirty-seven years old, six years older than Paul. She had devoted her entire youth to suffrage. She was growing weary and missing home. Paul knew she was running out of time.

■ ■ ■

On Election Day, November 7, 1916, the Wilsons drove to the Princeton firehouse early in the morning so that the president could cast his vote; the first lady was there to watch. New Jersey had suffrage on the ballot and Wilson told Americans he would vote in favor of it, not as president or the leader of his party, but as an individual. After voting, the president and first lady retreated to Shadow Lawn, a local mansion that served as a summer White House for the Wilsons. They had a quiet dinner and the family played Twenty Questions. At 10 p.m., Wilson's daughter Margaret took a call from a friend in New York offering her condolences; the early returns did not look good for the incumbent. But Margaret was unwilling to concede just yet. The polls were still open in the West, she said, so it was too soon to call the race. Dr. Grayson arrived at the mansion to report that the *New York World* was predicting victory for Hughes. The president phoned his secretary, Joseph Tumulty, who confirmed that Wilson would lose.

"Well, Tumulty, it begins to look as if we have been badly licked," Wilson said without any sadness in his voice.

Wilson decided to wait until morning before sending a congratulatory telegram to Hughes, a man the president believed would surely drag America into the war. At 10:30, Wilson had a glass of milk and said goodnight. "I might stay longer but you are all so blue," he said to his family. Edith joined him upstairs a few minutes later and sat on his bed, holding his hand.

"Well, little girl, you were right in expecting we should lose the election," he said. "Frankly, I did not, but we can now do some of the things we want to do." Sleep came quickly.

At CUWS headquarters, Paul and her colleagues waited for the election results, too. Their reports also indicated a win for Hughes. The overnight tallies had New York, Pennsylvania, New Jersey, and Illinois solidly for the Republican, who had also taken Minnesota and Delaware by narrow margins. The race came down to California and its thirteen electoral college votes. Two days later, officials were still counting. While the nation waited anxiously, the Wilsons passed the time with golf. The president was on the eighth tee when Dr. Grayson reported that the state was leaning in his favor. The following day, on November 10, Wilson won California by 3,806 votes. He became the first Democrat elected to a second consecutive term since Andrew Jackson in 1832.

■ ■ ■

The national election was interpreted to be bad news for suffrage, and the results in the states were equally disheartening for the cause. Their strategy of backing Republicans had not worked as well as they had hoped. New Jersey, Massachusetts, Pennsylvania, and even New York rejected their state initiatives to give voting rights to women. Across the country, suffragists wailed over their defeat. But Paul cried victory. She knew that Democrats had heard their message and did not want to go through another election with suffrage hanging around their necks.

The election was not the only devastation the month of November wrought for the CUWS. Two weeks later, on November 25, Milholland's body succumbed to what had been diagnosed as "pernicious anemia," or a lack of vitamin B12. She was thirty years old. Members of the CUWS were devastated—and vigorously angry. Had Wilson supported federal suffrage sooner, Milholland might still be alive. They decided to channel their grief into action.

On December 5, six women who worked closely with the CUWS and the NWP waited for the House chamber doors to open. Elizabeth Rogers of New York, whose sister was married to the U.S. war secretary Henry Stimson; Anna Lowenburg of Pennsylvania; Dr. Caroline Spencer of Colorado; Florence Bayard Hilles of Delaware, her father had been secretary of state under President Grover Cleveland; and Mabel Vernon, a friend of Paul's from Swarthmore who was also from Delaware, positioned themselves so they could nab front-row seats in the House gallery. Their seats were to the left of the big clock, which loomed behind the Speaker's desk, where the president would read his fourth annual congressional address. Vernon sat in the middle. Burns sat behind that first row and waited.

The women had been tipped off that Wilson, once again, would not mention suffrage in his speech. They sat patiently. When he arrived and began to speak, Vernon—covered by a long cape—unpinned a large yellow sateen banner from her skirt and waited for the right moment. They heard Wilson call for an eight-hour workday for railroad workers. He then mentioned greater freedom for Puerto Rican men, providing the perfect moment for the women's grand reveal. Each of the suffragists held a tab at the top of the banner and flung the sign over the balcony with a snap.

MR. PRESIDENT, WHAT WILL YOU DO FOR WOMAN SUFFRAGE?

The women held perfectly still, gripping the sign with all their might. The president looked up, hesitating for a moment before continuing. The Speaker was immobilized by his position on stage but all other heads turned to see what was unfolding. Guards attempted to rush upstairs but were blocked by other members of the CUWS deliberately clogging the stairwell. A page leapt upward from the floor, arms outstretched, and tore the banner from the women's clutches. The president managed to finish his address and depart while the congressmen finally permitted themselves a full swivel toward the gallery. The women had accomplished some measure of success. The next day, the story of the suffrage banner was on the front page of every major newspaper, stealing Wilson's headlines.

The following week, the Judiciary Committee sent the Federal Suffrage Amendment to the House of Representatives. While this small legislative action in her favor may have been a reason to celebrate, Paul was preoccupied planning a memorial service for Milholland.

The Capitol Building's Statuary Hall was a cavernous space lined with stone flooring and figures of prominent men and two neoclassical feminine monuments: Liberty, standing with her eagle; and Clio, the muse of history, perched on top of a clock. It was Christmas Day. Paul chose this time and place to honor Milholland and elevate her status from mortal to martyr. She enlisted decorating help, softening the echoing room with boughs of festive greenery, suffrage flags on every chair, and velvet drapes behind the dais. Capitol officials, concerned about security, reminded Paul of the various areas that were closed to the public. She thanked them for letting her know and then pressed them into service assisting her in hanging purple, white, and gold pennants between every pillar; she nagged the men until the flags were hung straight. Paul was equally successful at convincing a recalcitrant volunteer to deliver the memorial address. Maud Younger was from a prominent San Francisco family and had become an activist after working in New York's settlement houses. Paul was impressed with Younger's dedication to suffrage and asked her to give a speech for Milholland.

"I can't," Younger said. "I don't know how to do it."

"Oh, just write something like Lincoln's Gettysburg address," Paul told her dryly.

Younger, like most of the women in Paul's orbit, did what Paul told her to do. When it was time to address the mourners, she was nervous but prepared, as was Statuary Hall. The space had been transformed into a suffrage cathedral. Thousands of guests assembled silently in their seats and tucked into nooks as the organ opened with "Ave Maria." When the piece came to an end, they heard a distant song, growing steadily louder and closer. A boys' choir appeared in the doorway and marched through the hall, chanting:

Forward out of darkness,
Leave behind the night.
Forward out of error,
Forward into light.

A woman in white carried a banner with the same words, followed by divisions of women, each carrying a banner.

GREATER LOVE HATH NO MAN [THAN] THIS
THAT HE LAY DOWN HIS LIFE FOR A FRIEND

WITHOUT EXTINCTION IS LIBERTY
WITHOUT RETROGRADE IS EQUALITY

Burns held a sign with Julia Ward Howe's "Battle Hymn of the Republic" that said:

AS HE DIED TO MAKE MEN HOLY
LET US DIE TO MAKE MEN FREE

The banner holders assembled behind the stage and the choir sang again. The acoustics of the space made it sound as if the quartet's "Thou,

Whose Almighty Word" came from heaven above. When the music stopped, Younger began her tribute.

> There where the sun goes down in glory in the vast Pacific, her life went out in glory in the shining cause of freedom. . . . They will tell of her in the West, tell of the vision of loveliness as she flashed through her last burning mission, flashed through to her death, a falling star in the western heavens. . . . With new devotion we go forth, inspired by her sacrifice to the end that this sacrifice be not in vain, but that dying she shall bring to pass that which living she could not achieve, full freedom for women, full democracy for the nation.

After the last song, the audience did not move. They strained to hear the final lyrics, growing more distant. Then, like a trumpet call to battle, the defiant anthem "La Marseillaise" burst from the organ.

Although Milholland's memorial service concluded beautifully, it was not the last of her remembrances. From coast to coast, suffragists organized other memorials. Despite all of the signature collecting they had already achieved, suffragists used these events to ink even more for amendment petitions. Three hundred volunteers assembled to deliver the documents at the White House on January 9, 1917, holding banners with Milholland's last public words: "How long must women wait?"

Mabel Vernon led the suffragists into the East Room and when the doors opened, Wilson entered, surrounded by Secret Service agents. He smiled and shook Vernon's hand. She said hello and gave him the resolutions. Then came Sara Bard Field, once again their chosen speaker.

"The same maternal instinct for the preservation of life—whether it be the physical life of a child, or the spiritual life of a cause—is sending women into this battle for liberty with an urge that gives them no rest night or day," she said to Wilson. "Every advance of liberty has demanded its quota of human sacrifice, and, if I had time, I could show you that we have paid in a measure that is running over. In the light of Inez Milholland's death, as we look over the long backward trail through which we have sought our political liberty, we are asking, how long, how long, must this struggle go on?"

Wilson's eyes flashed from cordial to cold, and when she finished speaking there was an icy stillness in the room before the president spoke.

"Ladies," Wilson said. "I had not been apprised that you were coming here to make any representation that would issue an appeal to me. I had been told that you were coming to present memorial resolutions with regard to the very remarkable woman whom your cause has lost. I therefore am not prepared to say anything further than I have said on previous occasions of this sort. I do not need to tell you where my own convictions and my own personal purpose lie, and I need not tell you by what circumscriptions I am bound as leader of a Party."

As the leader of a political party, he continued, "my commands come from that Party, and not from private personal convictions. I do want to say this: I do not see how anybody can fail to observe from the utterance of the last campaign that the Democratic Party is more inclined than the opposition Party to assist in this great cause, and it has been a matter of surprise to me, and a matter of very great regret, that so many of those who are heart and soul for this cause seem so greatly to misunderstand and misinterpret the attitudes of Parties. In this country, as in every other self-governing country, it is really through the instrumentality of Parties that things can be accomplished. They are not accomplished by the individual voice, but by concentrated action, and that action must come only so fast as you can concert it. I have done my best, and shall continue to do my best to concert it in the interest of a cause in which I personally believe."

Wilson paused and gave the women a frosty glare before abruptly leaving the room. The Secret Service, reporters, and aides followed close behind.

The women slowly made their exit from the East Room and returned to their new headquarters. After four years of toil and hardship in the damp basement on F Street, the CUWS, NWP, and the movement Paul reignited were finally in a sunlit space, in a place of prominence. Cameron House stood at 21 Madison Place, on the edge of Lafayette Park—the green space in front of 1600 Pennsylvania Avenue. The building—a wide, three-story, brick townhouse—had several benefits.

First, it was visible and just two hundred steps away from the White House; the Wilsons could see the suffrage flag fluttering from its perch on the third-floor balcony. Second, there was ample space to work and entertain guests—from tourists and strangers walking in off the street to catch a glimpse of the women, to those attending ever-expanding fundraisers. There were also bedrooms to accommodate Paul and others, eliminating their daily commute. Paul was now using Susan B. Anthony's old desk, a Victorian cylinder rolltop that Anthony's secretary had donated to the NWP.

When the indignant suffragists walked through Cameron House's front door, they entered into a great hall with a large staircase and a fireplace that burned eternal. Paul was there, waiting for them, ready to stoke their anger as they dropped into comfortable chairs in front of the flames and asked the question again: How long must we wait?

With the women assembled in front of the fire, Paul pitched a carefully orchestrated idea, which she asked Blatch to present.

"We have got to take a new departure," Blatch told them. "We have

Cameron House.

got to bring to the President, day by day, week in, week out, the idea that great numbers of women want to be free, will be free, and want to know what he is going to do about it. We need to have a silent vigil in front of the White House until his inauguration in March. Let us stand beside the gateway where he must pass in and out so that he can never fail to realize that there is a tremendous earnestness and insistence in back of this measure."

So far, with Paul as their leader, the women had marched four years earlier, in 1913, in one of the largest and most outrageous protests America had ever seen. They had assembled an eighty-car brigade to deliver signatures from all over the nation. They had testified, editorialized, and reorganized. They had formed their own political party. They held May Day parades in nearly every state in the union. They raised funds and actively worked to defeat Democrats. They had a booth at a global exposition, collected a miles-long scroll of signatures, and drove it cross-country from San Francisco. They dropped leaflets from the sky and a banner from the House chamber's balcony. And they had sacrificed one of their own. On this day, in front of the crackling fire at their new headquarters, with the White House at their backs, they may have been exhausted, but they were neither depleted of ideas nor the passion to continue the struggle.

They listened as Blatch offered a new form of protest. In America, pickets had become a common union tactic, typically ending in violence. But suffragists had been employing the practice as well. Blatch had used pickets in her Votes for Women campaign with the New York Legislature in 1912, so when she delivered her final plea to the women of Cameron House, they stirred.

"Will you not," she asked, "be a 'silent sentinel' of liberty and self-government?"

CHAPTER THIRTEEN

The Silent Sentinels

By 1917, Alice Paul's plan to picket the White House was taking shape. Inside Cameron House, a dozen or so suffragists bundled themselves into wool coats, hats, and gloves and draped purple, white, and gold sashes across their chests. As they braced for the bitter January chill, they were fortified, not just with their warmest street clothes—which included heavy tights beneath their three-quarter-length skirts—but with Paul's advice: don't be provoked into a physical or verbal confrontation, don't make eye contact with angry bystanders, stay quiet, and keep your backs to the gate for safety and to make sure the public can read the signs. "If the police press you further," Paul said, "go out to the curb and stand there. If they press you still further, move your lines into the gutters. If they won't allow you to remain there, get in parade formation and march around the grounds, going from gate to gate. Don't come back until your time is up."

"Gee, whiz. How about eating?" one of the protesters joked as they began to walk. "I'm hungry already."

The group, led by Mabel Vernon, marched across Lafayette Park in single file, the barren trees a tracery against the dead-of-winter sky. Paul stayed behind to manage the protest from headquarters, which provided a clear view of the women, carrying colorful silk banners on tall poles, like luminous sails. She watched as they made their way toward the White House—some excited and others scared.

The first suffrage picket line leaving the National Woman's Party headquarters to march to the White House gates on January 10, 1917.

"What are we going to do if we can't even talk?" one suffragist asked another as they walked. "That leaves us in a fierce position."

They arrived outside 1600 Pennsylvania Avenue and took their positions, six on either side of the east and west iron gates in front of the White House. The geographic split was a deliberate metaphor, employed to highlight the gap between the women of the West, who could vote, and those in the East, who could not. They stood silently and held their signs, which begged for answers to tired questions:

MR. PRESIDENT, WHAT WILL YOU DO FOR WOMAN SUFFRAGE?

HOW LONG MUST WOMEN WAIT FOR LIBERTY?

The sentinels had been in position for only forty minutes when Woodrow Wilson appeared, returning home from golf. His arrival was so sudden and unexpected that the women did not notice him until after his car had passed by. Smiling broadly but ignoring them, he zipped through the gates and out of sight. Nonetheless, the president must have been shocked to discover such a scene on his doorstep; never before in the history of America had anything like this happened in front of the White House.

The public response was easier to read—government clerks, tourists, diplomats, school children, and pedestrians of every kind were stunned to stumble upon the protesters. Their reactions were transparent, but varied; some laughed at the spectacle, making a mockery, while others demonstrated respect or admiration.

Keep it up, they said. That's the way to get it.

An elderly man paused to read their signs. He removed his hat, exposing his white hair, and bowed to the first group of six women; he repeated this act of chivalry with the second group before quietly shuffling away. A local man stopped with his children and told the youngsters that they were witnessing history.

Visiting the White House from Oklahoma, a group of Comanches studied the scene with curiosity and some confusion, unclear as to what they were witnessing. "What are you doing?" they asked. The women stuck to their silence.

The first lady came and went several times throughout the day, without engaging the pickets. Seeing the Silent Sentinels was especially jarring for Edith, who had not had the privilege of wading slowly into politics. In the thirteen months since marrying Wilson after a swift courtship, she had been thrust into the role of first lady without time to develop a thick skin. She hated the fish bowl of the White House and was dismayed to see the constant political pressure her husband felt. Without experience or coping mechanisms to distance herself personally from politics, Edith took the protests as a personal affront. And although she had always been firm in her own opinions, now she was protective of her husband's positions, as well. Neither of them supported a federal amendment and neither thought it was proper for women to be protesting at the gates on Pennsylvania Avenue. There was, however, at least one woman in the White House who was in favor of women voting: Wilson's daughter Margaret waved cheerfully at the sentinels as she passed through the wrought iron gates.

White House officials were unsure how to handle the situation. Reporters covering the protest asked Major Raymond W. Pullman, the superintendent of police, what he intended to do about the suffragists. Pullman elucidated that they did not need a permit if they were not advertising anything and that, as of now, there was no violation of the law. In fact, the police walking the beat seemed sympathetic. "It's going to be much colder tomorrow," one officer warned the suffragists. "We'll bring hot bricks for you to stand on."

The sentinels stood there, peacefully, until early afternoon. Although the temperature had climbed to forty degrees, the women were still frigid when replacements arrived from Cameron House to begin their shift; they would stay until dark. Back at headquarters, Paul informed the press that the pickets would continue this silent protest from 10 a.m. to 6 p.m. daily, except for Sundays. She promised that their numbers would grow with each appearance and by March 4—the president's inauguration—they hoped to have enough protesters in place to completely surround the White House. But, she said, the protest was designed to continue until the Susan B. Anthony Amendment passed.

The news of this ongoing protest had an immediate effect, overwhelmingly negative, even among suffragists. Carrie Chapman Catt told the *Washington Times*, one of many major papers splashing the details of the protest across their front pages, "I think the Congressional Union is beginning at the wrong end when it seeks to embarrass the President." The National Association Opposed to Woman Suffrage called the picketing "a menace to the life of the president—a silent invitation to the assassin," and said "it is impossible to follow the mental processes of the women who devised the picket idea. As an argument it ranks with the small boy's thrusting out his tongue. As a demonstration of fitness for the vote it is idiotic."

Even close allies were upset by the brazenness of it all, now veering toward socially inappropriate. Paul's own mother, familiar with her daughter's single-minded focus and stubbornness, wrote to her with a Quaker plea: "I hope thee will call it off." Harriot Stanton Blatch, one of the Congressional Union for Woman Suffrage's (CUWS) hardiest volunteers, thought using women from states that already allowed women to vote was offensive; after all, they had no reason to protest. She resigned from the executive committee over the issue, but remained a member. One organizer told Paul to "use your own splendid talents for something besides circus tricks!" Even as a slew of women quit the CUWS, Paul refused to adapt or apologize; she was unremitting, responding to her critics with copies of *The Suffragist*, so they could "learn what we are attempting to do."

On the second day of the pickets, the protesters were better prepared to withstand the cold because many of them wore fur coats. Elizabeth Kent drove over in her coupe to serve them hot cocoa and delivered boards for them to stand on, to prevent their feet from freezing. Strangers were eager to shake their hands or hold a banner for a few minutes. Men digging ditches in the street said they would make them benches, but the women declined, reminding them that the whole point of being a sentinel meant they needed to stand at their posts. The Treasury Department sent a verbal invitation to the women to warm up inside their building; that, too, was declined.

Even the Wilsons seemed to feel sorry for the women. As the president and first lady were leaving the White House for lunch, he turned to the head usher and said: "Hoover, go out there and ask those ladies if they won't come in and get warm, will you? And if they come, see that they have some hot tea or coffee." The Wilsons watched him walk down to the gates and return quickly.

"Excuse me, Mr. President," Ike Hoover said, "but they indignantly refused." The Wilsons continued with their afternoon, but the president was impressed by their resolve. This time he tipped his hat to them as he drove by.

Well beyond that second day of protests, the Silent Sentinels persevered, helped by warm clothing drives at Cameron House, wheelbarrows full of warm bricks that the janitor and a helper brought from headquarters, and a rotation of volunteers organized by state or association. The New York delegation carried banners using words copied from Wilson's book *The New Freedom*: LIBERTY IS A FUNDAMENTAL DEMAND OF THE HUMAN SPIRIT. On another occasion, a woman held a banner that said: DENMARK ON THE VERGE OF WAR GAVE WOMEN THE VOTE. WHY NOT GIVE IT TO AMERICAN WOMEN NOW?

At the end of each day, all of the pickets would step down from their clay perches, on command and in perfect synchronicity. One observer said they looked like "statues stepping from their pedestals." If it was raining, sleeting, or snowing, the protesters adhered to a rotation of two-hour shifts. Their commitment amplified their notoriety while softening the opposition. Even the most hardened anti-suffrage forces felt sorry for these shivering, dripping women. One congressman who had been against the pickets at first later shouted his support: "Don't let us forget you for a moment," he said. Another congressman told a picket that there was "something religious" about the Silent Sentinels. "To me," he said, "it has already become a part of the modern religion of this country."

Support came from men and women of all ages: the very young—schoolboys from Massachusetts who told the women they deserved the vote—and the very old. A ninety-year-old former senator who had been a friend of Susan B. Anthony's and made the first pro-suffrage speech in the chamber navigated along the picket line with his crutch and a stick to encourage them. A group of old Confederates in town for a reunion gathered in front of the picket line. One of the soldiers told the sentinels, "I have been through wars, and I know. You-all got to have some rights."

Of course, not everyone believed that. A young groom, walking with his bride, stopped to speak with one of the women. "I think this is outrageous," he said. "I have no sympathy with you whatever. I wouldn't anymore let my wife—"

"Oh, do you mind if I hold one of those banners for a while," his wife interrupted.

"No, if you want to." And so she stood there holding a pole, beaming.

As for Wilson, he refused to be held hostage by this new tactic. He resumed his walks when he could. When he strolled through the gates and passed the women and their signs, he now tipped his hat sarcastically at them. The truth was, Wilson had other issues to worry about.

CHAPTER FOURTEEN

Fighting for Democracy

On the last day of January in 1917, Joseph Tumulty, Woodrow Wilson's private secretary, brought a bulletin to the president from German Ambassador Johann Heinrich von Bernstorff. Wilson had been waiting for weeks for a response to his pleas for peace. As his eyes quickly scanned the page, the president's face darkened and lips tightened. Germany, the letter said, was announcing a new policy of unrestricted submarine warfare. They would sink any ship—even neutral ones or those carrying civilian passengers without arms or other wartime contraband—found in the war zone around Britain, France, Italy, or the eastern Mediterranean.

Wilson's most recent attempt to broker an end to the war unfolded the month before, when he sent a "peace note" to the Allies, consisting of Britain, France, Italy, and Russia and those fighting against them, the Central Powers consisting of Germany, Austria-Hungary, Bulgaria, and the Ottoman Empire. Wilson's letter asked all of the factions what it would take to stop the conflict. In late January, in an address to Congress, Wilson went one step further, asking both sides in the Great War to agree to a "peace without victory." He did not believe there should be a winner imposing terms on a loser; that would lead to more conflict. "Only a peace between equals can last," he said in that address.

Although many considered the sinking of the *Lusitania* an aggression toward Britain, despite the deaths of innocent Americans,

Germany's new submarine warfare policy suddenly placed all U.S. vessels and citizens at risk. Not only out on the seas, but potentially close to the coast of the homeland, the nation could be attacked at any time. With his hope for peace dwindling, Wilson went to Congress to announce that he was severing diplomatic ties with Germany and told their ambassador he was no longer welcome in America. It was the first step of a slow march toward war.

Wilson was also struggling on the domestic front. America was on edge. Nationalism, a global epidemic, had spread to the United States, and people were suspicious of immigrants from Central Power countries. Congress wanted to stop the flow of immigrants into America and passed a sweeping act that required prospective citizens to take a literacy test and barred those from the Asia-Pacific zone. Wilson vetoed the legislation but on February 5, the House and Senate overrode him. Indeed, everywhere Wilson looked, including from his own windows, there was trouble.

Outside, the Silent Sentinels continued to hold their banners high throughout the first month of the year. Inside the White House, there was chaos as well. In February, Edith's sister had died unexpectedly and her mother was so distraught that the first lady moved the matriarch into the executive mansion to care for her. On top of that, the family was preparing for the second inauguration, with the Wilson women scrambling to select their gowns. The president, his problems ranging from the massive to the minute, was so overwhelmed that he was skipping Sunday church service to stay in bed. He could not hide under the covers forever.

On February 28, with the Silent Sentinels nearing their second straight month of protest, Wilson agreed to meet with a delegation of peace activists, including Jane Addams, who was a well-known suffragist, and William Isaac Hull, a historian and former student of Wilson's. They wanted Wilson to keep trying, to do anything to prevent U.S. soldiers from fighting in Europe.

"Send an appeal to the German people," Hull said. "Circumvent the military."

"Dr. Hull," Wilson responded, "if you knew what I know at the present moment, and what you will see reported in tomorrow morning's newspapers, you would not ask me to attempt further peaceful dealings with the Germans." Wilson dismissed his guests.

The next day, the news was as grim as he predicted. Germany had asked Japan and Mexico to join their alliance against America and in return, Germany would reward Mexico financially and help the country reclaim Texas, New Mexico, and Arizona. Unity, of thought, purpose, and now even geography, was more at risk than it had been since the Civil War.

■ ■ ■

As for Paul, she knew unity would be essential to her efforts, too. On March 2, the CUWS and National Woman's Party (NWP) gathered in Washington, D.C., for a scheduled convention. Paul proposed collapsing the CUWS into the NWP, and keeping the latter's name because it represented political power. Members approved the move and she was voted party chairwoman. The women were also distracted by the looming war, how it would affect their cause, and what they should do about it. As a Quaker, Paul believed in nonviolent solutions and saw how the National American Woman Suffrage Association's (NAWSA) intensifying patriotism would likely put that organization's suffrage work on hold, just as Susan B. Anthony had done during the Civil War, and many British women's suffrage organizations had when the Great War erupted. In the end, the NWP agreed on a resolution to be sent to the president explaining how the fight for democracy at home and abroad were inextricably linked. Their message read:

Whereas, the problems involved in the present international situation, affecting the lives of millions of women in this country, make imperative the enfranchisement of women,

Be it resolved that the National Woman's Party, organized for the sole purpose of securing political liberty for women, shall continue to work for this purpose until it is accomplished, being unalterably convinced that in doing so the organization serves the highest interests of the country. And be it further resolved that to this end we urge upon the President and the Congress of the United States the immediate passage of the National Suffrage Amendment.

Paul also made it clear that NWP members could support the war effort if they wanted to, but the NWP would not.

■ ■ ■

The rainy weather in early March matched Wilson's mood as he left the White House for his swearing-in at the Capitol, with the public pomp and circumstance scheduled to take place the following day. Only Wilson, his wife, and an entourage of about thirty officials gathered for a simple ceremony in the President's Room, an ornate space adorned with gilt and Italian frescoes near the Senate chamber. At noon, the clerk of the Senate handed the president the same Bible used to swear him in four years earlier, and as governor of New Jersey before that. Chief Justice Edward D. White administered the oath of office while Edith, the only woman present, watched with watery eyes and a little smile.

With the formalities complete, the Wilsons traveled back to the White House under heavier-than-usual security. The president had been getting anonymous death threats for weeks—some wanted war, others were against, and tensions were high among everyone—but a recent letter was more explicit, saying there was a plot to throw a bomb at him from a rooftop along the inaugural route. As the Wilsons' Pierce-Arrow rolled away from the Capitol, they saw Secret Service on top of every building. The first lady was especially nervous and when the motorcade slowed near the Peace Monument, she was jolted by a thud on her lap. For a split second, she thought it was an explosive, but looked down to discover a bouquet of flowers that someone on the street had thrown through the window.

Across town, it began to pour again. Inside Cameron House, a rubber company quickly set up shop to outfit nearly one thousand suffragists with raincoats and boots. Outside, the women assembled into formation with Vida Milholland in the lead. After her sister's death, Vida had quit her career as a singer to devote herself completely to suffrage. And on this day, she carried to the White House not just the weight of her personal sacrifice but also a banner with her sister's last words: MR. PRESIDENT, HOW LONG MUST WOMEN WAIT FOR LIBERTY?

Behind her, a woman carried an American flag, an important symbol meant to show that those protesting during the president's inauguration were patriots, too. The rest of the line, making its way to surround 1600 Pennsylvania Avenue on Wilson's first official day of his second term—was organized alphabetically with each of the forty-eight states represented, with Arizona in front. In the North Dakota section, Beulah Amidon, voted by her colleagues as the "prettiest girl on the picket line," carried an especially heavy banner, the one Inez Milholland had carried in the New York suffrage parade: FORWARD OUT OF DARKNESS; FORWARD OUT OF NIGHT; FORWARD OUT OF ERROR; FORWARD INTO LIGHT.

Despite the raincoat sales, many of the women were not properly dressed and some sloshed around in puddles wearing suede shoes. The only man who participated held an umbrella for one of the women carrying a banner. As they made their way across Lafayette Park toward the White House, five thousand people, most of them inaugural visitors and many lured by posters advertising the protest, lined the sidewalks and cheered them on from behind a cordon and beneath their rain gear. There was none of the chaos of the previous inaugural protest but police, as if trying to protect themselves, stayed inside the White House fence, watching the scene unfold peacefully. The protesters circled the White House four times, each lap representing a year that they had pressed for a federal amendment.

The Wilsons were back inside the White House as the protesters had them surrounded. Anne Martin of Nevada lead the deputation to the main gate to deliver their resolution to the president. All of the protesters were considered part of this visitation, intended to be the largest ever to go to a president. That gate, like every other one they checked, was locked. She thrust her arm through the fencing and asked a police sergeant to take a handwritten note explaining that the women had come in person to deliver the resolution, a printed version of which was included.

"I can't present these until I go off duty," the sergeant told Martin. "And I can't assure you when they will reach the President."

Just then, the eastern gate opened and the president and first lady drove out. The marchers cleared a path to let the car through and stared down the Wilsons, who in turn refused to acknowledge them. Soaked to the bone, their hands blue from the cold and sticky with varnish from the poles after two hours in the rain, the suffragists walked back to Cameron House. Amidon, who had struggled mightily to hold her banner in the wet wind, collapsed as soon as she arrived and was taken to the hospital. While she was being treated for "shock," the rest of the women assembled at the National Theater. The gathering was meant as a closing rally and, as always, a fundraiser. Alva Belmont, who'd already committed to raising a half million dollars for Paul and donated many thousands more of her own wealth, was sick and could not attend, but she still pledged another $15,000, a fact that Paul touted to encourage others to donate. That night, Paul collected an additional $9,000 from the audience. The funds were enough to keep the NWP operating for a while, at least. The event ended with Milholland, bracketing her day of service, leading the crowd in singing "The Women's Marseillaise."

> Arise! Ye daughters of a land
> That vaunts its liberty!
> May restless rules understand
> That women must be free
> That women will be free. . . .
> March on! March on! Face to the dawn
> The dawn of liberty.

When the music ended, the suffragists filed out, restored and ready to picket again. Amidon also recovered quickly and reflected on her experience by writing a poem, published a few days later in *The Suffragist*:

On the picket line

> The avenue is misty gray,
> And here beside the guarded gate

We hold our golden blowing flags
And wait.

The people pass in friendly wise;
They smile their greetings where we stand
And turn aside to recognize
The just demand.

Often the gates are swung aside:
The man whose power could free us now
Looks from his car to read our plea—
And bow.

Sometimes the little children laugh;
The careless folk toss careless words.
And scoff and turn away, and yet
The people pass the whole long day
Those golden flags against the gray
And can't forget.

■　■　■

The protesters were not the only ones pouring out the words. Wilson was locked up in the private quarters of the White House with his wife, who told the staff they should not be disturbed, except to bring them lunch. The president needed quiet to draft his war message. He was writing his ideas in bursts of shorthand, which he then corrected in long-hand, before typing them himself on his Hammond typewriter. While he toiled over the speech, the first lady was decoding messages that had come for the president, a process that intentionally involved her as the intercept. She also blocked unwanted visitors, relayed important messages as a "blind" operative, and attended meetings with the cabinet. Her duties even included driving the president through the park for a break from his mounting stress. But there was no escaping the war and the tension it produced, no matter where or how fast Edith commanded the car. Throughout the month of March, the president was sullen and then depleted by a cold. The mansion itself seemed darker, with low embers dying in the fireplaces and the shadows of death looming everywhere.

On April 2, Washington hummed liked a machine. The 65th Congress opened for a special war session, which Wilson had asked for, and both chambers would swear-in their new members. Among them was suffragist Jeannette Rankin, a thirty-seven-year-old from Montana who was the first woman ever elected to serve in the House of Representatives. Before Congress convened, NAWSA and the NWP hosted a breakfast for Rankin at the Shoreham Hotel, with Paul seated to her left and Catt to her right, an arrangement that also reflected their three places on the political spectrum. Catt had been pressuring Rankin, a known pacifist, to support the war, whereas for Paul, war was never an option. It was an awkward scene and the audience openly gossiped about it. After the breakfast, some joined Rankin's escort to Capitol Hill. Paul made sure there were Silent Sentinels at the House entrance to welcome the congresswoman, as well as pickets at 1600 Pennsylvania Avenue, where this time, police greeted them warmly.

"Glad to see you're back," one of the officers told them. "We missed you."

"When is the President coming out?" one of the women asked.

"I guess you'd like a dollar for every time people ask you that," another said.

"I'd rather have a dollar for every time they ask 'when are the suffragists coming out?'"

The suffragists' rapport with the police and the public had grown in the nearly three months of picketing. Having made it through the harshest season, their colorful presence was as welcome as the matching spring landscape, white hyacinths, purple azaleas, and gold forsythia mirroring the tricolor suffrage banners. The women stood on the picket line all day, until about 6 p.m., with no sign of the president. They also stood silently at the Capitol all day, where pacifists, dressed in white, and warmongers swirled around them.

Due to scheduling issues with the House, the president's speech to Congress was delayed until 8:30 p.m. When the Wilsons reached the Capitol, they were amazed by what they saw. For the first time ever, the dome was lit by electric light. Despite a light rain, all around the building, the crowd, which had come to witness history, was orderly but almost as dense as on Inauguration Day. Security was tight; the enemy could be anywhere.

Inside the House chamber, the first lady took her seat in the front row of the gallery with her mother and Margaret. The room was so still and tense that Edith could hear people breathing all around her. As the senators entered, they carried or wore small American flags. Two members of the Cavalry in dress uniform with sabers drawn greeted Wilson as he entered the House chamber. Everyone stood and applauded him, and the first lady felt her heart skip a beat. The audience sat quickly as the president began his speech. Wilson looked and sounded nervous, with a quavering voice and shaking hands. Six paragraphs in, he hit upon a key line: "We will not choose the path of submission." Chief Justice White, who had served as a Confederate soldier, dropped his hat on the floor and stood to cheer with his hands above his head. The rest of the chamber followed. The sound was deafening. Wilson waited for the roar to subside and then continued:

> Our objective is to vindicate the principles of peace and justice in the life of the world as against selfish and autocratic power and to set up amongst the really free and self-governed peoples of the world such a concert of purpose and of action as will henceforth insure the observance of those principles. . . . *The world must be made safe for democracy.*

A steadily building applause interrupted him again.

> Its peace must be planted upon the tested foundations of political liberty. We have no selfish ends to serve. We desire no conquest, no dominion. We seek no indemnities for ourselves, no material compensation for the sacrifices we shall freely make. We are but one of the champions of the rights of mankind. We shall be satisfied when those rights have been made as secure as the faith and the freedom of nations can make them.

When Wilson was done, the joint session roared in praise. After the president left the chamber, Wilson, a child of war, sat in the cabinet room looking pale. An aide handed him a supportive note from the editor of the *Springfield Republican*. Wilson read the letter, mopped his eyes, laid his head on the table, and wept. When he composed himself, he spoke softly. "Think what it was they were applauding," he said. "My message today was a message of death for our young men. How strange it seems to applaud that."

The next steps belonged to Congress. A couple days after Wilson's address, again beneath the electrified dome, two major issues stood before the Senate: the Susan B. Anthony Amendment, which had been reintroduced, and the war. The chamber set suffrage aside, for now. There was no such delay on the question of fighting the Germans. The Senate voted 82 to 6 in favor.

Paul, knowing the House would take up the war debate the following morning, went with a Montana member of the NWP to see Rankin. "I assure you we speak as individuals, not as members of the National Woman's Party," Paul told Rankin, referring to the constituent standing beside her. "We thought it would be a tragedy for the first woman ever in Congress to vote for war; the one thing that seemed to us so clear was the women were the peace-loving half of world and that by giving power to women we would diminish the possibilities of war." As the women spoke, Rankin gave them her full attention.

The following morning the House began debate. One hundred and fifty members addressed the issue. During the first roll call, one voice could not be heard clearly. It was Rankin's. NAWSA had been lobbying the Democrat all day to demonstrate that women could support a war, while the NWP had been urging her to vote for peace. Representative Joseph Cannon, a Republican from Illinois and former Speaker of the House, walked over to her.

"Little woman, you cannot afford not to vote. You represent the womanhood of the country in the American Congress," Cannon said. "I shall not advise you how to vote, but you should vote one way or the other—as your conscience dictates."

The clerk called the roll again. This time, Rankin was sure to be heard. "I want to stand by my country," she said, tears welling in her eyes. "But I cannot vote for war. I vote no." The last word was barely audible. Her colleagues, even those who favored the war, applauded her.

She was, in more ways than one, in the minority. It was after three in the morning on April 6, when all the votes were tallied. "On this motion, the ayes are 373 and the noes are 50," Speaker Champ Clark said. He banged his gavel and the chamber fell silent. It was Good Friday. At noon, an aide brought the president a printed copy of the resolution, signed by the vice president and the Speaker of the House. Edith handed Wilson a gold pen he had given her. He signed his name with it. Hoover, the White House usher, pressed a button to notify the Navy, and the aide picked up the phone to call the press waiting in the executive offices. America was now at war.

While all of this was happening, the Silent Sentinels stood outside, in view of the president. Most assumed the protesters would do their patriotic duty and go home. Some did hang up their sashes in deference to the war, spending their volunteer time working in knitting teams to provide woolen garments for the battlefront, planting war gardens to produce food, attending canning demonstrations to learn how to preserve their crops, and distributing food pledge cards to encourage Americans to economize by promising to eat local food, in smaller portions, with little wheat or waste. The first lady brought out her sewing machine, one of the few items she moved into the White House from her townhouse, to make pajamas, surgical shorts, and other items for the Red Cross.

The idea of women being pressed into service, even if it was as a volunteer, and carrying other burdens of war—waving good-bye to their husbands and sons—had another effect: it generated sympathy for suffrage. Within weeks, Michigan, Rhode Island, and Nebraska granted equal voting rights to women. This war, one that Wilson had framed around the intangible ideals of democracy, encouraged Americans to be accountable to these principles as well. If young men were willing to die for liberty on the other side of the ocean, the least Americans could do was grant all of their citizens suffrage.

CHAPTER FIFTEEN

The Russians

The train rolled to a clanging, chuffing, grinding halt at Washington's Union Station. Despite the smoke of the engine and the crush of other passengers climbing off the railcars, the eight Russians were easy to identify on this fine June day in 1917. There was Ambassador Boris A. Bakhmetieff, with his distinctive white mustache; military officials in uniforms of khaki coats, navy pants, and black knee boots; Russia's ministers of finance and foreign affairs; and several of their wives. The American delegation, along with regular travelers who happened to be in the station, greeted the Russians with cheers. The U.S. contingent, comprised of Secretary of State Robert Lansing and his assistants, also brought with them two Cavalry troops, mounted police, and members of the Secret Service, offering protection in addition to hospitality.

The genuine welcome was comforting to the Russians. For the last three years, their country had been locked into a brutal war they were not prepared for and could not sustain. Their population had been decimated, with 1.7 million people killed and 5 million wounded. Peasants were starving and freezing due to food and fuel shortages. The army was in revolt, and a man named Vladimir Lenin, a champion of the working class, was leading his Bolshevik Party in protests against a corrupt and ineffective monarchy. And he was succeeding. Just three months before this Russian mission had arrived in Washington, the

Bolsheviks had forced Czar Nicholas II to abdicate his throne, replaced with a provisional government led by Prince Georgy Lvov.

In the five weeks it had taken this Russian mission to journey to America, however, the situation back home had deteriorated further. The Russian army, in a desperate act of self-preservation, was putting all of its focus into a new and risky strategy: fighting German soldiers burrowed into trenches along the Austro-Hungarian line. The enemy, protected by machine gun nests, sniper hideouts, and a vast network of communication tunnels, would be difficult to defeat. Now that America's fate was aligned with the Russians, this intense campaign, known as the Brusilov Offensive, had the United States on edge, hoping the Russians would win a badly needed victory on the Eastern Front. Meanwhile, America was supporting Russia in other ways, sending money and supplies for the war effort and dispatching diplomats, including Elihu Root, who had been secretary of state under Theodore Roosevelt, to meet with the new government. Root had arrived in St. Petersburg the previous week.

Now that the Russians had pulled into Washington, the United States was proud to show off its own government's stability and congratulate the guests on revolting against a monarchy to establish liberty and democracy, just as America had done in 1776. But Russia's revolution had produced one outcome that the United States' had not. In the weeks after Lvov had been installed as the country's new leader, forty thousand women clogged the streets of St. Petersburg and demanded voting rights. Lvov, facing a popular uprising, granted them suffrage the next day.

Alice Paul was happy that Russia had joined the handful of other nations where women could vote, including Finland, Iceland, Sweden, Norway, Denmark, New Zealand, and Australia. Canada was considering extending the vote to wives, widows, mothers, and sisters of soldiers serving overseas, as well as nurses and other women directly working in the war effort. And in England, Prime Minister Asquith—the same man Paul had confronted at the House of Commons and Guildhall— was now favoring woman suffrage. Progress toward voting rights was the only positive emerging from a horrible war. But Paul thought it was wrong for the Wilson administration to praise Russia on its new freedom without acknowledging the disenfranchisement of half the population of America. And she thought the issue was worth a public conversation. As the Russians left Union Station in a motorcade to attend some official events—they were expected at the White House the following day—people waved and applauded enthusiastically at them. Paul, meanwhile, was planning a different kind of greeting.

The next day, a car dropped off Lucy Burns, Dora Lewis, and their heavy cargo in front of the White House about an hour before the Russians were expected to meet with Woodrow Wilson at 12:30. The women unfurled their ten-foot, hand-stenciled cloth sign, stretched between two wooden posts, shuffled into position, and straightened the banner between them. The crowd, many of them on their lunch hour, slowed to read the wordy message:

TO THE RUSSIAN ENVOYS

PRESIDENT WILSON AND ENVOY ROOT ARE DECEIVING
RUSSIA. WHEN THEY SAY "WE ARE A DEMOCRACY, HELP
US WITH THE WORLD WAR SO THAT DEMOCRACY MAY
SURVIVE," WE, THE WOMEN OF AMERICA, TELL YOU THAT
AMERICA IS NOT A DEMOCRACY. TWENTY-MILLION AMERICAN
WOMEN ARE DENIED THE RIGHT TO VOTE. PRESIDENT
WILSON IS THE CHIEF OPPONENT OF THEIR NATIONAL
ENFRANCHISEMENT. HELP US MAKE THIS NATION REALLY
FREE. TELL OUR GOVERNMENT IT MUST LIBERATE ITS
PEOPLE BEFORE IT CAN CLAIM FREE RUSSIA AS AN ALLY.

As pedestrians processed the words—some scribbled to transcribe the banner—the situation grew tense. To attack the president so directly in front of diplomatic guests was an unprecedented outrage not only for those witnessing the protest from inside the White House, but for many who saw it happening on the street. Murmurs rippled through the crowd and cars stopped to take in the scene.

The Russians, arriving by motorcade, passed quickly through the gate, but with enough time to see the sign. Bystanders—men and women alike—were enraged that the delegation had seen the protest.

"Take down that banner or I'm through with woman suffrage for life," one man screamed at Burns. Lewis argued with the man as he stormed off and ignored her.

"You are a friend to the enemy, and a disgrace to your country," one woman sneered at the protesters.

"Why don't you take that banner to Berlin? You are helping the enemy!"

Another man, a local builder driving by, stopped to read the sign. "Let's tear the damn thing down!" he shouted.

"It's treasonable, and I'm with you!" one man, a visitor from New York, shouted back.

"Come on boys! Let's tear that thing down," said another.

A police officer who had just arrived was jotting down the message on the banner and asked the gelling mob to slow down. "Wait until I finish transcribing this," he huffed.

But the men, so agitated by the sight of these women holding a sign, could not be held back any longer. They grabbed it, punched it, shredded it, pushed Burns, and left the women stunned but standing. Others shredded what remained, leaving one tiny piece of fabric dangling from the post. The officer and two other security guards who had been inside the gates ran toward the scramble. From across the street, near the NWP headquarters, suffragists watched in horror as the men closed around their colleagues. All they could see was the top of the poles and people in straw hats surging this way and then that way. They held their breath as the guards approached to break up the scene.

Burns and Lewis stood still, clutching their wooden poles, when another man leapt between the officers to pull off the last bit of fabric. The police caught him but they let him go when he handed over the remnant with a smile.

"You are giving just as bad an impression by standing around here as these people are," one of the guards said, speaking to the crowd as he pointed to the suffragists.

"Are you going to pinch them?" a man asked.

"No," he said. "We won't give them the satisfaction." There would be no arrests that day.

Although the police tried to shoo away the crowd of about 250, those watching were in no rush to leave. Even Burns and Lewis stayed a few minutes longer, perhaps hoping to be arrested. When it was clear the trouble had passed, the suffragists walked calmly back to headquarters. Meanwhile, bystanders gathered around the attackers to shake their hands and congratulate them as the media closed in for interviews.

"It's a shame," one of the men told the *New York Times*, "that we have to give our sons to the service of the country and be confronted by such outrageous statements at the very White House gates."

Americans were outraged that the women were not hauled off to jail. They told the press and wrote letters to Wilson declaiming what they thought was a double standard: if the pickets had been men, they would have been cuffed for provoking a riot.

Another man was so proud to have confronted the women that he raced home to write a letter bragging to Wilson about the incident:

Permit me to inform you that today at about 1 p.m. I defended your admirable name and honor against disgraceful statements made at the White House gates. After a suffragette had remarked that you are a hypocrite and opposed to their enfranchisement I expressed my extreme indignation and with the assistance of a little group of "real men," tore down all the banners which had been placed in front of the White House. Col. Bryan was leaving at the time and smiled. I love this country and the American flag and in the name of the group of men who helped me to defend your good name I appeal to you to put an end to these offensive and outrageous doings. A distinguished Russian congratulated and informed me that if the women in Russia would do such a thing they would immediately be spanked on the street. . . . [M]illions of young men must leave for France and die for this country's honor . . . is it justice to them that at the same time females who are no [*sic*] women are permitted to disgrace and insult the government and the manhood of this country?

Most Respectfully yours,
John C. Fheurer

Meanwhile, police picked up the strips of material and carried them into the White House, where D.C. police superintendent Pullman huddled with Joseph Tumulty, Wilson's right-hand man, about how to respond to the situation. The Wilsons were angry. Edith was especially indignant that these women were causing a scene and embarrassing her already emotionally wrought and exhausted husband. After conferring with the administration, Pullman agreed to find some excuse, however flimsy, to arrest the suffragists "if the thing was attempted again." They made sure Paul and the press knew there would be no tolerance for picketing anymore.

The threats of arrest did not scare Paul. She told the press that she planned to repeat the Russian protest the next day. "We have ordered another banner with the same wording and we intend to show it in the same place," she said. Sure enough, within twenty-four hours, a new batch of Silent Sentinels were back at their posts, carrying signs that read:

WE DEMAND DEMOCRACY AND
SELF-GOVERNMENT IN OUR OWN LAND

and

MR. PRESIDENT, WHAT WILL YOU DO FOR WOMAN SUFFRAGE?

No one bothered these women and they completed their shift. But as news of the Russia banners rippled across America, everyone seemed to have an opinion about the demonstration. Was it patriotic or not? Was this form of protest helpful to advance suffrage or would it create more opposition? In England, the suffragists had put their cause on hold to support the war effort. In America, the suffragists had opposing opinions.

The war had only intensified the NWP's protests, whereas Anna Howard Shaw and Carrie Chapman Catt, once again, publicly criticized Paul's approach, telling the press: "We feel that our men in Congress should not wait another minute to submit to the legislatures the Federal amendment for woman suffrage. Nevertheless, we are not in the least in sympathy with the method that has been used by the White House pickets."

Citizens telegrammed the White House immediately, registering a range of reactions from outrage to admiration over the picketing. Letters came from all over, from New York to Colorado. The Woman Suffrage Party of Albany said it wished "to convey its absolute disapproval" of the protests. Meanwhile, the NWP branch in Utah urged Wilson to pass the amendment as a war and preparedness measure.

Publicly, members of Congress, even those who supported suffrage, told the press that the banner protest made them reconsider their position. Representative Edward Keating of Colorado, one of the leaders in the House on suffrage, criticized both sides. "We must condemn the exhibition of such a banner on this occasion," he said.

> There is no defense for that. This picketing maintained by one of the suffrage organizations has been unwise, and I have disapproved it from the outset. On the other hand I do not like to see an exhibition of mob spirit. If the suffragists were violating a law they should have been stopped in an orderly manner. It would have impressed the Russian envoys very favorably no doubt had the offending pickets and banner been removed in an orderly way and without aid of a mob. A mob should never take charge of things in this country.

Another representative reserved judgment. "I don't want to discuss it now," Jeannette Rankin said. "I will think it over, but I don't think I shall have anything to say."

Paul, at headquarters planning her next steps, was not shy about their plans and publicly committed to continue the protest. Knowing the picketing would become more intense, Paul rallied the toughest women she could find. She telegrammed Katharine Morey, a protester from a prominent family in Brookline, Massachusetts, who had been organizing protests on Boston Common, and explained that she would likely be arrested if she picketed.

"I am willing," Morey said.

The day after the Russia protest, on June 21, Burns and Morey left headquarters carrying a duplicate banner to the White House gate. They stormed across the park but before they arrived at their post, a group of boys grabbed their sign and tore it apart. About one thousand people who had gathered in the park in the hopes of witnessing the second day of this spectacle watched as the police did nothing. The two women returned to headquarters and the NWP sent out replacements, Hazel Hunkins of Montana and Catharine Heacox of Washington. These suffragists were able to take their positions and stand firm, each holding their own sign. But very quickly, they attracted trouble. A woman named Dee Richardson, who worked in the War Department and had been boasting that morning in her office that she was going to assault the protesters, moved toward Hunkins and Heacox.

"I'll spit on those banners if you men will follow me," Richardson shouted to the crowd. But when no one else came forward, she barked at the women for being treasonous, ripped the banner from Heacox's hands, broke one of the poles and stomped on the cloth. Hunkins scrambled up a stone ledge that supported the White House fence and held her banner as high as she could. As Richardson rushed her, Hunkins moved to throw her sign over the railing but Richardson grabbed her by the waist and dragged her to the sidewalk along with the banner. By this time, the crowd was yelling encouragement at Richardson, who was in a frenzy looking for her next move. Morey, eating lunch back at headquarters, "heard a great roar" outside. She ran out of Cameron House toward the White House and saw Richardson running near the northwest gate, the crowd trailing behind her. Richardson was making a beeline for two Silent Sentinels, Catherine Lowry and Lillian Crans, who placidly held a sign that said WHAT WILL YOU DO FOR WOMEN, MR. PRESIDENT? Richardson went for the banner but a plainclothes policewoman who had been running behind her grabbed the government employee by the neck and arrested her.

Meanwhile, the police called for backup officers, who arrived to a chaotic scene. The mob charged the pickets and destroyed their banners. Crans ran to headquarters for another sign, and told her colleagues what had happened. Mabel Vernon was furious. She grabbed her purple, white, and gold flag and rallied three other women to march out of Cameron House for a post at the gates. Their faces ranged from pale with fear to fierce with determination. When the crowd saw them, they quieted and let them pass. Even the police were chastened by how out of control the situation had become and, hoping to create calm, they escorted the replacements to their stations and cleared the sidewalk of those looking for a show.

Back at headquarters, Morey and Burns regrouped. They decided to be photographed standing outside Cameron House holding a replacement Russia banner. The police, however, were waiting for them on the other side of the threshold and when the women stepped out, the officers confiscated the sign, saying they wanted to prevent a riot.

Inside the White House, the administration was searching for a solution that would end the protests without giving the women the glory of more publicity. Someone in Wilson's inner circle sent a reporter to NWP headquarters to tell Paul that the president could be assassinated by someone in the crowds and pleaded with them to stop out of safety concerns.

"Is the Administration willing to have us make this [information] public?" Paul asked the intermediary.

"Oh, no!" he said.

"The picketing will go on as usual," she told him.

After word reached the White House that the NWP planned to protest again, Superintendent Pullman called Paul. This, he said, was her last warning.

"If anybody goes out again on the picket line, it will be our duty to arrest them," he told her.

"We have been picketing for six months without interference," Paul said. "Has the law been changed?"

"No, but you must stop it."

"But Major Pullman, we have consulted our lawyers and we know we have the right to picket."

"I warn you, you will be arrested if you attempt to picket again."

"Well, we think it is our duty to continue to go out," she told him.

As she hung up, the sentinels were still on duty. They were able to finish their shift without incident. In fact, it was so serene outside the White House, one of them was able to knit sweaters for soldiers in the battlefield. But the calm would not last.

The next morning, on June 22, Paul picked up the cone-shaped receiver from the tall black telephone stand and leaned into the mouthpiece. She had called Pullman to give him advance notice that the pickets were heading to the White House soon. It did not take long for rows of policemen to assemble outside Cameron House. Suffragists came and went without issue. None carried a banner. On this day, the sentinels took a sneakier approach. Vernon left headquarters carrying a box under her arm. She crossed the park and sat down on a bench. Then Burns left the building and walked leisurely in one direction, while Morey headed off along a different path. At 9:45 a.m., these three women met at the east gate of the White House, where Vernon pulled from her box the banner and gave it to Burns and Morey to hold.

The sign contained Wilson's own words, those he spoke in his war message to Congress on April 2:

WE SHALL FIGHT FOR THE THINGS WHICH WE HAVE
ALWAYS HELD NEAREST OUR HEARTS—FOR DEMOCRACY—
FOR THE RIGHT OF THOSE WHO SUBMIT TO AUTHORITY
TO HAVE A VOICE IN THEIR OWN GOVERNMENT.

It took a few minutes for anyone to notice that the suffragists were there. But once they did, six policemen and one policewoman surrounded them.

"The little devils!" one officer shouted when he saw it. "Can you beat that!"

"My God, man, you can't arrest that," another officer said when he read the sign. "Them's the President's own words."

Nearly ten minutes passed as the officers debated whether to arrest them. Finally, they did.

"You have no right to touch our banner," Burns said.

"Miss Burns," the policewoman said, "wouldn't you rather give this up peaceably than be arrested?"

"We don't intend to give it up," Burns said. "You have no right to take it. Our position is logical and constitutional and yours is illogical and unconstitutional."

They were steely but nervous as they were brought to jail. The officers guided them into the backseat of a squad car and before closing the door, handed Burns the banner. Once inside the district station, the women sat down and waited for their fate to be decided by Pullman and the chief of detectives, Inspector Clifford Grant, both of whom were still at the White House. When the two men arrived at the station, Burns asked what the charge was. Grant was not ready to answer her.

"Let me see the banner you are carrying," he said.

Burns unfolded the sign and showed it to him.

"My, those are the President's own words!" Grant said.

Pullman, attempting to recover from Grant's verbal mistake seemingly legitimizing the sign, said the charge would come under Section 5 of the police regulations, which forbade blocking traffic and unlawful assemblage. Burns argued that she and Morey were nothing but peaceful and had the right to advance their cause by means of a reasonable argument. "Surely you consider the President's own words 'reasonable argument,'" Burns said. "Moreover, peaceable picketing is allowed by national laws."

Pullman was in a bind. On the one hand, the authorities were trying to stop the pickets. On the other, they knew that if the women were charged and—worse—sent to prison, they would be instant martyrs. Pullman took a middle path, releasing them on personal recognizance. As the women returned to headquarters, they saw that Cameron House was a hive of excitement and work. Paul, still busy managing staff, members, and mail, was bombarded with questions and telegrams—one of which stood out.

"Congratulations," her still besotted friend William Parker wrote. "Stick to it."

Parker had been living in Washington since the previous year, working as a statistician in the U.S. Department of Commerce. He came by Cameron House occasionally, and sometimes succeeded in taking Paul out. But now that the United States was at war, and Parker was eligible to be drafted, any communication between them could be their last.

Parker's note gave Paul a much-needed boost. She was once again exhausting herself with work. In addition to orchestrating the pickets, she was managing the NWP's publicity operation, which issued a three-page press release that not only explained the details of what happened but included a copy of a letter Paul had received the day before from a Russian named N. A. Nessaragoff.

To Miss Alice Paul:

I just read in the New York Times about the "deplorable incident" at the White House. From all my heart and soul I am proud of the courage of American women who so boldly defend real liberty and democracy. I pray all good forces in the world to give you the courage to stay unshaken, find in the high ideals [an] unlimited source of joy, helping you not to fall down spiritually.

I am proud of Miss Burns and Miss Lewis who stood so courageously despite the angry crowd.

In Russia, a different kind of oppressors did the very same things the American police do now. Yet a real liberty was won at last, and there are not forces on earth which could deprive humanity of it.

With deepest respect and admiration,
N. A. Nessaragoff

The press printed the letter and took it to Ambassador Bakhmetieff, who was still visiting in Washington. Bakhmetieff, said the writer, living in New York for the last two years, had served as an artillery officer under the previous regime. He made sure to publicly state that the man was not connected with the new government in any way. Still, the timing was awkward for the Russian envoys; the ambassador was scheduled to address Congress the next day.

Capitol Police were eager to show off the legislative chambers to Bakhmetieff and give him a proper stage to talk about the war effort. They did not want a repeat performance of the suffrage demonstration that the NWP had staged during Wilson's 1916 annual address to Congress. And they had good reason to be worried. Guards throughout the building searched for women with unusual bulges under their dresses and checked all visitors at the door. Knowing it would be impossible to smuggle in a sign, three NWP members took a different approach. Vernon, Virginia Arnold, and Florence Youmans positioned themselves outside on the steps and quickly opened their Russia banner: WE SHALL FIGHT FOR THE THINGS WE HAVE ALWAYS HELD NEAREST OUR HEARTS, FOR DEMOCRACY, FOR THE RIGHT OF THOSE WHO SUBMIT TO AUTHORITY TO HAVE A VOICE IN THEIR OWN GOVERNMENT. They were only there for a few moments before Capitol Police were on the scene. They seized the sign, arrested Vernon and Arnold and ushered them inside for questioning. The police told Youmans they would not arrest her because her hand had not been on the sign pole.

Police cleared the steps just in time. The Russian delegation arrived and were escorted inside the House to rousing applause. Speaker Champ Clark, a Missouri Democrat, welcomed the group, praised their determination to create a republic, and reminded them about America's own experiment in democracy, which operated "not by conquering armies, not by the [chain]mailed hand, but by the wholesomeness of our example; by teaching all creation the glorious fact that men can govern themselves."

When Bakhmetieff took the podium, men, women, and children cheered and waved their handkerchiefs. They cheered again when he said Germany was a menace, and they cheered even louder when he said Russia would stay in the war until there was "a firm and lasting peace" with all countries. They would not negotiate a peace just to release themselves from the war. "The triumph of German autocracy would render such peace impossible. It would be the source of the greatest misery, and besides that, a threatening menace to Russia's freedom," he said. It was precisely what the Americans wanted to hear.

After his address, Congress organized a receiving line that included Representative Rankin. When she was introduced to Bakhmetieff as the first woman elected to federal office in the United States, he was fascinated and "paid her extra attention."

Meanwhile, across town, in front of the White House, Lewis and Gladys Greiner were continuing the protest there. But police did not allow them to stand outside for long. They arrested the pickets and, once again, released them on their own recognizance. It had been an eventful Saturday.

The next morning, Cameron House was quieter than usual, even for a Sunday, the Silent Sentinels' one day off of every week, now in their sixth month of protest. Overnight, someone had broken into NWP headquarters and pilfered their typewriters. The thieves did not ransack the place. Rather, they directed their attack to the machines that churned out statements to the press and produced *The Suffragist*. Without the typewriters, there was no click, clack, ding punctuating the air. But the theft did not get in the way of Paul pushing out the story she wanted told. Nor did she have to go far to report the crime. Just beyond the front door, the press and the police were waiting, hanging around in case something else happened. Paul stepped out to give them all an update, explaining not just the theft, but that—more importantly—the NWP would never stop picketing. In fact, she said, the organization had put out a call for reinforcements from Maryland, Pennsylvania, Connecticut, and other states to replace any women who were arrested and these women were on their way to help. Paul went back inside and waited for her troops to arrive. When they did, she prepared them for the picket line.

The following day, police, without any real charge, arrested twelve suffragists outside the White House, including repeat offenders such as Vernon, Burns, Greiner, Morey, Lavinia Dock, and Arnold. Police drove them away in unmarked cars so as not to give them any more publicity. There was a growing sense in the coverage that the escalation in picketing and arrests was feeding into Paul's strategy. The protesters seemed to want to be arrested and locked behind bars so that they could go on a hunger strike. Concerned about that larger scheme, the police processed the women at the station and then let them go.

By morning, nine suffragists—many from the previous day's batch—were picked up outside the White House again. The last six arrested were brought to jail for the night and required to appear in district court at nine the following morning. Those facing the judge were not just radical young women. They were respected professionals, such as Dock, a sixty-year-old, internationally known expert in nursing who had worked in the Henry Street Settlement house in New York; Annie Arniel, a widowed factory worker from Delaware in her mid-forties; Arnold, a former school teacher who helped establish NWP branches in the West; Maud Jamison, a forty-six-year-old former teacher and businesswoman from Virginia; Morey, whose mother was also an active suffrage organizer in the Boston area; and thirty-four-year-old Vernon, Paul's classmate at Swarthmore who came from a prominent Delaware family and was considered one of the best organizers of the NWP, where she had worked since it was founded.

After spending the night locked up, Vernon told her colleagues she would defend herself and them in court; it was a tactic to turn the courtroom into a forum for publicity, which Paul had learned in England. When the women assembled before the judge, Vernon asked a policeman to fetch the suffrage banners as evidence. Those in the courtroom waited quietly but they burst out laughing when the officer returned, struggling with the signs, which trailed all over the floor as he dropped poles and fabric everywhere. Eventually, he managed to open one banner, which read:

MR. PRESIDENT, YOU SAY "LIBERTY IS THE FUNDAMENTAL DESIRE OF THE HUMAN SPIRIT."

After a technical discussion about the width of the sidewalks, Vernon produced a photo of the scene, showing they were deserted at the time of the arrests. The police corroborated this fact when Vernon cross-examined them.

The judge, Alexander Mullowney, was not convinced. "If you had kept moving, you would have been alright," he said. "I find these defendants guilty as charged of obstructing the highway in violation of the police regulations." He imposed a fine of twenty-five dollars each or three days in prison. The women surprised Judge Mullowney by choosing prison over the fine.

In order to seek maximum exposure for their sacrifice, the women refused to ride in automobiles to prison, instead choosing the police transport van, known as a "black Maria"—slang among veteran criminals. They arrived and settled in their first-floor cells, each with a cot and toilet and towel. For a brief time they were allowed in the common area, which had an organ. Vernon sat down to play "God Be with You Till We Meet Again." While her colleagues huddled around the organ, about forty others, most of whom were black, collected in a staircase and sang along. After a few songs, the NWP inmates held a suffrage meeting, which ended with a "Votes for Women" chant. Before they went to bed, the prison allowed a reporter to call Vernon and see how the group was doing. She told him they were "very comfortably fixed. We had shoulder, kale, bread and tea for supper."

After three days, the women walked out of prison and returned to Cameron House. There, one hundred suffragists representing many states gathered to celebrate over breakfast, sharing praise and encouraging each other about the days ahead. While regular citizens were planning their escape from Washington's sultry summer, this group had other plans for July and August. For one thing, the pickets would continue.

CHAPTER SIXTEEN

The Bastille Day Protest

T he war had cast a shadow over Washington. On Independence Day of 1917, rather than launch fireworks, the city organized less celebratory events to show its patriotism. There was a drive to recruit soldiers, and at 10 a.m., House Speaker Champ Clark gave a speech at the Washington Monument with the Marine Band playing and the Boy Scouts serving as ushers to the British and French dignitaries attending. Woodrow Wilson skipped all of it. He was exhausted. The previous week had been intensely stressful as the first U.S. troops arrived in France after an agonizing transatlantic journey with U-boats lurking underwater. All anyone could speak of in Washington was how miraculous their safe arrival was, but many more had yet to make the perilous journey. Rather than stay at the White House in a constant state of dread, Wilson and his family motored down the Potomac on the presidential yacht, the *Mayflower*. While Wilson rested on board and stayed informed about the war through the wireless, there was no holiday at Cameron House.

Just before 1 p.m., with the sun blazing, five sentinels marched from headquarters to the White House, flying their tricolor banners. Vida Milholland took the lead and Helena Hill Weed, a forty-one-year-old Washingtonian, brandished a sign inspired by the Declaration of Independence: GOVERNMENTS DERIVE THEIR JUST POWER FROM THE CONSENT OF THE GOVERNED.

This time, the pickets followed the judge's advice and kept moving, collecting a trail of angry people—mostly men in straw boaters—and police behind them. Paul had advertised the picketing in advance and the crowd was waiting, hot and agitated, for the show to start. As soon as the protesters crossed Pennsylvania Avenue, a riot erupted. A mob tore the flags from the women's hands. A War Department clerk, Charles E. Morgan, offended when New Yorker Kitty Marion tried to sell him a copy of *The Suffragist*, grabbed her papers and the two began to scuffle. She managed to connect several punches before she, Morgan, and the rest of the protesters were arrested. Hazel Hunkins, who had rushed over from headquarters, got into the mix and tried to take back a banner from one of the attackers, but police caught her, too. As the officers put all of the suspects in cars, another group of six protesters—including Burns, who seemed reenergized by these more physical protests—filled the void on the sidewalk briefly before they were arrested as well, charged with unlawful assembly.

The court hearing was a farce. The suffragists successfully demanded that their torn banner—GOVERNMENTS DERIVE THEIR JUST POWER FROM THE CONSENT OF THE GOVERNED—be hung from the bench. And with that as her backdrop, Burns cross-examined the witnesses, asking why it was legal to protest on June 21 but not on July 4.

"An order came later," one officer said, "to not allow picketing."

The judge banged his gavel and declared that all but Hunkins and Marion were guilty.

"I hate to do it," the judge insisted. "But under the law there is nothing else for me to do. I can fine you $25 but that's nothing. I know it's not going to make you quit marching in front of the White House. And I know you don't care if I fine you." It was an accurate assessment. The sentinels chose to go to district jail for three days. They sang in the prison van as it carried them from the courthouse to their cells.

The suffragists seemed almost titillated by their predicament, perhaps enamored with the novelty. Paul's insistence on keeping the operation running, however, was taking a heavy toll on her. The NWP's funds were depleted; donations had dropped sharply after the United States entered the war because women everywhere were economizing and shifting their contributions to causes such as the Red Cross. For months, Paul had been frantically seeking donations. Income for May was $2,000 less than the same month the previous year and a $6,000 drop from January's prewar level. In addition to soliciting donations in a series of in-person meetings across the Northeast and sending out written appeals, Paul had been managing the frenzy of pickets and press interviews. She was as depleted now as the NWP's bank account. Her limbs frail and her face gaunt, Paul's already big eyes appeared even more dramatic, emphasized by their hollowed-out sockets. Her digestive issues, the very ones she developed in England, were wreaking havoc again.

Shortly after the Independence Day protest, Paul was busy at work on the next idea, a protest to be held on July 14, Bastille Day, France's annual celebration marking the turning point in the French Revolution. But before she could complete the logistics for the event, Paul collapsed at Cameron House. Her colleagues rushed her to a hospital in Washington where Dr. Cora Smith King, a suffrage supporter best known for carrying a "Votes for Women" banner to the top of Mount Rainier eight years earlier, was practicing.

King ran a series of tests and when the results came back, her diagnosis was grim: Bright's disease, the same kidney affliction that had taken the life of the president's first wife, Ellen. The news was even more shocking because Dr. King said she was concerned that Paul might not live two weeks. The NWP's executive board raced to the hospital to make solemn arrangements, believing they would never see Paul again. They gathered around her bedside, offering sympathy, encouragement, and to pay Paul's medical bills. Paul was uncomfortable with the attention, refused the financial help, and handled the rest of the meeting professionally as the group agreed to appoint Burns as the acting chairwoman. Meanwhile, Lewis thought the diagnosis—and its awful treatments of colonic irrigation and electric shocks therapy—was inaccurate. She convinced Paul to transfer to Johns Hopkins, another institution with Quaker roots, where Lewis's brother was a doctor. Paul agreed to go for a second opinion. This time, the news was much better. Paul did not have a kidney disease, she just needed to rest for two months. Relief rippled through the ranks as Paul followed the doctors' orders and took the train to Moorestown.

When Paul's would-be paramour heard the news, he sent a letter right away.

"I am very sorry to hear that you are more than temporarily retired to a sanatorium or hospital (!) *Je ne sais quoi*, and not especially surprised. I had so absurd a reason for being obliged to rush away the last time I saw you I hesitated to interpose it. Of course, had I known you were really in need of a word or a hand you would have had them," William Parker wrote. "I venture to congratulate you and the Party again and hope the amendment will soon go thru and that you will come back. . . . Sincerely your friend, W Parker."

■ ■ ■

Meanwhile, in Paris, the annual Bastille Day pageantry was more poignant than usual. The Central Powers were locked in battle in France along the German and Belgian borders. The five hundred–mile Western Front had worn down the Allies; the French army had lost more than a million men since the war began in 1914 and some divisions were now in mutiny, refusing to do battle at impregnable enemy positions. Which was why the sight of the American troops, called doughboys, marching a bit sloppily down the Champs-Élysées on July 14, 1917, was such an emotional moment. Dressed in their khaki uniforms and broad-brimmed hats, bayonets slung jauntily over their shoulders, the Americans looked young and fresh, and for good reason. Having only disembarked a few weeks earlier in the French port of Saint-Nazaire, these fourteen thousand soldiers had not yet entered the theater of battle. As they made their way through Paris as part of the Bastille Day pomp and circumstance under the direction of the American military commander-in-chief John J. Pershing, the American forces were smaller in number than the desperate French had hoped for. Nonetheless, they were highly celebrated.

With Parisians waving flags from the jammed sidewalks, the Army walked shoulder to shoulder from the Arc de Triomphe to Picpus Cemetery. There, they paid their respects at the tomb of the Marquis de Lafayette, a French aristocrat who, with his soldiers, had fought alongside George Washington during the Revolutionary War and helped win his country's support for the end of British colonialism in America. Many saw the U.S. involvement in the Great War as a favor owed the French for 140 years. It was a welcome payback.

At the same time that the doughboys were completing their parade, back in the United States, Wilson was attending a noon wedding away from the White House. His absence from 1600 Pennsylvania Avenue made no difference to Paul. Her vision for a different kind of Bastille Day event began to unfold. Three groups of pickets marched from Cameron House toward the White House with their suffrage banners and a sign expressing the French national motto: LIBERTY, EQUALITY, FRATERNITY.

Missing from the sentinels that day was Mary Church Terrell, even though the NWP had invited her to participate. Terrell, the prominent African American activist who had marched in the inaugural protest, lived in Washington, D.C., where her husband was a municipal judge. Paul frequently called on her to participate in the picketing and Terrell almost always obliged. "As a rule I complied with the request and several times [my adult daughter] Phyllis would come with me to swell the number," Terrell later wrote. But on this day, Terrell had to decline the invitation. It was a fateful decision.

Those who did participate faced a large crowd on Pennsylvania Avenue. At first, nothing happened. But the police moved in as soon as the second group had made it to the lower gate. The third group marched forward and police arrested them, too.

All sixteen women, many from prominent families, were booked for "unlawful assembly." The defendants included Alison Hopkins, whose husband, John, had helped finance Wilson's campaign; Anne Martin, the daughter of a Nevada state senator; Matilda Gardner, whose husband, Gil, was the Washington correspondent for the national newspaper chain Scripps, which was delivering the story to small-town America; Mary Ingham of Pennsylvania, whose grandfather had been treasury secretary during the Andrew Jackson administration; and Elizabeth Rogers, sister-in-law of the former war secretary Henry Stimson. At the police station, they refused to answer any questions, were released on bail, and told to appear in court the following week.

On Monday, Judge Mullowney sat down in his red throne in front of a stuffy courtroom overflowing not just with suffragists, but with prominent supporters. One of them was Dudley Field Malone, a lawyer and Wilson appointee as the collector of the Port of New York, who, despite being married to the daughter of Senator James O'Gorman, was having an affair with Doris Stevens, one of the women on trial. The other supporters there included Frederic C. Howe, commissioner of immigration of the Port of New York; Frank P. Walsh, an international labor leader; and John Hopkins, chairman of New Jersey's Progressive Party.

"Silence in the courtroom," barked the bailiff. The room went quiet. After dispatching with the weekend's other arrests, the proceedings turned to the suffragists. The prosecution called as witnesses the police and a clerk who proved that, yes, there was a White House, a sidewalk, and some protesters who carried banners and were arrested. Then it was the suffragists' turn to take the stand.

"This is what we are doing with our banners before the White House," said the thirty-two-year-old Martin. "Petitioning the most powerful representative of our government, the President of the United States, for a redress of grievances; we are asking him to use his great powers to secure the passage of the national suffrage amendment. As long as the government and the representatives of government prefer to send women to jail on petty and technical charges, we will go to jail. The right of American women to work for democracy must be maintained. We would hinder, not help, the whole cause for freedom if we surrendered right now. Our work for the passage of the amendment must go on. It will go on." People whispered to each other in the court as she took her seat. Then, Rogers, a descendant of Roger Sherman, a man whose signature is on the Declaration of Independence, stood to testify.

"We believe the president is the guilty one and we are innocent," she said.

"Your honor, I object!" the government's lawyer shouted.

"There are votes enough and there is time enough to pass the national suffrage amendment through Congress at this session," Rogers said. "More than 200 votes in the House and more than 50 in the Senate are pledged to this amendment. The President puts his power behind all measures in which he takes a genuine interest. If he will say one frank word advocating this measure it will pass as a piece of war emergency legislation."

Rogers finished her testimony, but many others took the stand during the two-day trial, hotly demanding the right to vote. After a short recess, the bailiff called the courtroom back to order. The judge returned to issue his ruling.

"Sixty days in the [Occoquan] Workhouse in default of a $25 fine," the judge said. "You had better pay your fines. You will not find prison a pleasant place to be."

The women, unprepared for such a severe punishment for an obstructing traffic offense, huddled with each other in the courtroom. After whispering among themselves for a few moments, they turned to announce their decision. They would submit to the harshest punishment that any picket had faced: two months behind bars in a Virginia workhouse an hour away from Washington.

Malone and Hopkins were stunned. They stood as the judge left the courtroom and watched as the women they cared about were rounded up into a pen with other prisoners. They said their good-byes. As the suffragists were escorted out of the courtroom, Malone drove directly to the White House. The president agreed to meet with him for five minutes. Instead, they argued for three-quarters of an hour, and Malone threatened to quit. He stormed out of the Oval Office so angry that he forgot there was a cab waiting for him and he walked past the car to the Shoreham Hotel.

CHAPTER SEVENTEEN

Behind Bars

The sentinels were led out of the courtroom and mixed with other convicts into black wagons with tiny windows. This was the first leg of the prisoners' journey to Occoquan Workhouse, where they would serve sixty-day sentences, the whole summer of 1917, in prison. The drivers brought the women to the train station where some friends were waiting to say good-bye and slip them contraband fruit or sweets. Superintendent W. H. Whittaker, a thin old man, herded the women onto a railcar using a long stick. It was late on Tuesday and dusk was falling fast on Washington. The train pulled away slowly. As it traveled south the sky dimmed even more and by the time the women arrived at a tiny station in the country, it was dark.

Three vans waited for them. The prisoners were sorted by skin color; whites filled the first two and blacks the third. They all bumped along a rocky dirt road surrounded by a forest of poplar trees. Up ahead, they saw the lights of Occoquan Workhouse twinkling on the hill. The facility, a group of white buildings nestled into fields filled with cows and crops, had opened about five years earlier as a penal experiment to see if fresh air and hard work, such as sewing clothes or farming, could reform criminals.

The women were funneled into a well-lit intake room. A matron named Mrs. Herndon sat at her desk and called each person forward individually to collect their eyeglasses, jewelry, toiletries, letters, and anything else they had with them. When she completed the process, Herndon brought the inmates to a bare dining room, the table serving as a color line with whites and blacks sorted onto opposite sides, and told them to sit down but they were not allowed to speak, smile, or laugh during mealtime.

The protesters obeyed. They were hungry. It had been a long day and an even longer weekend. But when the workhouse staff served them sour soup and a crust of rye bread they could barely eat it. After the meal, the matron ushered them into a long dormitory lined with cots. She ordered the suffragists to take off all of their clothes and walk to a bathing area where they were given tin buckets and scraps of dirty soap. They asked for toothbrushes, combs, and handkerchiefs, but Herndon only scoffed at their request. Once they had showered, the suffragists were given the clothes off the backs of the black inmates: coarse muslin chemises, petticoats made of ticking fabric, Mother Hubbard–style dresses, and heavy dark blue aprons to top it all off. The African American prisoners were given patched rags as a replacement for the clothes they were forced to give up. The workhouse staff also gave the suffragists muslin underwear and tortuous shoes that were the same for each foot and only came in size large or small. Luckily, prison-issued footwear was in short supply and some were able to keep their own shoes. The inmates were also each given one small rough towel to tuck into their aprons; workhouse rules allowed inmates to have only what they could carry.

Once the suffragists were dressed, they were asked to line up again. As they waited in silence, Superintendent Whittaker burst through the door with an unidentified man beside him. The men whispered, nodded, and laughed to each other as they looked at the women.

"Well, ladies, I hope you are all comfortable," Whittaker said. "Now make yourself at home. I think you will find it healthy here. You'll weigh more when you go out than when you came in. You will be allowed to write one letter a month to your family. Of course we open and read all letters coming in and going out. Tomorrow you will be assigned your work. I hope you will sleep well. Goodnight."

The women stayed quiet and cast glances at each other as the warden and his guest left the room. Then they were brought to their cots, covered in dirty sheets. Although there was a separate sleeping wing for the black prisoners, all the women were consolidated into the same room. They slept fitfully, awakened often by many disruptions in the room: bright lights flashing across the ceiling, a woman talking loudly in her sleep, and others shuffling to the open toilets that could only be flushed from the outside by one of the male guards; there was no toilet paper.

At dawn, the suffragists went to the dining room and tried to force down another inedible meal with greasy black coffee. They sat in an uncomfortable silence afterward. Meanwhile, Washingtonians eating breakfast at home devoured a sensational story—written by Whittaker's unnamed guest from the night before—in the morning paper. The dispatch purported to be the inside story about the protesters behind bars, and noted that the food was "delicious." Not everyone believed it. Gil Gardner and John Hopkins bolted to see their wives at the workhouse. After a brief couple's visit in the reception room with Herndon scolding the women to stay seated, the men were angry. Hopkins, friendly enough with the president to have recently brought his wife to dinner with the Wilsons, left the workhouse and went straight to the White House.

The inmates, meanwhile, were sent to the sewing room, where they turned hems on sheets and pillow slips using machines. There, the black prisoners who had not yet met the suffragists asked in a whisper what their crime was.

"Why, I held a purple, white and gold banner at the gates of the White House," one of them replied.

"Oh, yes. I've seen your parades, meetings, everything. I know where y'all live, right near the White House. You're alright. I hope you get it. Women certainly do need protection against men like Judge Mullowney. He has us all the time picked up and sent down here. They send you down here once and then you come out without a cent and try to look for a job and before you can find one a cop walks up and asks you where you live and you don't got a place yet, because you ain't got a cent to rent one with, and he says, 'Come with me, I'll find you a home,' and hustles you off to the police station. . . . I hope you all get a vote and fixes up some things for women!"

Another prisoner who had been listening joined the conversation. "You see that young girl over there? Well, Judge Mullowney gave her thirty days for her first offense and when he sentenced her she cried out desperately, 'Don't send me down there, Judge! If you do I'll kill myself.' What do you think he said to that? 'I'll give you six months [in prison] in which to change your mind.'"

The wardress heard the women talking and reprimanded them.

"You must not speak against the President," she said. "You know you will be thrashed if you say anything more about the President; and don't forget you're on government property and may be arrested for treason if it happens again."

The suffragists thought the woman was bluffing about being whipped. But those who had been there longer told them it was true. "Old Whittaker beat up that girl over there just last week and put her in the 'booby' house [meaning insane asylum] on bread and water for five days."

"What did she do?" Stevens asked.

"Oh, she and another girl got to scrapping in the blackberry patch and she didn't pick enough berries." The wardress interrupted their whispers by calling them to lunch. They carried their heavy chairs with them to the dining room as the staff counted their heads. The gray walls and vile odors made the awful food even less appetizing and the women barely ate, again.

Later, at the end of the day, the inmates spent forty-five minutes sitting with their chair backs against the wall in the "recreation" room, watching two other prisoners pick lice out of each other's hair. To distract themselves, they started to sing, and everyone joined in before they were sent to bed.

■ ■ ■

John Hopkins and Woodrow Wilson, two men who had worked together for years, joined in the common cause of Progressive politics, were at loggerheads.

"How would you like your wife to sleep in the dirty workhouse next to prostitutes?" Hopkins asked Wilson.

The president, taken aback by the heat and content of Hopkins's question, stalled. "What might be done?" Wilson asked.

"In view of the seriousness of the present situation," Hopkins said, "the only solution lay in the immediate passage of the Susan B. Anthony Amendment." He told the president there were enough votes in both chambers for it to pass. Wilson, turning defensive, said he would take his own poll to find out if that was true.

Hopkins gave a curt bow and marched out of the Oval Office. But he was not the only one objecting to the suffragists' prison term. Telegrams poured into the White House, as well as the NWP headquarters, from those upset by the harsh punishment these women had received. Wilson struggled over what to do.

The next day, golfing with the first lady and Dr. Grayson, Wilson swung his club and asked his wife for her thoughts. Edith had been seething all year over the picketing, and she was especially angry at Dudley Field Malone's resignation offer, which the president had refused to accept. She told Wilson that the most important thing was that the women not be made into martyrs. They finished their game and made up their minds: a pardon was the best solution. When Wilson got back to the White House, he told his closest aide the plan.

■ ■ ■

On their third morning at Occoquan, the women were brought one by one to the warden's office for interviews. Are your parents insane? Do you drink alcohol, and if so, how much? Do you smoke or chew tobacco? Are you married or single? Do you have children? What's your religion? The women answered the questions and then Superintendent Whittaker called them into a semicircle in front of him. He said the Department of Justice had called the workhouse with news that he had to relay.

"Ladies, there is a rumor that you may be pardoned," he said.

"By whom?"

"For what? We are innocent women. There is nothing to pardon us for."

"I have come to ask you what you would do if the president pardoned you," Whittaker said.

Several women said they would refuse to accept it unless the president had changed his mind and would push for an amendment.

"I shall leave you for a while to consider this. Mind! I have not yet received information of the pardon, but I have been asked to ascertain your attitude."

Whittaker left and the women discussed the situation. They all agreed that since they had not committed a crime, there was no reason for a pardon. They told Whittaker this when he returned.

"You have no choice," he said. "You are obliged to accept a pardon."

Shortly after this conversation, Malone arrived at the workhouse. He told the women he was as surprised as anyone to hear that Wilson had offered the pardon; the president had not consulted with him despite the fact that he was the women's attorney. He explained that while they could not be forced to accept the pardon, the attorney general would kick them out of the workhouse anyway and that the public would interpret the outcome as if they had taken the president's offer. That's exactly what happened.

"Ladies," Whittaker said. "You are free to go as soon as you have taken off your prison clothes and put on your own." Some of the black prisoners helped the suffragists change back into their own clothes. When the protesters were ready to leave, Whittaker showed them to the exit, where Lucy Burns and two men—Malone and Gardner—waited for them.

"Now that you women are going away," Whittaker said angrily to Burns, "I have something to say and I want to say it to you. The next lot of women who come here won't be treated with the same consideration that these women were."

"What did you just say?" Malone asked. "Repeat yourself." Whittaker said it again. Malone told him the women had rights and they would be respected.

"I was not speaking to you," Whittaker said. "And I will not speak to you."

Everyone piled into a lineup of cars waiting to take them back to

Washington, to home or headquarters; for some, they were one and the same. As the women caromed down the rocky road, they were happy to be out of the workhouse, but they still did not feel free.

After an hour's drive, they arrived at Cameron House for a welcome party, organized by Malone and John Hopkins. The press, dawdling around headquarters, was eager for a statement. Hopkins put his conversation with the president on the public record, saying he predicted Congress would pass the Susan B. Anthony Amendment in the current session if they had an opportunity to vote on it and that the president was interested in polling the House and Senate on the issue. The mood was positive, but not celebratory.

Paul, still recuperating in the hospital, missed their welcome. A reporter for the *Baltimore Sun* found her there in bed, sitting up straight, and asked her for her thoughts about the day's events.

"We're obliged to the President for pardoning the pickets," she told the reporter.

But we'll be picketing again next Monday. Picketing will continue, and sooner or later the president will have to do something definite. Oh, yes, picketing has accomplished just exactly what we wanted it to accomplish, and picketing is going to end in forcing the issue. The pickets have brought the issue before the eyes of the world and put Wilson in the final corner. Now he has got to the point of practically declaring for the federal suffrage amendment, and we have placed him where he will be obliged to do something to prove that. Monday he had a conference with Dudley Field Malone. Tuesday he, of necessity, reviewed the votes which the federal amendment can lay claim to in Congress.

He has pardoned the pickets. A second pardon if they are arrested again will gain him no respite. He will have to find a new course. The sentence was monstrous—sixty days for blocking the traffic! And we didn't block it! If we could only have appealed the case! Mr. Malone took it up for us but there was nothing irregular about the trial upon which he could base an appeal, in spite of the gross injustice.

The reporter scribbled Paul's every word and departed. Left alone, Paul knew it was time for her to get back to work, even if she was still not feeling well. The same sentiment was true for the women who had just been released from the workhouse.

The morning after her pardon, Alison Hopkins was bursting with energy and emotion. She channeled her thoughts by writing a letter to the president, a man she no longer held in high regard: "You pardoned me to save yourself the embarrassment of an acute and distressing political situation," she wrote. "As you have not seen fit to tell the public the true reason, I am compelled to resume my peaceful petition for political liberty. If the police arrest me, I shall carry the case to the Supreme Court if necessary. If the police do not arrest me, I shall believe that you do not believe me guilty." When she put down her pen it was 5 p.m. Instead of preparing for dinner, she carried a banner to the White House gates and stood there for ten minutes holding a sign that read: WE ASK NOT PARDON FOR OURSELVES BUT JUSTICE FOR ALL AMERICAN WOMEN.

A large crowd gathered around Hopkins, but nobody bothered her. While she stood there, the president passed through the gates, tipping his hat at her as he went by.

■ ■ ■

Inside the White House, Wilson took off his hat and got to work. There was a stack of correspondence, taller than usual, for him to address. The mail included a letter from the new owner of the *Washington Times*, Arthur Brisbane. Brisbane wrote that he did not think the women deserved attention in the press. "I have an idea that if the ladies were allowed to parade harmlessly, the public would forget them. The trouble has really come from their illegal and stupid acts in putting up a poster for the benefit of the Russians denouncing the United States. But that would not have amounted to anything if it had been ignored." Brisbane went on to write that "what this paper intends to do is *whatever will be desired by the president* [emphasis his]. If you will be good enough to give me a suggestion it will be followed to the letter."

Wilson, who cared deeply about favorable coverage, told Joseph Tumulty, his secretary, to write to accept Brisbane's proposal:

There is a great deal in what Brisbane says about the entire silence on the part of the newspapers possibly provoking the less sane of these women to violent action. My own suggestion would be that nothing that they do should be featured with headlines or put on the front page but that a bare, colorless chronicle of what they do should be all that was printed. That constitutes part of the news but it need not be made interesting reading.

The President

The National Woman's Party (NWP) public relations operation had grown to a six-woman team that Burns had led for nearly two years, relentlessly churning out press releases in addition to publishing *The Suffragist* weekly. The volume of news they generated, combined with the party's tactics, made it nearly impossible for newspapers to ignore what the protesters were doing. But the press was hungry for war headlines now that U.S. troops were finally on the ground in Europe and marching toward the front lines.

The war, now in its third year, had the globe locked in a sprawling conflict that was so complex that a headline in the *New York Times* at the end of July 1917 spanned the width of the page and ran four levels deep: "British Victory at Vimy Ridge, French Forward Movement in Champagne, and Germany's Counteroffensive There—Rumania's Collapse Before Teutonic Onslaught—Capture of Baghdad by British Mesopotamian Army—Italy's Advance Toward Trieste—Russia's Revolution, Resumption of Offensive, and Military Debacle." The ten-month Battle of Verdun, the longest, largest, and most horrific battle the world had ever experienced, had ended six months earlier with no winners. The French and the Germans both lost approximately the same number of soldiers on the field, totaling nearly one million. Since then, the French and British had held their ground. And now the Americans had arrived, willing to fight for democratic ideals.

At the same time as U.S. troops were fanning out across Europe, Washington was in its summer stupor. When the daily suffrage picket resumed in late July, Burns knew that signs alone would not be enough to keep the cause on the front page. Envoy Root had returned from his mission to Russia and was expected at 1600 Pennsylvania Avenue. She and Dora Lewis decided to greet him with a protest sign:

TO ENVOY ROOT: YOU SAY THAT AMERICA MUST THROW ITS MANHOOD IN THE SUPPORT OF LIBERTY. WHOSE LIBERTY? THIS NATION IS NOT FREE. 20,000,000 WOMEN ARE DENIED BY THE PRESIDENT OF THE UNITED STATES THE RIGHT TO REPRESENTATION IN THEIR OWN GOVERNMENT. TELL THE PRESIDENT THAT HE CANNOT FIGHT AGAINST LIBERTY AT HOME WHILE HE TELLS US TO FIGHT FOR LIBERTY ABROAD. TELL HIM TO MAKE AMERICA FREE FOR DEMOCRACY BEFORE HE ASKS THE MOTHERS OF AMERICA TO THROW THEIR SONS TO THE SUPPORT OF DEMOCRACY IN EUROPE.

ASK HIM HOW WE COULD REFUSE LIBERTY TO AMERICAN CITIZENS WHEN HE HAS FORCED MILLIONS OF AMERICAN BOYS OUT OF THEIR COUNTRY TO DIE FOR LIBERTY.

For two hours, the pickets held the banner and attracted their largest crowd yet, clogging two blocks of Pennsylvania Avenue. But police, under orders to stop the cycle of arrests, managed the crowds well; there was no violence, no heckling, no charges. So the women considered using more aggressive rhetoric.

On August 10, Burns designed a sign comparing the president to Germany's unpopular, blundering king, Kaiser Wilhelm II. Anticipating that the sign would be attacked, she had extras made and then marched with forty women from NWP headquarters to the White House carrying their most antagonistic banner yet:

KAISER WILSON

HAVE YOU FORGOTTEN HOW MUCH YOU SYMPATHIZED WITH THE POOR GERMANS BECAUSE THEY WERE NOT

SELF-GOVERNED? 20,000,000 AMERICAN WOMEN ARE NOT
SELF-GOVERNED. TAKE THE BEAM OUT OF YOUR OWN EYE.

The pickets held their ground in long shifts over two days, taking turns holding the signs. Public tension mounted but the picket
remained peaceful, for now. On the third day of these pickets, Paul
was released from the hospital and headed back to Washington, where
tensions increased with the temperature. The banner language stoked
suspicions that the NWP was being financed by the Germans. One
government clerk, so outraged by the sign, assaulted the women and
shredded the banner. When police moved in to arrest the aggressor, men
in Army and Navy uniforms rushed to protect the counterprotester
from the officers. Someone threw a punch at the cop and the situation
spiraled out of control.

At that precise moment, the Wilsons drove through the gates on
their way to a military event in Fort Myer. As people tried to flee the
scuffle with police, they ran into Lafayette Park, toward Cameron
House, following suffragists who needed fresh flags and signs. The
women ran inside and locked the doors behind them. One uniformed
soldier grabbed a ladder, leaned it on the headquarters, and climbed
high enough to grab onto a flag hanging above the door. Burns ran upstairs just as the Stars and Stripes was ripped down. From her position,
she unfurled a tricolor suffrage banner and held on to it as the mob
threw eggs, tomatoes, and apples at her. Shots were fired into the air.
More men climbed the ladder, and there was a tug of war over the
suffrage flag, which Burns lost. Other women charged upstairs with
a replacement while two other suffragists marched back to the White
House holding a fresh Kaiser Wilson sign. No one noticed those
pickets for seventeen minutes. But when they did, a mob dragged the
women to the pavement and ruined their banners in front of police.
The melee would not end. Into the early evening, men were trying to
climb over the back fence of the garden to get into Cameron House.
Counterprotesters destroyed twenty-two lettered banners and fourteen tricolor flags that day. The suffragists regrouped inside Cameron
House and kept watch through the windows. Paul, who had just settled

back into her bedroom there, did not sleep that night. Neither did anyone else.

A few days later, on August 15, the pickets were back at their posts. This time, Paul went with them. Police were nowhere to be found when a crowd assembled and became agitated. A soldier struck Elizabeth Stuyvesant and destroyed her flag. A sailor threw Beulah Amidon down on the pavement and stole hers. Paul was knocked down three times before a sailor brutally dragged her thirty feet along the White House sidewalk trying to tear off her suffrage sash, gashing her neck. New flags and new pickets kept appearing; the organizers ever hopeful that the president would see them when he left at 5 p.m. It was all for naught. He sneaked out through a rear gate. Similar scenes played out day after day with more pickets, more attacks, and finally, more arrests. On August 17, six women were sentenced to month-long confinements at the workhouse.

Events throughout September led to a new intensity in the campaign.

First, Burns, carrying a sign that said, MR. PRESIDENT, HOW LONG MUST WOMEN BE DENIED A VOICE IN THE GOVERNMENT THAT IS CONSCRIPTING THEIR SONS, was one of thirteen pickets arrested and sentenced to sixty days at Occoquan. While her friends had previously faced the same sentence, Burns knew that she might actually serve the full time. She was ready. Next, Malone finally quit over Wilson's inaction in the face of such sentences, and his letter to the president— elevating him to hero status within suffrage circles—said it was time for men to advocate for women. Meanwhile, in Maine, male voters rejected a state referendum on woman suffrage by a two-to-one margin, with newspapers blaming the White House pickets for driving conservatives to the polls.

The pickets had another unexpected effect. They softened Carrie Chapman Catt, of the more conservative NAWSA, who called the protesters' actions "noble" and, for the first time publicly, supported a federal amendment, all while pushing for a New York referendum on voting rights for women. In a frenzy of fall campaigning, Catt sent NAWSA members to knock on the doors of farmhouses in the country and tenements in the city, collecting more than a million signatures for a petition and delivering millions of leaflets. She also convinced Wilson to voice his support for the state-level measure. She felt confident suffrage would win on New York's ballot in November.

At the federal level, the suffrage logjam seemed to be loosening as well. In Washington, Senator Andrieus Jones, chairman of the Woman Suffrage Committee, went to Occoquan to investigate the deplorable conditions there. When he returned, he told his committee to take favorable action on the suffrage bill, which had been on hold for six months. The House, which had always been a few steps behind the Senate on the issue, finally created their own suffrage committee by a vote of 181 to 107, numbers that Wilson surely noted.

The protesters kept up the pressure. By the end of September, two dozen suffragists were confined to Occoquan Workhouse. Although the situation created a shortage of pickets—women were either scared away or the most committed were already locked up—new members and donations poured into the NWP. Paul continued to ask for money and volunteers, but she was frank with potential protesters: be prepared to go to prison for up to six months.

CHAPTER EIGHTEEN

The Hunger Strikes

The New York Giants were playing the Chicago White Sox in the first game of the World Series at Comiskey Park. A patriotic image of Woodrow Wilson throwing a pitch was on the cover of the Fall Classic program. As Game 1 was getting under way, on October 6, 1917, Congress was winding down its last day of the session, giving them a break until December. In Europe, the American Expeditionary Forces continued their slow arrival into France, a pace hindered by two issues: the troops needed to be trained first and there was a shortage of ships to transport them across the Atlantic. Only a small number of U.S. soldiers had fought in battle. That would change by spring. With the nation distracted, Alice Paul made one more desperate attempt to capture the nation's attention. She walked out of Cameron House with a procession timed for when government employees concluded work for the day. Her face glowed with purpose as she held a white banner above her head: MR. PRESIDENT, WHAT WILL YOU DO FOR WOMAN SUFFRAGE?

She led ten other women, ranging in age from twenty-one to forty, carrying the suffrage banners toward the White House gates. As they took their positions, a crowd quickly formed around them. One young man yanked Paul's sign down and left her standing there holding the naked pole. And that was it. The women held their ground silently until the police wagon arrived. The crowd scattered as the officers hauled the pickets to the station. Once in court, Paul and the rest of the protesters refused to enter pleas, call witnesses, or be sworn in.

"We do not consider ourselves subject to the court since as an unenfranchised class, we have nothing to do with the making of the laws," Paul said.

Judge Alexander Mullowney knew the women were looking for a harsh sentence. But he refused to give them what they wanted and released them on parole, believing the picketing would stop during the congressional recess. He was wrong.

On October 20, while Wilson was having his portrait painted by John Singer Sargent inside the White House, Paul was outside breaking parole. She put on her fur coat, which swallowed her frail frame, and led three pickets to the west gate. Her banner carried the president's own words: THE TIME HAS COME TO CONQUER OR SUBMIT. FOR US THERE CAN BE BUT ONE CHOICE. WE HAVE MADE IT.

Following behind Paul was Dr. Caroline Spencer of Colorado, who had organized that state for the NWP. Spencer, a fifty-six-year-old physician, had chronic asthma and was in poor health. Her banner used the

Alice Paul marches to the White House. Dora Lewis stands behind her.

motto of America's revolutionaries in 1776: RESISTANCE TO TYRANNY
IS OBEDIENCE TO GOD. Gladys Greiner, a twenty-four-year-old from
Baltimore whose father was a member of the Elihu Root mission to
Russia, and Gertrude Crocker, a young government worker who served
as treasurer of the NWP, carried suffrage banners.

Police waited until a large crowd gathered before arresting the pickets, processing their alleged crimes, and telling them to come back for
trial in a few days.

While they were waiting to be sentenced, Burns was grasping for
new ways to cause dissidence inside Occoquan. Inspired by Socialist
Party tactics, she led a campaign for prisoners to refuse work and be
treated as political prisoners. She also committed to a hunger strike if
their demands were not met, which they weren't. The inmates secretly
circulated a petition among themselves, smuggled it out, and had it presented to the district commissioners. The crackdown was swift. Every
woman signing the petition was transferred to the district jail, where
they were put in solitary confinement. News of Burns's strike broke on
the same day Paul was expected in court.

Before leaving to appear before Judge Mullowney, Paul prepared
for a long stay behind bars. She asked her old friend Lewis to manage
the NWP and Virginia Arnold to handle the administrative work. She
also wrote to her mother: "Do not worry. It will merely be a delightful
rest." Perhaps Paul believed her own words, laying out a plan to read
five newspapers a day and dictate orders once a week to Arnold and a
stenographer. With her affairs in order, she gathered some books, including a volume of Elizabeth Barrett Browning's poetry, grabbed her
fur coat, and left to appear before Judge Mullowney's bench.

It was a speedy trial. He sentenced Paul and Spencer to seven months
in jail; the other two pickets were offered the choice of a five-dollar fine
or thirty days, and, of course, they chose to do time. As Paul was led
out of the courtroom, people lined her path. Some of them hissed and
some of them cheered. Reporters asked her for comment on receiving
the harshest sentence yet of any suffragist.

"I am being imprisoned not because I obstructed traffic, but because
I pointed out to President Wilson the fact that he was obstructing the

cause of democracy and justice at home, while Americans fight for it abroad." She said she expected to be treated as a political prisoner.

Paul disappeared into the van and was taken to the old district jail, where Burns and the others had just been released from solitary confinement. The three-story facility, built in 1872, was decrepit and surrounded by a rickety picket fence. Although conditions were terrible, most of the suffragists thought it was better than the workhouse. For one thing, they could wear their own clothes, buy food in the canteen, and receive gifts of fruit.

But the cells, with steel cots and mattresses infested with bed bugs, were so narrow that the women could touch two parallel walls at the same time. Each cell had an open toilet—flushed only from the outside—and it stunk. Rats scampered around and fresh air was in short supply, especially on the top floor, where most of the suffragists were kept, away from the regular inmates. The windows, small portholes with bars, were closed from late afternoon until morning. Even though it was late October, it was stuffy and dusty inside the jail, dangerous conditions for Spencer's asthma. As Paul entered the cell block, women began asking her for help with the windows. She and another suffragist grabbed a rope to pull one open. When the prison matron yelled for them to close it they ignored her and male guards came running. They grabbed the rope away from Paul as she resisted being dragged to her cell by holding tightly to some bars; more guards joined the effort and succeeded in dragging her away.

The windows were about twenty feet away. Paul, reminded of her time in Holloway Gaol, told the women to throw everything they could find, from tin cups to lightbulbs, at the panes in an attempt to break them. Paul even threw her book. They persisted for three hours, only cracking the glass. Finally, the matrons opened a few windows, but the rebellion landed Paul and the others involved in solitary confinement, locked up twenty-four hours a day without mail or visitors.

The next day, as the guards swept dust into the cells. Paul told the other women to fill their replacement tin cups with water and throw it through the bars so the damp floor would be impossible to sweep. They hung blankets for privacy, which guards quickly tore down. They were fed inedible, raw, wormy salted pork, a liquid that was either coffee or soup, some bread, and occasionally molasses, which they saved to "distribute the nourishment" throughout the day. Ten days into this routine, with no exercise and little food, Paul was growing weak.

On November 3, Burns and several others from the Occoquan group, having served their sentence, were released from the district jail. A big group of suffragists were outside to greet them with cars and banners flying. Burns told the press that Paul was frail and that the jailers were intentionally making the women unwell so they would be forced to pay and admit guilt to get out.

Now that there was a smaller group of suffragists in jail, the guards felt they were better able to manage the women. They unlocked their doors and encouraged them to get some air in the yard. But Paul did not get out of bed; she did not have the strength. Rose Winslow, who had been incarcerated a week earlier than Paul, fainted as soon as she went outside. Both of them were brought on stretchers to the prison hospital. Staff offered them fresh milk and eggs but the women refused, saying all of the suffragists in jail should have access to such food.

When word spread outside the prison that Winslow and Paul were in the hospital, a group of suffragists sneaked up to the facility and gathered outside their window. Vida Milholland sang "Marseillaise" to them while the other women did a roll call for the inmates to hear. Before the guards swooped in and shooed them away, the visitors were able to share some news: there was an influx of monetary donations to the NWP and forty-one women had committed to protesting the next day over the imprisonment.

Paul and Winslow, lying next to each other in the ward, were encouraged by the support. It was just what they needed to muster a hunger strike. The jail staff, worried about their condition, called Paul's doctor, Cora Smith King, to come check on her. Dr. King was shocked to see how thin Paul was but she knew she could not convince her to stop the hunger strike, and left to tell the press the protest would continue.

The following day, while Paul and Winslow fasted, New York made history, becoming the first eastern state to pass a woman suffrage referendum. Women throughout New York and beyond celebrated. For Alva Belmont and hundreds of others gathered at the Ritz-Carlton in Manhattan to mark the occasion, there was no time to rest. They passed around a petition, which they planned to send to Wilson immediately, demanding a federal amendment. Now that they were voters, perhaps he would listen to them. Malone gave a short speech that was well received, although the crowd hissed when he mentioned the president's name.

The National American Woman Suffrage Association's veneer of respect for the president had worn thin. Catt, Shaw, and other leaders from the National American had been urging the president for weeks to meet in person. He finally agreed to receive them on November 9 at the White House. For the first time, they urged Wilson face-to-face to press for the federal amendment. He said no.

While Paul and Winslow would have been cheered by the news out of New York, they were on their third day of a hunger strike, and they were limp. The staff, which had assumed the women would eat once they were truly hungry, became concerned and persistent.

"You will be forcibly fed immediately if you don't stop," the doctor, J. A. Gannon, said, his face close to Paul's. She laid in bed silently. "You will be taken to a very unpleasant place if you don't stop this."

In the morning, a psychiatrist walked into her room, trailed by a stenographer taking shorthand and a prison hospital attendant who stood a few paces away.

"Does this case talk?" the psychiatrist asked the attendant.

"Why wouldn't I talk?" Paul asked.

"Oh these cases frequently will not talk," he said.

"Indeed, I'll talk," said Paul. "Talking is our business. We will talk to anyone on earth who is willing to listen to our suffrage speeches."

"Please talk," said the doctor. "Tell me about suffrage. Why have you opposed the President?"

Paul propped herself up in bed to deliver what she later said was one of the best speeches of her life. She recited the history of suffrage, political theory, and the status of their fight.

"But," the doctor interrupted in an attempt to provoke her, "has not the President treated you women very badly?"

She launched into a dissertation on Wilson's political predicament. "We oppose President Wilson," she said, "merely because he is President. Not because he is Woodrow Wilson."

"But isn't President Wilson directly responsible for the indignities which have been heaped upon you?"

"How would we know whether the President knows about any of this?"

The doctor picked up a small light and shone it in her eyes. Later, with other staff in the room, including the district commissioner, he asked her to repeat her thoughts on Wilson.

"Note the reaction," the doctor said anytime Paul mentioned the president's name. It was then that she realized they were trying to prove she was crazy.

"I will not give up the hunger strike," she said.

The psychiatrist and commissioner agreed that Paul should be fed by force. "Go ahead, take her," the commissioner said as he stormed out of the room.

The attendants put her on a stretcher and took her to the psychiatric ward, to a big, square room with a metal grate door and two windows the doctor ordered covered. Paul saw a man on a ladder outside, peering through her window. He told her he was in jail for drinking but had never seen anyone treated so cruelly as the suffragists. He apologized as he nailed a board over the panes.

Nurses were ordered to observe Paul throughout the night, shining a light in her face hourly. They told her they felt sorry for doing so. "We know you're not insane," a nurse said.

After she and Winslow went seventy-two hours without food and only intermittent sleep, the doctor came to draw Paul's blood. She objected—there was no reason to do it. But he pushed the needle into her vein anyway.

"You know you're not mentally competent to decide such things," he said.

Whatever test result he was seeking was a prelude to the horrors of

Alice Paul's boarded-up jailhouse hospital window, upper right.

what came next: forced feedings. The staff, including a new doctor and nurse who were both sympathetic, strapped Paul down, stuck a tube up her nose, and funneled milk and raw eggs down her throat. She thrashed and sprayed the attendants with puke. The ghastly ritual occurred three times that day. Winslow, subjected to the same treatment, could be heard throughout the jail screaming. She had developed a painful irritation from the tube and fainted often. The feedings triggered a severe headache, an aching throat, and uncontrollable sobs.

Although news reports quoted Dr. Gannon as saying both women took the nourishment without protest, Paul and Winslow smuggled out their own more accurate accounts. Outrage mounted. On November 10, forty-one women protested outside the White House about Paul and Winslow's treatment; thirty-one were arrested, including Lewis and Burns, who had been released from prison only a few days before. The pickets were sentenced to varying terms at Occoquan Workhouse; Burns received the harshest penalty: six months.

Malone, with so many legal issues swirling, made Paul his top priority. He was granted a court order to see her. When he arrived, he barked at the staff to take her out of the psychiatric ward and remove the board from the window. The same inmate who had boarded up the window took it down.

"I thought when I put this up America would not stand for this long," he told her. Paul, faint and feeble, was carried on a stretcher to the hospital section. There, the forced feedings continued for the next two weeks.

The pickets most recently arrested, including Burns and Lewis, arrived at Occoquan on November 15. Whittaker was not there to meet them because he was in a secret meeting at the White House. The suffragists demanded to be treated as political prisoners and refused to answer any intake questions, saying they would only speak with the superintendent. Mrs. Herndon kept the women in the front office until Whittaker arrived.

The women waited for hours until Whittaker burst through the door with a group of men. The suffragists, lying or sitting on the floor, were startled. Lewis stood up and wasted no time with her demand to be treated as a political prisoner.

"You shut up!" Whittaker shouted. "I have men here glad to handle you! Seize her!"

Two men dragged Lewis out of the room. Next they grabbed Mary Nolan, a white-haired former teacher from Jacksonville who was frail and in her seventies.

"I will come with you; do not drag me. I have a lame foot," she shouted. But they dragged her down a flight of dark stairs, outside, across a field, and into a building whose small light illuminated an American flag flying outside.

"Damn you! Get in there!" a man with a stick shouted at Nolan. The guards did the same with the other women. Lewis hit her head on the wall and crumpled to the floor, motionless. The other women thought she was dead and began to wail. Lewis regained consciousness. Burns, described as "worth her weight in wild cats," fought two guards the whole way to the cell. She was thrown in with Dorothy Day, an activist and social worker. Burns began calling the roll to see if everyone was okay. The guards ordered silence but she paid no attention to them.

"Where is Mrs. Lewis?"

"They have just thrown her in here," Alice Cosu told Burns.

"If you speak again," the guard said, "We'll put you in straitjackets."

Burns continued, so they handcuffed her wrists above her head to the cell door. They threatened her with putting a gag buckle over her mouth. Julia Emory, in the cell across from Burns, held the same position in solidarity. Cosu had a heart attack and vomited throughout the night. Another woman from their group was locked up with the male prisoners, who were told that they could do whatever they wanted with her.

The next day, sixteen of these women went on a hunger strike. The superintendent, targeting the ringleaders, ordered the forced feeding of Burns and Lewis first, followed by Elizabeth McShane, a twenty-six-year-old Vassar graduate. Burns, always quick to fight, refused to open her mouth. So the staff inserted a glass tube up her nostril, causing significant bleeding and pain. McShane did not take the tube feeding well, either. She developed stomach ulcers and a gallbladder infection.

The workhouse staff tried tempting the other women with fried chicken and fresh eggs and coffee for breakfast. No one succumbed to the food. Burns slipped a note around that said: "I think this riotous feast which has just passed our doors is the last effort of the institution to dislodge all of us who can be dislodged. They think there is nothing in our souls above fried chicken."

But fasting was not easy. On the first day, they felt weak. The second day there was slight nausea and headaches; the third day, fever and dizziness, dry, peeling skin and swollen lips. The situation was dire. At headquarters, Doris Stevens, trying to manage so many issues at once, was in a panic. But increasingly, so was Whittaker. Four days into the hunger strike, he called Stevens and asked her what to do. She told him the women wanted to be treated as political prisoners and he should oblige them. But when Whittaker brought this demand to the district commissioners, not only did the Wilson appointees nix the idea, they sent a detachment of U.S. Marines from their camp at Quantico, Virginia, to guard the workhouse grounds and prevent any communication from leaking out.

Matthew O'Brien, a lawyer working with Malone, got a court order allowing him into the workhouse to check on his clients. O'Brien made the trip to Occoquan with Katharine Morey, frantic about the health of her mother, Agnes, who was there. Whittaker tried to turn them both away. It was only when O'Brien showed him the order that the warden let him in. As for Morey, he ordered a Marine to escort her back to the car.

"I am sorry to do this," the Marine said. "But we are under military orders."

"What would you do if I refused to obey your orders?" Morey asked.

"I cannot say what I would do, but I have strict orders."

Inside the workhouse, O'Brien found Burns in bed in her dark cell, wrapped in a blanket as her clothes had been violently stripped from her. It was all the proof he needed to argue that the suffragists were being subjected to cruel and unusual punishment. At a hearing a week later in U.S. district court, with Burns and Lewis in the room but too weak to testify, Judge Edmund Waddill ordered all suffragists transferred from Occoquan to the district jail, where Paul was. O'Brien was relieved by the decision, but he also told Waddill there should be an investigation into the conditions at the workhouse. The judge snapped at the attorney:

"If these women, who are highly educated and refined, picket in front of the White House, what will other classes of extremists do if given the same liberties?" Waddill asked. "There is no telling what the dangers and consequences might be. The President is entitled to all the protection that can be given him, and I have never seen anybody who believed that the women did the right thing when they picketed the White House."

Concerns about the president's safety were real. The assassination that triggered the Great War was still fresh in America's mind and three U.S. presidents—Abraham Lincoln, James Garfield, and William McKinley—had been fatally shot. An attempt to shoot Andrew Jackson left him unscathed but Theodore Roosevelt, shot while campaigning against Wilson, carried the bullet in his chest for the rest of his life.

Although Wilson's political appointees, including Waddill, were trying to defend the president, they were doing him more harm than good, according to the torrent of letters and telegrams flowing toward the White House. Some writers made plain to Wilson that Democrats would lose the next election over the maltreatment issue. Tammany Hall operatives in New York were especially alarmed now that women could vote there. As Calvin Tomkins, chairman of the New York State Businessmen's Campaign Committee, said in a note to Tumulty, "the picketing issue has brought to the support of the Suffragists the labor element . . . and the consequences of this will soon be obvious." Others blamed Wilson for the prison mess. But the president dug his own trench. He told his aides to respond to complaints by saying the women were lying about their conditions behind bars. In a note to Tumulty on November 21, he wrote:

> I think your present reply . . . ought to be to the effect that no real harshness of method is being used, these ladies submitting to the artificial feeding without resistance; that the conditions under which they are made to work are being thoroughly investigated for the second or third time, and that any abuses that may exist will certainly be corrected but that none has yet been disclosed, there being an extraordinary amount of lying about the thing.

Perhaps it was political pressure getting to the judge or perhaps it was the right thing to do under the law, but when Malone took up the next legal challenge a week after the Waddill hearing, all the women were granted release. By November 28, Paul, Burns, and twenty other protesters were freed. Now it was Wilson who was handcuffed in a difficult position.

CHAPTER NINETEEN

The Watch Fires of Freedom

At high noon, on January 8, 1918, Woodrow Wilson stood at the podium in the House chamber eager to deliver to Congress a foreign policy speech that he had been working on for days. It was his Fourteen Points for peace, a road map to end the Great War, nine bloody months into America's involvement. While the speech itself came together fairly quickly, the exhaustive research supporting it had not. A team of 150 social and political scientists—called "The Inquiry"—had been gathering information in secret and produced 2,000 reports and documents as well as at least 1,200 maps to help analyze the economic, social, and political facts that could arise during peace talks.

The president only gave Congress thirty minutes' notice that he would address them. Surprised and rushed, the elected officials settled into the chamber quickly and hushed as soon as he appeared. Then, Wilson began his argument.

"What we demand in this war," he said, "is nothing peculiar to ourselves. It is that the world be made fit and safe to live in; and particularly that it be made safe for every peace-loving nation which, like our own, wishes to live its own life, determine its own institutions, be assured of justice and fair dealing by the other peoples of the world as against force and selfish aggression."

Wilson was concerned that England and France were plotting to redraw the maps of Europe in their favor, and in secret. His speech told

Congress—and the world—that there should be no "private international understandings of any kind but diplomacy shall proceed always frankly and in the public view." His points for peace called for freedom on the seas and open trade; a reduction in armaments; an "adjustment" of colonial claims; the enemy evacuation of Russia, Belgium, and France; the redrawing of Italy's borders; the sovereignty of Turkey; and an independent Poland. He saved his boldest point for last: to create "a general association of nations" that would guarantee fairness throughout the world.

His broad vision for peace, so clearly articulated, sent a pulse of hope and loud cheers through the chamber. And then, just as quickly as Wilson had arrived, he darted from the House. With such monumental work to do, he had no time to waste.

The next day, Wilson absorbed the joyful responses to his peace plan; European leaders were thrilled, with the exception of Germany. But the president had pressing domestic matters he needed to focus on as well. The House was about to vote on woman suffrage and eleven congressmen, most of them Democrats, descended upon his office in the evening to discuss the matter. The representatives of California, Kentucky, Arizona, Texas, Kansas, Utah, Maryland, Ohio, and Colorado explained that an anti-suffrage group had gone to great expense to print and circulate a booklet filled with the president's statements opposing the federal amendment. The House was scheduled to vote on the Susan B. Anthony Amendment within twenty-four hours, and the men wanted to know where Wilson really stood on the issue. Lately, he seemed to be supporting it, but the booklet proved otherwise. For forty minutes, they explained the situation in their own states and then asked the president for his thoughts. Wilson said that his personal position had not changed—leaving the states to decide would be the "proper and orderly way of dealing with the question." But, he said, America, and the world, had changed. There was growing public sentiment in favor of votes for women, and the nation's stature as a beacon of democracy had grown.

The men, astonished by Wilson's reply, asked if he would write it down so they could share his thoughts accurately with the press. Wilson

called a clerk for a pencil and paper, pulled up a chair, and produced
the following statement, which he did not attribute directly to himself:

> The committee found that the President had not felt at liberty to
> volunteer his advice to members of Congress in this important
> matter, but when we sought his advice he very frankly and earnestly
> advised us to vote for the amendment as an act of right and justice
> to the women of the country and of the world.

Congressman Edward T. Taylor, a Democrat of Colorado, took
the statement and said he would make copies of it for the newspapers.
Representative John E. Raker, a California Democrat, was elated over
what he had just witnessed. He left with a huge smile on his face, and
was met by a small group of suffragists standing in the light snow on
Pennsylvania Avenue where they had been waiting for news.

"The President," Raker told them, "has declared for the Susan B.
Anthony Amendment, and will stay home from his game of golf tomorrow morning to see any Congressman who wishes to consult him
about it." The women cheered. Over at the National American Woman
Suffrage Association (NAWSA) headquarters, everyone was ecstatic,
including Anthony's niece, Lucy, who, when she heard the news,
shouted "Washington! Lincoln! Wilson!" At the National Woman's
Party (NWP), Paul, mostly recovered from her last hunger strike, was
also upbeat. In a statement to the press, she said, "It is difficult to express our gratification at the President's stand. For four years we have
striven to secure his support for the national amendment, for we knew
that this, and perhaps it alone, would ensure us success." But despite
her comments, Paul had a secret poll that showed that the House still
lacked votes. An amendment needs a two-thirds majority vote in both
the House and the Senate in order for the proposed change to be sent
to the states, three-fourths of which (thirty-six of forty-eight states at
that time) also need to ratify the amendment (a simple majority in
each legislature is required for approval) for it to become part of the
Constitution.

The following day, suffragists darted to the House gallery. Some were there early enough to greet the cleaning staff still scrubbing floors. Chamber staff ushered NAWSA women, including Carrie Chapman Catt and Anna Howard Shaw, to prominent seats in the Speaker's Gallery overlooking the crescent rows of desks on the floor. Members of the NWP filled the gallery on the opposite side, Paul among them. The debate began at 11 a.m. when Speaker Champ Clark walked in and settled the chamber as if a religious ceremony were about to begin.

There were the usual speeches, pro and con. Congresswoman Jeannette Rankin, whose desk was decorated with flowers, opened the debate and led it for the Republicans. Her argument was typical of those who supported the amendment: "How shall we explain to [women] the meaning of democracy if the same Congress . . . refuses to give even this small measure of democracy and justice to the women of the nation?"

Representative Jacob Edwin Meeker of Missouri argued for the opposition. He mocked the wives of those in the House, saying they would withhold sex if the men did not vote for suffrage; he called this the "no votes, no children" ultimatum. The suffragists snickered while Meeker glared up at them. As the debate wore on, those from the NWP sneaked lunches out of their bags and ate quietly. Paul, however, did not have the appetite to listen anymore. Or perhaps she sensed how the vote would split, so she left the group and returned to headquarters to work.

At around 4 p.m., a set of doors swung open dramatically in the House chamber. It was Congressman James R. Mann, an Illinois Republican, who had dragged himself in from the hospital to participate in the historic event. Mann was welcomed with resounding cheers; as was Tennessee Democrat Thetus Sims, who arrived late with his yet-unset broken arm in a sling, injured in a slip on the ice. A congressman from New York, whose suffragist wife had died the day before, also made it to the chamber. Their votes were critical. After roll call, there were 274 yeas to 136 nays, exactly the two-thirds margin required for the Susan B. Anthony Amendment to pass. A closer look at the results showed the president, now working behind the scenes on the phone, in letters, and in telegrams, had swung six votes toward suffrage. Republicans favored the measure four to one. Democrats were divided, with those from the South generally against it.

At the bang of a gavel, women wept with joy and spilled into the halls singing "Glory, Glory, Hallelujah" and "Praise God, from Whom All Blessings Flow." Their voices reverberated through the halls and beneath the massive dome, on top of which the bronze statue of Freedom gazed east. For the NWP, it was a fulfilling way to mark the one-year anniversary of the start of their White House protests.

When the NWP returned to headquarters, they found Paul at her desk. It was the eve before her thirty-second birthday. She looked up at her friends and said: "Eleven [votes needed] to win before we can pass the Senate."

The scene at NAWSA was joyful, not just over the outcome in the House, but because they believed that they had helped push the president to change his mind. In recent months, Wilson had aligned himself more closely with the women of the National American, and appreciated their stated commitment to the war; he even appointed NAWSA vice president Helen Gardener to his Civil Service Commission. After the House suffrage vote, Joseph Tumulty told Gardener that he would send the president's penciled press statement to her as a thank you for her hard work. Gardener was thrilled, and asked Tumulty if he could get Wilson to sign it, include a photo, and please not fold the paper. It was an important document, she wanted it to be pristine for the record.

With the House vote behind them, suffrage supporters turned their attention to the Senate campaign. Like running the last leg of a marathon uphill, this effort would require all the determination and stamina Paul could muster. Burns, still determined to reclaim a normal life, had been offered a teaching position in Brooklyn, in the English Department of Bay Ridge High School. She was home considering the job when Paul begged her to return. Once again, Burns answered Paul's battle cry, but asked to remain in the Northeast, to campaign in places where senators were against the amendment. She traveled throughout New York as well as Massachusetts, where Republican senator Henry Cabot Lodge was as intransigent as anyone from the South on suffrage.

Paul also dispatched a handful of others to contentious states. The logistics were enormous. With the Senate expected to vote in the spring, there was a mad dash to cover ground in all directions without budget earmarked for the job. But Paul drew on an important tool: a primitive database that she, Burns, and other members of the lobbying committee had developed over the years. The files, comprised of index cards in long wooden boxes, had information on where elected officials stood on the issue, among many other personal details.

Beulah Amidon, Lillian Ascough, Abby Scott Baker, Sarah T. Colvin, Doris Stevens, and Mary Winsor were unleashed upon America. Lucy Branham had a particularly important assignment: Tennessee, where the governor was challenging the incumbent senator John K. Shields, who opposed suffrage but supported the war and Wilson.

The Senate campaign began just as the NWP moved into its new headquarters at 14 Jackson Place, directly across Lafayette Park from Cameron House. The suffrage work animated the huge building. In the white entrance hall, a young woman sat at the busy switchboard. To the left was the frantic press department. Upstairs, near a three hundred–seat ballroom, was Paul's office, with gold woodwork and purple velvet upholstery. There, she would give interviews, read letters,

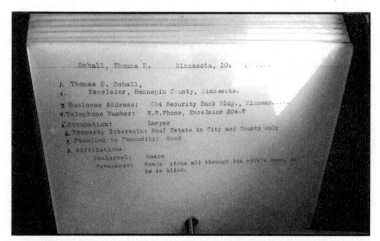

Replica of the NWP's card catalog at the Belmont-Paul House in Washington, D.C.

dictate dispatches, ask questions, eat off a tray, or do all of these things simultaneously. In the other offices, there were two dozen typists and stenographers, all clacking away at great speed.

The place was so big that Paul asked for donations to furnish it. The gifts, mostly from upper-class white women, ranged from pianos to Duncan Phyfe antiques, gilt mirrors, and oil paintings. She was grateful, but did not concern herself with material items or personal possessions. Her own bedroom was as sterile as a hospital room—painted white—and in addition to her bed, the only piece of furniture that she owned was a simple wooden desk.

As winter melted into spring, the Senate votes were not changing as much as they needed to. Wilson and Tumulty, concerned about how Democrats might fare in the upcoming midterm elections, personally reached out to influential lawmakers in states such as Texas, Kentucky, and Tennessee, urging them to embrace suffrage. Senator John C. W. Beckham, a Kentucky Democrat, gave Wilson a respectful but firm no.

"In the matter of woman suffrage," Beckham wrote to the president, "I cannot see this as you do. In the first place, I am very much opposed to any federal action on suffrage questions, and believe that they should be left entirely to state control. In addition, I have such deep seated convictions against Woman Suffrage that I cannot, under any circumstances, vote for it." Wilson received a similar response from Senator Benjamin R. Tillman, a South Carolina Democrat. "When the women of South Carolina want the vote," he said, "the men will give it to them."

The Senate, sensing defeat of the measure, postponed the debate scheduled for May 10. This deferment concerned the White House, where the administration worried about broad political damage for Democrats in the upcoming elections, especially in the West, if Congress did not take action on suffrage. Losing congressional seats to the GOP could shift the balance of power Wilson had been enjoying.

The NWP had done enough research to know who the opposition was and how they might be convinced to change their minds. Now that Wilson appeared to be supporting suffrage, they offered to meet with the administration to discuss their shared goal of forcing a vote in the Senate. But Tumulty refused to arrange a meeting between the president and three members of the NWP, telling Wilson the women were "militant."

"Mrs. Catt, Mrs. Gardener and the women of the other branch have been cooperating with the Administration in the most loyal way," Tumulty said. "It strikes me that Mrs. Kent and her friends may be seeking certain notoriety in asking for this appointment, and if it meets with your approval, I will advise them that it is impossible for them to see you owing to the pressure of other business." Wilson agreed to decline the meeting.

Catt, who had worked as an activist for eight years abroad, applied pressure in her own way, calling on her domestic and foreign friends for help. Catt also pressed the president personally and gave him talking points for his conversations with reluctant Democrats. Her helpful language included the fact that "the only Parliaments in the world which have turned down bills for extending suffrage have been those of the Central Powers," which consisted of Austria-Hungary, Germany, Bulgaria, and the Ottoman Empire.

But the president stayed mum. And the Senate stayed firm, putting off the vote again, this time until the fall. The only good news for the NWP in that spring of 1918 was that a federal appeals court declared unconstitutional the arrests and detainment of all of the White House suffrage pickets.

■ ■ ■

The American troop count in Europe had grown, thanks to a draft, to nearly one million; it needed to if Wilson had any chance of swaying the outcome of the war. But as the armed forces sucked up every able man to go and fight, any seemingly eligible man left behind was suspect. Were they draft evaders? Were they the enemy? Congress passed legislation to outlaw offensive speech and the expression of opinion that cast the government or the war effort in a negative light. Called the Sedition Act, it expanded on the previous year's Espionage Act to forbid the use of "disloyal, profane, scurrilous, or abusive language" about the

U.S. government, its flag, or its armed forces. The war was forcing a militaristic uniformity on the culture, leading to regressive policies and new behaviors.

The Wilson administration, in an effort to influence public opinion, created a Committee on Public Information to instruct the public on how to detect pro-German sympathies. At the Justice Department, a twenty-two-year-old official named J. Edgar Hoover oversaw a program that photographed, fingerprinted, and interrogated five hundred thousand suspects. And newspapers published the names of people who were not buying war bonds or otherwise supporting the war. People were fired for not being enthusiastic enough about the war.

Vigilante organizations performed so-called slacker raids, where citizens were legally allowed to pull people off the street they suspected of being unpatriotic or avoiding conscription. Sometimes the raids turned violent; one man was tarred and feathered, another hung from his neck from a tree. One New York City raid, carried out by the American Protective League, a quasi-public organization that Wilson's Justice Department authorized in June, netted ten thousand people who were questioned and, if warranted, tried. The event, like all of these vigilante actions, was marred by a lack of due process. People were seized on suspicion, not evidence. The mere hint of a European accent could trigger an attack or an arrest. While vigilantism was occurring in many cities, Washington was especially tense because of the political environment and the fact that the district was crawling with soldiers and sailors, who were either passing through or camping out along the Potomac as a security detail.

Knowing that the public could be easily provoked by any act that seemed unpatriotic, Paul planned the date of her next protest intentionally, August 6, which was Inez Milholland's birthday. On that day, at half past noon, one hundred suffragists emerged from headquarters and fell into single-line formation, carrying purple, gold, and white banners. Crowds cheered and saluted as Hazel Hunkins, holding a U.S. flag, led the group across the park toward the eponymous bronze statue of France's Marquis de Lafayette. The heroic monument was a symbolic one for the suffragists, evocative of revolutionary ideals, democracy, and the idea that some causes are worth the ultimate sacrifice.

At the statue, on the corner closest to the east gate of the White House, two women stood on the pedestal and held their banners so Wilson might see them. Even though the president seemed to be supporting suffrage, he was not pushing the Senate to vote and they needed to keep pressuring him to act.

The protest was designed to embarrass Wilson. One suffragist carried a sign with Milholland's last words: HOW LONG MUST WOMEN WAIT FOR LIBERTY? The other banner brought home their point:

WE PROTEST AGAINST THE CONTINUED
DISENFRANCHISEMENT OF AMERICAN WOMEN, FOR WHICH
THE PRESIDENT OF THE UNITED STATES IS RESPONSIBLE.
WE CONDEMN THE PRESIDENT AND HIS PARTY FOR
ALLOWING THE OBSTRUCTION OF SUFFRAGE IN THE SENATE.
WE DEPLORE THE WEAKNESS OF PRESIDENT WILSON
IN PERMITTING THE SENATE TO LINE ITSELF WITH THE
PRUSSIAN REICHSTAG BY DENYING DEMOCRACY TO THE
PEOPLE. WE DEMAND THAT THE PRESIDENT AND HIS PARTY
SECURE THE PASSAGE OF THE SUFFRAGE AMENDMENT
THROUGH THE SENATE IN THE PRESENT SESSION.

As the other women gathered around the monochromatic statue, wrapping its base in color, Lewis stepped toward the pedestal. The police drew near as well.

"We are here," she said, "because when our country is at war for liberty and democracy—"

But before she could finish her sentence, the police arrested her, along with the others who had not said a word. There was a pause of complete silence until Hunkins leapt to the center.

"Here, at the statue of Lafayette, who fought for the liberty of this country, and under the American flag, I am asking for the enfranchisement of American women!" Hunkins shouted. Then she was arrested. In total, the police took nearly four dozen women, including Burns, who was back in town, to jail. When an officer spotted Paul, who had been organizing reinforcements from some distance, he took her away, too. When the women asked what they were being charged with, the police refused to answer.

"Do not tell them anything!" one said.

Hunkins would not let go of her flag as she was placed in the police van. All of the women were released on bail. They marched back to headquarters behind Hunkins.

The protests persisted in the days ahead. Another sixty-eight were arrested. On August 15, Paul, Burns, and the rest of the women from the initial demonstration were tried. Paul refused to recognize the proceedings and would not speak any further. The rest of the women followed her lead. They sat, silently knitting, reading, or sleeping, while the judge decided their fate. And they refused to stand when the charges came down. Flustered by their courtroom behavior, he convicted them of "climbing a statue" or "holding a meeting on public grounds" and sentenced them to ten to fifteen days in the district workhouse. The facility was worse than Occoquan.

At this District of Columbia workhouse in Lorton, Virginia, the cells were mostly subterranean and dark, so cold it made their teeth chatter, despite the blazing summer heat. Once again, they asked to be treated as political prisoners, but the authorities said no. Two dozen of the women began hunger strikes. Those who were still drinking water noticed something foul about it. And as they began to ache and suffer from nausea and the chills, they suspected lead poisoning. With so much attention on the cause, a steady stream of elected officials came to see the women and reported to the public on their conditions. Outrage sped up the prisoners' release, and they walked out five days later, on August 20, before completing their sentences.

Paul once again barely paused as she got back to work, filling out an application for a permit to make speeches in the park two days later. C. S. Ridley, chief of engineers of the U.S. Army, telegrammed back with approval. "You are advised good order must prevail," he said. But so many of the suffragists were sick from their time in the workhouse, Paul had to postpone the demonstration.

The NWP received a tip that the Senate would not take up suffrage during the current session. That news superseded reports out of the White House that day: Catt had met with the president, along with a group of women from the West and South, and he had told them he was "heartily in sympathy with you. I have endeavored to assist you in every way in my power and I shall continue to do so. I shall do all that I can to assist the passage of the Amendment by an early vote." For the women of 14 Jackson place, Wilson's words were hollow, and so they marched yet again, this time with their permit in hand, from the headquarters to the statue of Lafayette.

As the women assembled around the base of the statue, Berthe Arnold, a kindergarten teacher from Colorado Springs, appealed to the monument.

"Lafayette, we are here!" she cried. The phrase had become an unofficial motto of the Great War after an aide to John Pershing called out the sentence as he toured Lafayette's tomb in Paris on July 4, 1917.

We, the women of the United States, denied the liberty which you helped to gain, and for which we have asked in vain for sixty years, turn to you to plead for us. Speak, Lafayette! Dead these hundred years but still living in the hearts of the American people. Speak again to plead for us, condemned like the bronze woman at your feet, to a silent appeal. She offers you a sword. Will you not use the sword of the spirit, mightier far than the sword she holds out to you? Will you not ask the great leader of our democracy to look upon the failure of our beloved country to be in truth the place where everyone is free and equal and entitled to a share in the government? Let that outstretched hand of yours pointing to the White House recall to him his words and promises, his trumpet call for all of us to see that the world is made safe for democracy.

The police, following orders not to bring more attention to the suffragists by arresting them, smiled and nodded as if they were watching a play. The gathering crowd applauded. Branham stepped forward with Julia Emory beside her, holding a flaming torch, which she said represented their burning indignation over the Senate filibuster.

"We want action," Branham said, paraphrasing the Pankhursts' motto, "not words."

Branham held a card with Wilson's statement to Catt from earlier in the day—"I shall do all that I can . . ."—and she burned it.

"We, therefore, take these empty words, spoken by President Wilson this afternoon, and consign them to the flames," Branham said

Branham's speech generated applause and the crowd began passing donations to the women. As this was going on, the suffragists saw a car drive up to the White House door. The president got into the vehicle, and instead of exiting toward the statue, the driver turned around and left in the opposite direction.

Before the month was over, something shifted in the Senate and the chamber took up the amendment again. For three days, beginning on September 26, they debated the legislation before it was clear that they

Lucy Branham burning the president's words at the statue of Lafayette.

were at an impasse. There was only one hope left and that was to have Wilson address them.

The last day of the month brought the president and his cabinet to the Senate. "Look," said one correspondent watching from above in the press gallery, "he's brought all his heavy artillery with him." At 1 p.m., Wilson took to the podium and, perhaps sensing the hostility in the audience, he began to read slowly from a fifteen-minute speech:

I tell you plainly, as the commander-in-chief of our armies and of the gallant men in our fleets, as the present spokesman of this people in our dealings with the men and women throughout the world who are now our partners, as the responsible head of a great government which stands and is questioned day by day as to its purposes . . . I tell you plainly that this measure which I urge upon you is vital to the winning of the war and to the energies alike of preparation and of battle. And not to the winning of the war only. It is vital to the right solution of the great problems which we must settle, and settle immediately, when the war is over. We shall need then in our vision of affairs, as we have never needed them before, the sympathy and insight and clear moral instinct of the women of the world.

After the speech, the Senate gave Wilson respectful applause and he left immediately. When he returned to the White House he wrote a note to Catt offering "earnest hope that the amendment may pass." But his effort, just as suffragists had been complaining all session, was too little, too late. The next day, the votes came down: 34 nays to 62 yeas, two votes shy of the required two-thirds majority. Hundreds of suffragists, Paul included, sat silently in the chamber watching the vote tally as a wave of shock washed over them. Then they put on their hats and left. In the hall, Paul grabbed a friend. "Come," she said, "we must . . . go into the election campaign at once."

For the rest of October and into November, when elections would be held, the NWP shifted its protest location from the White House to the U.S. Capitol and Senate Office Building. Inside, they lobbied southern senators. Outside, they picketed and were arrested in the face of civilian harassment. In a revolving door of bookings and releases, the suffragists would not surrender.

■ ■ ■

In Europe, a war of attrition raged on. On the same day that the Senate took up the last suffrage vote, Pershing launched the largest military offensive in U.S. history, deploying 1.2 million troops along the Western Front in France in the Battle of the Meuse-Argonne. The American Expeditionary Forces had one objective: end a war so devastating that it had claimed ten million soldiers and many more civilians. The battle was especially horrific. Unlike the British and French, who typically fought from the trenches, cocky, fresh-faced American doughboys ran straight into the machine-gun fire, mustard gas, flame throwers, and the worst thickets of muddy forest hiding the enemy. It cost them dearly. Over the course of forty-seven days, 26,277 Americans died, making the Battle of the Meuse-Argonne the single deadliest conflict that the United States had ever fought. The Germans fared even worse, losing 28,000 men in the attack. As news of the bloody battle traveled back to Germany and it became clear that the German forces were irreparably broken, its sailors mutinied and its citizens took to the streets demanding the end to Kaiser Wilhelm's rule. On November 9, the Kaiser fled to the Netherlands and abdicated the throne. Two days later, in a secret meeting in a train car in Compiègne, France, at 5:12 a.m., the Germans signed an armistice agreement. The temporary pact called for the war to end at the eleventh hour of the eleventh day of the eleventh month of 1918. Word reached Washington at around 3 a.m., when a series of cables arrived from Colonel Edward M. House, who was in France. Edith and the president decoded his telegrams together.

"Autocracy is dead," House's final cable said. "[Long live] democracy and its immortal leader."

People flooded the streets of New York, Paris, and London to celebrate. They wept, mostly with joy. One German soldier, recovering in a European hospital from a temporary blinding, heard the news and cried over a defeat he could have never imagined. His name was Adolf Hitler. On the last day of the war, 2,738 more men died before the clock struck

11 p.m. In total, the Great War had claimed eighteen million people, and another twenty-three million were wounded.

For Wilson, this was his chance to implement the principles of peace that he had outlined in his Fourteen Points. He and Edith prepared to leave for France. But there was one thing he needed to do before embarking on the transatlantic trip. In his annual address to Congress, Wilson uttered the words Alice Paul had been asking of him from the beginning. He urged the House and the Senate to pass the Susan B. Anthony Amendment:

> And what shall we say of the women—of their instant intelligence, quickening every task that they touched; their capacity for organization and cooperation, which gave their action discipline and enhanced the effectiveness of everything they attempted . . . the least tribute we can pay them is to make them equals of men in political rights as they have proved themselves their equals in every field of practical work they have entered.

At the NWP, the women likely viewed the president's remarks in much the same way Pershing viewed the end of the Battle of the Meuse-Argonne: grateful for the win, bitter there had to be a fight at all, and anxious over whether a lasting peace was even possible.

CHAPTER TWENTY

The Amendment

The president and first lady traveled to Europe in early December of 1918 to begin peace talks. They embarked on the *George Washington* for their transatlantic journey, pulling away from the pier in Hoboken, New Jersey. As the music and fluttering flags receded with the shore, the president withdrew as well. Worn out, he had a quick lunch and retired to his state room, sleeping for hours. Edith enjoyed the smooth sail, and made a note in her diary about the Secret Service men who had been overcome by seasickness during the nine days on the open ocean.

When the ship steamed into Brest Harbor on France's western coast, it was surrounded by a light fog, imposing warships, a blimp hovering above, and crowds of people waving flags on shore. The Wilsons disembarked and boarded an overnight train to Paris. They arrived the next morning in a city that was bubbling over with celebration. French president Raymond Poincaré; his wife, Madame Poincaré; his cabinet; and the U.S. embassy staff greeted the Wilsons on the station platform. A band played the "Star-Spangled Banner" and the sun shone on everyone. The two presidents climbed into one open-air carriage pulled by horses in fancy regalia. The women, their laps blanketed in bouquets, followed behind them. The Wilsons were led down the cobbled Champs-Élysées by the Garde Républicaine, gleaming from the top of their brass-spiked helmets to their steeds' polished hooves, the road

lined with French soldiers standing like sentinels. They passed under
the Arc de Triomphe and made their way to what would be their home
away from home: the Murat Mansion, walled in and heavily guarded at
28 Rue de Monceau.

Woodrow Wilson had only scheduled three weeks for the trip, hoping to return before the congressional session ended in ten weeks, on
March 4. But the peace talks were slow to develop and dignitaries across
Europe wanted the president to visit their country or tour a battlefield.
The Wilsons spent hardly any time at the Murat Mansion before de-
parting for London, then traveling north to Scotland. Next was Italy,
where Wilson was hailed as "the God of Peace," and, finally, back to
France. In America, the National Woman's Party (NWP) was tracking
his schedule closely and monitoring his every word, but only to use his
phrases against him in a new form of protest.

■ ■ ■

A wagon squealed to a stop in front of the White House, piercing the
quiet on New Year's Day 1919. Its driver climbed out and unloaded a
large stone urn filled with kindling and logs and set it down directly in
line with Wilson's front door. From the entry of the NWP headquarters,
Alice Paul looked across the park to her right and watched the wagon
pull away. This was her plan, the one that she had conjured while she
was supposed to be resting in bed for all of Christmas Day the week
before. She rang a bell, newly installed above the entry at 14 Jackson
Place, a clarion call for protesters and bystanders alike. This year would
begin with a protest. Prompted by the sound, Edith Ainge, Dora Lewis,
and several other veterans of the NWP pulled on their coats and hats
and walked toward the White House.

Ainge lit the fire and stoked the flames. Lewis stood next to her,
dangling small slips of paper between her fingers. One at a time, she
read the words on the scraps and dropped them into the urn to inciner-
ate. These were bits of Wilson's speeches, words he had spoken publicly
since he and the first lady had disembarked in Europe.

At a speech in Manchester, England, Wilson had said: "We will
enter into no combinations of power which are not combinations of all

of us." Lewis let that sentence fall into the flames. In a toast at Buckingham Palace, the president had said: "We have used great words, all of us. We have used the words 'right' and 'justice,' and now we are to prove whether or not we understand these words." Lewis burned that sentiment, too. Next was his speech from Brest, where he had been greeted by fans in black neck scarves who were packed onto a pier and waving Old Glory. "Public opinion," he had said there, "strongly sustains all proposals for co-operation of self-governing peoples." Again, Lewis watched as his turn of phrase turned to ash. The president's words to those who were injured—"I want to tell you how much I honor you men who have been wounded fighting for freedom"—were the last to disintegrate. The bell at Jackson Place continued to toll.

While Lewis stood over the flames, two other suffragists held a wide banner that read:

> PRESIDENT WILSON IS DECEIVING THE WORLD WHEN HE
> APPEARS AS THE PROPHET OF DEMOCRACY. PRESIDENT
> WILSON HAS OPPOSED THOSE WHO DEMAND DEMOCRACY
> FOR THIS COUNTRY. HE IS RESPONSIBLE FOR THE
> DISENFRANCHISEMENT OF MILLIONS OF AMERICANS. WE IN
> AMERICA KNOW THIS. THE WORLD WILL FIND HIM OUT.

Although the president had publicly stated he supported suffrage, the NWP still did not believe him. What was he actually doing to help it pass? And so they kept up the pressure, with their flames and their bell, and they drew an audience, soldiers and sailors among them who paused, ran their eyes over the protesters' sign, and listened to their speeches. But these men were easily provoked. During one protest, they kicked over the urn, broke it, and stomped on the flames. Two other suffragists holding torches dipped them in the embers to light them and held them high. As the chaos intensified, the crowd spotted flames across the street. They turned to see Hazel Hunkins in the park, holding a suffrage banner and hanging off a raised bronze urn containing another fire. Paul and Julia Emory stood by the vessel's heavy stone base. As the police rushed over to arrest them, the suffragists in front of the White House nurtured the first fire back to life. And on it went. It was all part of Paul's vision, an endless cycle where Wilson would give a speech on democracy and the NWP would burn his words with an eternal flame fed by wood, symbolically delivered from every state.

In all, four suffragists were arrested and released. But they would not let the flame extinguish. Paul left jail and returned to the watch fire, which was still burning despite a steady drizzle. Wearing seamen's slickers, she and two of her colleagues stood guard through the night. The next morning, she passed the literal torch to another group of friends. An endless cycle: as the protesters tracked Wilson's movement across the European continent, they burned his words, police would arrest them and try to douse the flames with chemicals, the women were sent to jail and went on hunger strikes, but their colleagues lit more fires.

As the protests neared a second straight week, the hostility against the women intensified. A group of men attacked 14 Jackson Place; they climbed the pillars near the front door, ripped off the suffrage flag, and threw the bell down onto the sidewalk. The men who attacked NWP

The women with the watch fire, outside the White House, January 1, 1919.

headquarters were not arrested, but the suffragists, including Lucy Burns, were.

For Paul, it would have been enough to keep up with the reports in Europe, manage staffing for the protests, continue fundraising, and stay on top of the legal affairs of the women who were incarcerated. But in the midst of all of this yet another momentous event was sweeping across America: prohibition. On January 16, 1919, Nebraska became the thirty-sixth of the forty-eight states to ratify the 18th Amendment prohibiting the sale of alcohol. The regulation was scheduled to take effect a year later. While many early suffragists, including Susan B. Anthony, wanted alcohol banned, the NWP did not focus on the issue. However, the passage of Prohibition did make one thing clear. Congress just proved they could change the Constitution if they really wanted to.

■ ■ ■

As was the case with Paul, Wilson had little time to ponder Prohibition. After traveling around Europe for three weeks the peace talks were finally beginning in the French Foreign Office on the Quai d'Orsay. But agreement was elusive. European leaders were bogged down in misunderstandings and suspicion of each other. They could not even agree on what language to speak during the negotiations, or whether to open a window in the stifling salon. David Lloyd George, Paul's old nemesis, now British prime minister these last three years, wanted to crush Germany for good and did not agree with Wilson's more balanced plan for peace. Neither did France's prime minister Georges Clemenceau or British foreign secretary Arthur Balfour. These men were making their own secret deals dividing the spoils of war. Everyone had an agenda and everyone wanted Wilson to embrace their view.

That was also true of those who were not given a seat at the negotiating table. In late January, a delegation representing the working women of France went to see Wilson. They urged him to include woman suffrage as one of the foundations of the peace plan. Despite the in-depth, scholarly research that Wilson's aides had used to develop the Fourteen Points, their recommendations for creating stable post-war democracies did not include voting rights for half of the population. Wilson politely declined their idea and fell back on some familiar language in his response to them.

"That is necessarily a domestic question for the several nations," Wilson told them. "A conference of peace settling the relations of nations with each other would be regarded as going very much outside its province if it undertook to dictate to the several states what their internal policy should be."

The women left angry and told the press what Wilson had said. In Washington, Paul read those headlines with disgust. She clipped his quotes—more scraps to feed the flames. Wilson moved on quickly. He had set for himself one goal to achieve in Paris: to create an international body called the League of Nations to govern disputes all over the world and prevent any future wars. Wilson would have his chance to advocate for the League of Nations at an 8:30 p.m. meeting, after a full day of peace negotiations. As tired as he was, this was his chance to save the world.

■ ■ ■

WHY DOES NOT THE PRESIDENT ENSURE THE PASSAGE OF
SUFFRAGE IN THE SENATE TOMORROW? WHY DOES HE NOT
WIN FROM HIS PARTY THE ONE VOTE NEEDED? HAS HE
AGREED TO PERMIT SUFFRAGE AGAIN TO BE PUSHED ASIDE?
PRESIDENT WILSON IS DECEIVING THE WORLD. HE PREACHES
DEMOCRACY ABROAD AND THWARTS DEMOCRACY HERE.

This banner was one of many carried to the White House on the evening of February 9 from NWP headquarters. The group was led by a suffragist holding an American flag; one hundred others trailed behind, including those carrying logs for the fire. Sue Shelton White, the chairwoman of Tennessee's NWP branch, brought something more unexpected to the protest: Wilson's effigy, a three-foot-tall stuffed paper doll. Because Paul had advertised the demonstration, about two thousand people were there to watch as the wood went into the urn, followed by the three-dimensional caricature of the president. There was fire in the women's speeches, as well.

"We burn not the effigy of the President of a free people, but the leader of an autocratic party organization whose tyrannical power holds millions of women in political slavery," White said. "I have long been what is known as a Southern Democrat and the traditions of the democracy of Jefferson and Jackson are still strong in my heart; the stronger because I feel that it is what we are fighting for now." White said it was outrageous that while women in Russia, Hungary, Austria, and Germany could vote within the last year or so, the women of America could not.

Police moved in and arrested White, as well as any other woman who attempted to give a speech. As Paul sent out reinforcements with logs and banners, police arrested them immediately. In all, three dozen women were sent to prison and went on hunger strikes. The bell above the door at headquarters continued to toll.

The next day, the Senate took up suffrage again. The composition of the chamber had changed since the last vote on the Susan B. Anthony Amendment; Senator William Pollock of South Carolina, a Democrat, filled the seat of his predecessor, Benjamin "Pitchfork Ben" Tillman, a white supremacist and suffrage opponent who had died. When debate began, Pollock rose to explain his position.

"I come from the South," Pollock said. "I come from a state that has a majority of Negro population. Some men have said that they do not want to force anything on the South. I tell you, speaking for the new South, speaking for the real South, speaking for the American South, we want this privilege. We feel that the women are entitled to it and we know that we can handle any race question that comes up in this enlightened age. . . . You need not withhold your vote because you think that some of us down there do not want it."

The clerk called the roll. Pollock's pro-suffrage vote narrowed the gap, but it was not enough. The amendment lost by one vote, 33 nays to 63 yeas. The suffragists did not expect to win, but coming so close made the loss more painful. As they analyzed the results, they realized that if they could flip one of two senators, Frederick Hale of Maine, a Republican, or Edward James Gay of Louisiana, a Democrat, the next vote could go their way. To do this, the women had to keep up the pressure. So the NWP launched a new campaign focused on the states—not just in Maine or Louisiana, but any state that could be on the fence for ratification.

On February 15, Susan B. Anthony's birthday, twenty-two women from the NWP boarded a train they named the "Democracy Limited" and left Washington's Union Station. All of these suffragists—including the singing Vida Milholland—had served jail sentences and wore replica prison uniforms as part of the campaign. The train chugged south, from Charleston to Jacksonville, Chattanooga to New Orleans. Along the way, they spoke about their experiences, handed out pamphlets, and argued why suffrage was necessary. Their trip would take them through fifteen cities in a giant loop through America. From San Antonio to Los Angeles, Denver to Chicago, Syracuse, Boston, and New York.

■ ■ ■

As the women rolled south, the president and his wife steamed west, headed to Boston on the *George Washington*, reluctantly. Wilson had managed to draft a covenant for the League of Nations before he left, but he was unsure it would survive in his absence. Would England and France disregard his Fourteen Points? Although the seas were calm, doubts were swelling. He was even more upset when he read the ship's daily news bulletin, called *The Hatchet*. Its headline was blunt: "In Sensational Speech Borah Attacks League." The story explained that Senator William E. Borah, a Republican from Idaho, was already campaigning against everything Wilson had been working for in Paris. Once again, Wilson realized, the Senate was uncooperative. But so was Alice Paul.

When Wilson's ship arrived in Boston Harbor, Paul, wearing her too-big fur coat, was waiting for him at the piers. She and her crew stood out among the thousands. The NWP contingent broke through a line of Marines and pressed themselves near Wilson's reviewing stand. Katharine Morey carried an American flag, altered so its backside said: MR. PRESIDENT, HOW LONG MUST WOMEN WAIT FOR LIBERTY? Another carried a sign that read: MR. PRESIDENT, YOU SAID IN THE SENATE ON SEPTEMBER 20, "WE SHALL NOT ONLY BE DISTRUSTED BUT WE SHALL DESERVE TO BE DISTRUSTED IF WE DO NOT ENFRANCHISE WOMEN." The police caught up with the protesters and asked them to leave. When they refused, eighteen of them were arrested for loitering. Later that day, when Wilson gave a speech at Mechanics Hall, the NWP organized a watch fire demonstration on Boston Common and burned his words from that event. Thousands of people swarmed around the women, who held the center for three hours, until the police arrested them for public speaking without a permit. Twenty-one demonstrators spent eight days in the Charles Street jail. They would be the last women imprisoned for suffrage.

Wilson wrapped up the formalities in Boston as soon as he could and took the train to Washington. Back in the Capitol, he met with the Foreign Relations Committee, including Massachusetts' oppositional Senator Henry Cabot Lodge, to discuss the League of Nations. The group had many suggestions to change the covenants in the document, but Wilson hoped they could work out their differences. Next, Wilson met with Senator Andrieus Jones, chairman of the Woman Suffrage Committee. The president, feeling pressured politically to do more for suffrage, wanted to know where the Susan B. Anthony Amendment stood. He urged Jones to take up the vote before Congress adjourned on March 3. Jones refused. Overall, it was a disappointing trip home for Wilson. Before embarking on the long journey back to Europe, Wilson stopped at the Metropolitan Opera House in New York City to give a speech. It was his big chance to promote the League of Nations in America and begin to build support for the idea because he needed Congress's approval for it. Once again, Paul was on his tail.

Outraged that he would leave for Europe with the suffrage question unsettled, she drew foot soldiers from the NWP's local headquarters at 13 East Forty-First Street to march to the opera house. Two dozen women set out with their flags and banners, including one that said:

MR. PRESIDENT, AMERICAN WOMEN PROTEST AGAINST
THE DEFEAT OF SUFFRAGE FOR WHICH YOU AND YOUR
PARTY ARE RESPONSIBLE. WE DEMAND THAT YOU CALL
AN EXTRA SESSION OF CONGRESS IMMEDIATELY TO PASS
THE SUFFRAGE AMENDMENT. AN AUTOCRAT AT HOME
IS A POOR CHAMPION FOR DEMOCRACY ABROAD.

The goal was to burn Wilson's comments on democracy outside the opera. But the women never made it that far because they hit a wall of two hundred police officers at the corner of Fortieth and Broadway.

Assisted by soldiers and sailors, the police broke the banners and, without saying a word, clubbed the pickets ferociously. Some broke the sign posts over the cowering women's backs.

One of the suffragists, Margaretta Schuyler, was toward the front of the line carrying a silk American flag when a soldier pounced on her, twisted her arms until she cried, tore the flag from its pole, and then broke the pole over her head. Doris Stevens saw this and screamed to an officer to rescue Schuyler.

"Oh, he's helping me," the policeman said.

"Shame! Shame!" Stevens shouted. "Aren't you ashamed to beat American women in this brutal way? If we are breaking the law, arrest us. Don't beat us in this cowardly fashion!"

"We've only just begun," the cop barked back. The police arrested six women, including Paul, Elsie Hill, and Stevens. They were charged with disorderly conduct and released, only to reformulate a march to the opera house, with Hill holding a torch to burn Wilson's words. The police and public pounced on them again as Hill shouted to one of the soldiers: "Did you fellows turn back when you saw the Germans come? What would you have thought of any one who did? Do you expect us to turn back now? We never turn back either—and we won't until democracy is won!"

The police pushed back the crowd and the audience thinned. The pickets returned to the Manhattan headquarters. There, they found a mess. As Stevens tried to walk through the front door, she was knocked down by a man holding an NWP flagpole. The place had been ransacked and their banners burned in the street.

■ ■ ■

The Wilsons returned to Paris in March and settled into a different house. This one was on the Place des États-Unis, a street notable for its statue depicting Lafayette and George Washington in military uniforms shaking hands. The artistic gesture underscored the importance of foreign relations between the two countries, which was why Wilson was there. While he was gone, the Europeans' position on peace and the League of Nations suffered.

"All to do it over again," Wilson huffed to his wife.

The president reassembled the group of lead negotiators, this time in his study. There was Clemenceau, George, and Italy's representative, Prime Minister Vittorio Emanuele Orlando. They pinned maps all over the walls and talked all day and into the night. Wilson grew thinner and grayer. In late April, the strain became too much. He collapsed and was unable to get out of bed. Dr. Grayson examined the president and was concerned. He called for the advice of Dr. John Chalmers DaCosta, commander of the Naval Medical Corps, who happened to be in Paris. The doctors agreed that Wilson had suffered a small stroke and needed time to recuperate. The president and his doctors knew the negotiations would have to continue without him. And yet, as ill as Wilson was, he demanded regular updates on the peace talks. Even with Wilson working behind the scenes, it soon became clear that without him in the room to argue his point of view, the president's proposals, including the League of Nations, were losing momentum. Wilson was so furious that the negotiators would abandon his plans so quickly that he threatened to go home. The ultimatum succeeded in bringing support for Wilson's ideas back.

■ ■ ■

While Wilson struggled to rebuild his health and nurture the peace process, Paul was busy, too. In early May, she reviewed the poll of the most favorable noncommittal senators to determine where the NWP should focus its lobbying efforts. She decided on William J. Harris, a Georgia Democrat. Paul found out Harris was in Italy and reached out through intermediaries to try to arrange a meeting between him and the president. Her plan worked. Joseph Tumulty cabled Wilson and told him to invite Harris to Paris, where the president convinced him to vote for suffrage. Now that he had enough votes to pass the amendment, the president called for Congress to meet in a Special Session—on May 19—and sent them a persuasive cable:

Will you permit me, turning from these matters, to speak once more and very earnestly of the proposed Amendment to the Constitution which would extend the Suffrage to women and which passed the House of Representatives at the last session of the Congress? It seems to me that every consideration of justice and of public advantage calls for the immediate adoption of that Amendment and its submission forthwith to the legislatures of the several States. Throughout all the world this long delayed extension of the Suffrage is looked for; in the United States, longer, I believe, than anywhere else, the necessity for it, and the immense advantages of it to the national life, has been urged and delayed by women and men who saw the need for it and urged the policy of it when it required steadfast courage to be so much beforehand with the common conviction; and I, for one, covet for our country the distinction of being among the first to act in a great reform.

The day after Wilson sent his telegram to Congress, the House passed the Susan B. Anthony Amendment with 304 yeas and 89 nays, forty-two more than the required two-thirds majority, a much wider margin than its previous approval.

The Senate vote was scheduled for June 4. On that day, a group of suffragists from the NWP sat in the gallery to watch the historic moment they had all been waiting for. But the vote was so anticlimactic that Paul did not bother attending. She knew the amendment would pass—which it did, 56 to 25—and she was already busy working on the next step in the process.

With congressional approval, the legislation next required thirty-six states (a three-fourths majority) to ratify it. Paul's campaign strategy was designed for maximum momentum and speed because she wanted to change the Constitution in time for the 1920 presidential election. That meant lobbying the states whose legislatures were in session to vote right away, and to convince the rest to call a special session as soon as possible.

Wisconsin, Michigan, and Illinois voted yes on the same day, June 10; Wisconsin was technically the first state to ratify the amendment. A second burst of ratifications happened on June 16, with New

York, Ohio, and Kansas, which was the first state to call a special session. Pennsylvania approved the amendment on June 24, but not without a struggle. Dora Lewis, the state's NWP chairwoman, pressed every person in power she knew to lobby undecided lawmakers. Her work won the day in Harrisburg. Massachusetts followed. Then, on June 28, Texas became the first of the states controlled by Democrats to ratify it in a special session. As intense as the scene was in Austin that day, Wilson also faced a spectacular event on the outskirts of Paris.

■ ■ ■

The president and first lady arrived at Versailles with the sun shining down on them. There were jubilant people everywhere, on the streets leading to the palace, lining the entry stairs, and inside the Hall of Mirrors, packed with the international press corps, dignitaries, and anyone else who could get a ticket or con their way in. Inside the massive gilded gallery, lined with windows and adorned with sparkling chandeliers, Clemenceau took his seat at the table. Wilson and the other Americans sat on his right; George and the rest of the British were on his left. At 3:10 p.m., Clemenceau called the meeting to order. The Allies pressed their seals on the vellum treaty. As a marshal escorted in two Germans with downcast eyes, the room fell silent except for the sound of their footfalls, the click of cameras, and the buzz of motion picture machines. Edith, carrying a red rose the president had given her, noted that chills ran through her body when Hermann Müller and Johannes Bell, the stone-faced Germans, signed the treaty. Wilson, by contrast, beamed as he added his name to the document, followed by the other delegates, including the Italians and Japanese.

"*La séance est levée*," Clemenceau said. The meeting is closed. A cannon boomed to mark the moment, thirty minutes after the meeting had opened, and four years and 328 days since the war had begun. Now it was over. The Allies walked outside and down the back stairs, where thousands of people rushed forward to congratulate them. Planes buzzed overhead. After the men posed for pictures, it was time for the Wilsons to depart, first for Paris and eventually for home. Along the route out of Versailles, people waved banners that said: VIVE WILSON.

On the train to Brest, Wilson and the first lady looked out the window and watched the City of Light recede. "Well, little girl," the president said to Edith, "it is finished and, as no one is satisfied, it makes me hope we have just made a peace; but it is all on the lap of the gods."

The following day, the Wilsons boarded the *George Washington* one last time. On the pier, throngs of American soldiers, including black ones, waved and cheered. Wilson removed his top hat in their honor and stood on the bridge while a band played "The Star-Spangled Banner."

That final small sign of respect, the tip of his hat, was something the African American men who served in the war had been hoping for. For many of them, they had joined the armed forces because they believed they were fighting for democracy, an ideal they hoped would ultimately benefit them at home. So far, it hadn't. They faced great challenges during the war; most of them were kept off the battlefield to do less valiant work such as unloading ships, while those who did fight were segregated. In the case of one unit from New York named the Harlem Hellfighters, Pershing insulted them by making them fight under the French flag, something no other U.S. troops were forced to do. Still, these men believed that if they proved their patriotism in Europe, their own country would respect them more.

They could not have misjudged their country more. When the Hellfighters returned home, they found a nation embroiled in a race war. White soldiers wanted their jobs back and six years of segregation and rising prejudice had created a combustible mix in cities such as Chicago and Washington, the scenes of deadly riots in the summer of 1919, and in the South, where the Ku Klux Klan was resurgent.

Wilson's own return home was also a shock. While his arrival in the port at Hoboken had the veneer of triumph, America's domestic affairs were a mess. From coast to coast, there was economic and racial turmoil and a rising movement—both in the Senate and among the people—against the League of Nations. People did not want to get involved in other countries' problems anymore. And the Senate, whose approval of the treaty was required by the U.S. Constitution, did not want to, either.

The Vote

Woodrow Wilson was back in the White House, plotting how to save the unpopular League of Nations. He believed that if he could pitch the concept directly to the people, in a whistle-stop campaign crisscrossing the nation, they would understand and approve. Although he had recovered enough to sign the Treaty of Versailles, his health had deteriorated again. By late summer, Wilson's speeches rambled more and he found it difficult to hold a pen in his right hand. His wife and doctor were concerned and went to speak with him about his condition.

"I know what you have come for," Wilson told Dr. Grayson. "I do not want to do anything foolhardy but the League of Nations is now in its crisis, and if it fails, I hate to think what will happen to the world. You must remember that I, as Commander in Chief, was responsible for sending our soldiers to Europe. In the crucial test in the trenches they did not turn back—and I cannot turn back now."

And so on September 3, wearing a straw boater, blue blazer, and white trousers, Wilson and the first lady left Union Station to begin the campaign. The first stop was Columbus, Ohio, where he gave a speech to an overflow crowd and ignored his terrible headache. In Indiana, there was no microphone inside the Coliseum, yet he attempted to speak to twenty thousand people by shouting. Doing so wore him out and many people left in frustration, unable to hear him. In St. Louis, the city was full of Republicans and Germans, not his most enthusiastic audiences. Despite such challenges, Wilson, now sixty-two years old, carried on anyway, sometimes giving four speeches a day. The strain was too much, triggering asthma and fatigue. By the time he reached Spokane in mid-September, his terrible condition was obvious to the press.

In California, he received his most enthusiastic and largest welcome yet. But even such a turnout was not enough to buoy him. Wilson's train began a one-month journey back east, stopping in Pueblo, Colorado. There, he stumbled through his speech and had difficulty walking, but he brought his audience to tears with his emotional address, telling them of a cemetery he visited in France filled with soldiers from the Great War and saying he wished those opposing the League of Nations "could feel the moral obligation that rests upon us not to go back on those boys, but to see the thing through."

When they returned to the train that night, the Wilsons went to sleep in adjoining berths as usual. At 11:30 p.m., the president knocked on his wife's door. When she opened it, she found him sitting on the edge of his bed, resting his head on the back of a chair. He asked her to call Dr. Grayson. When the doctor arrived, he knew there was nothing he could do except keep the president comfortable. But even that was a challenge. Wilson was restless, only finding sleep at dawn as he sat in a chair. Edith looked at his face, lined and drawn, and knew their lives would never be the same.

"From that hour," she wrote, "I would have to wear a mask—not only to the public but to the one I loved best in the world; for he must never know how ill he was, and I must carry on."

Wilson's train rattled into Wichita. There, Joseph Tumulty told the reception committee that the president had to cancel his speech. The reporters traveling with Wilson called in the news flash and word spread along the route. People gathered near the tracks to bid Wilson goodbye, as if it were a funeral cortege. For the Wilsons, the journey back to Washington was long and dark. Edith had the shades down for the final leg of the trip, which dragged on for another forty-eight hours. She did not want anyone to see him like this.

On October 2, shortly after they arrived at the White House, Wilson was stricken again. As he sat up in bed, the president tried to reach for a water bottle on his nightstand. But his hand hung loosely. Edith saw him struggling and went to help him.

"I have no feeling in that hand," he said. "Will you rub it? But first help me to the bathroom." It was difficult but she walked him to the toilet and left for a moment to call Dr. Grayson. She rushed back when she heard a noise and found the president slumped on the floor, unconscious. She placed a blanket over her husband and a pillow under his head. When Dr. Grayson arrived, he could immediately see that Wilson had suffered a massive stroke, paralyzing the left side of his body. No one was sure if he would survive.

Edith called Wilson's daughters and the doctor summoned a specialist named Francis X. Dercum based in Philadelphia for a second opinion. The prognosis was tricky: there was no chance for a recovery unless the president was "released from every disturbing problem" while his body tried to heal.

"How can that be," the first lady asked, "when everything that comes to an executive is a problem? How can I protect him from problems when the country looks to him as the leader?"

Dr. Dercum leaned in closer. "Madame, it is a grave situation, but I think you can solve it. Have everything come to you; weigh the importance of each matter, and see if it is possible by consultations with the respective heads of the departments to solve them without the guidance of your husband," he said. "In this way, you can save him a great deal. But always keep in mind that every time you take him a new anxiety or problem to excite him you are turning a knife in an open wound. His nerves are crying out for rest, and any excitement is torture to him."

Edith asked if the president should resign and let Vice President Thomas R. Marshall take over.

"No," the doctor said. "For Mr. Wilson to resign would have a bad effect on the country, and a serious effect our patient. He has staked his life and made his promise to the world to do all in his power to get the treaty ratified and make the League of Nations complete. If he resigns, the greatest incentive to recovery is gone." Edith listened carefully as he went on. "Dr. Grayson tells me he has always discussed public affairs with you; so you will not come to them uninformed."

The first lady agreed to the doctor's orders. Wilson's aides told the press he was suffering from "nervous exhaustion" and that he just needed some rest. Meanwhile, Edith Wilson stepped in to serve as the de facto first female president of the United States, even if no one outside the White House knew it. She studied all the paper that came to the president and decided what to share with him—or not. No one was allowed to see Wilson. And no one outside of the inner circle knew just how incapacitated he was.

His absence from politics was not without consequence. Despite the momentum he had gained with voters in the West, the Senate rejected the Versailles Treaty on November 19. Edith was devastated, and worried that the news might kill her husband. When she told him at his bedside, he was silent, then said, "all the more reason I must get well and try again to bring this country to a sense of its great opportunity and greater responsibility."

■ ■ ■

Although neither Wilson nor his treaty were faring well, states continued to vote in rapid succession on the ratification of the Susan B. Anthony Amendment. The logistics of a campaign of this magnitude stretched the suffragists' resources. With so much ground to cover, so many travel expenses, and a vast network of new politicians who were not in their card catalog, Alice Paul had to focus wisely, often asking the most influential person—a governor or party leader—to try to favorably alter precarious situations. She took nothing for granted.

Throughout the summer, the South remained her biggest concern in the ratification campaign. She needed the southern states to move into the yes column in order for the amendment to make it. Georgia was among the first in question with a scheduled vote at the end of July. Paul dispatched her best suffragists to the state. Dora Lewis, Anne Martin, and Mabel Vernon campaigned there all month in the intense summer heat. Despite being bedridden, the president lobbied, too, concerned about the political ramifications if his party were to be blamed for blocking the amendment at this late stage. Unbeknownst to the public, he sent a letter to the governor of Georgia, but it had no effect. The state where Wilson spent his formative years rejected the amendment. There were, however, some wins that month. Arkansas and Montana passed the amendment and Iowa and Missouri ratified it in special sessions. In August, Nebraska did, too. In September, Minnesota, New Hampshire, and Utah approved the amendment. Alabama voted no, despite a plea from Wilson to the governor. And Virginia, meeting in special session, did not ratify the amendment even though the president urged the governor of his home state to pass it. So far, seventeen states had passed the amendment.

On November 1, California approved the amendment after the local NWP inundated the governor with telegrams to call a special session. In Maine, Paul personally traveled there to campaign because the vote was so tight. She asked national leaders of both the Democratic and Republican parties to cable legislators there to support the measure and the extra effort helped: lawmakers ratified the amendment by a narrow four-vote margin. Next, after a long siege by the NWP on the governor of North Dakota, that state ratified the amendment in a special session on December 1. Colorado was the last state to approve the amendment in 1919, bringing the total number of states that had ratified it to twenty-one.

The first month of 1920 was also a successful one for suffrage. Five states approved the amendment: Rhode Island, Kentucky, Oregon, Indiana, and Wyoming. In February, Nevada passed it in a special session. But New Jersey was problematic. Leaders of both parties there opposed suffrage. Paul swooped in with Alison Hopkins, the NWP's New Jersey chairwoman, to activate everyone they could find. Although political insiders had said the state could not be flipped, it ratified the amendment on February 10. The audience was so stunned when it happened, they were silent for a long pause before wild cheers filled the halls.

Next, Idaho, Arizona, New Mexico, and Oklahoma approved the amendment, followed by West Virginia and Washington in March. But there were also four defeats: Mississippi, South Carolina, Virginia (for the second time), and Maryland. The South was impenetrable.

Now that thirty-five states had ratified the amendment, the suffragists needed just one more for the win. They turned their attention to Delaware. Paul went there with nine colleagues to rally support, but the state rejected the amendment in early June. And then, when there was nowhere else to turn, a state no one thought would vote on the amendment was suddenly in play: Tennessee.

Sue Shelton White, the NWP's research director, arrived in Nashville by train, thrilled to be home. She rented a storefront on Sixth Street, within walking distance to the state capitol, and began organizing a scrappy campaign. She drew on her local knowledge, relationships forged during her early career there as a stenographer, and, more recently, her skills as a lawyer and role at the NWP. White sent her colleagues to Memphis, Chattanooga, and Johnson City to find support, but the reports back were alarming.

Many believed that an old provision in the Tennessee Constitution prohibited the state legislature from voting on the amendment. The language, written in 1870 after the 14th Amendment gave black men civil rights but punished Confederate soldiers by stripping their right to hold public office, was meant to prevent the state from having to vote on a federal law it did not like. Even though a recent U.S. Supreme Court case found that state laws could not prevent a federal amendment, many lawmakers were dubious.

White needed all the help she could get and asked Paul to come to Nashville from Washington. But the funds were so tight, there was no money to cover the expense. Instead, Paul marshaled every remaining resource available. In June, she sent protesters to the Republican National Convention in Chicago, followed by the Democratic convention in San Francisco. The NWP pressed both parties to include suffrage as a plank in their platforms and to sway state officials toward suffrage. When the GOP nominated Warren Harding as their presidential candidate, about two hundred women from all over the country, dressed in white and carrying tricolor flags, showed up on the lawn of his home in Marion, Ohio, and held a banner that said:

THE REPUBLICAN PLATFORM ENDORSES RATIFICATION OF
SUFFRAGE. THE FIRST TEST OF THE PLATFORM WILL COME
WHEN THE TENNESSEE LEGISLATURE MEETS IN AUGUST. WILL
THE REPUBLICANS CARRY OUT THEIR PLATFORMS BY GIVING A
UNANIMOUS REPUBLICAN VOTE IN TENNESSEE FOR SUFFRAGE?

The suffragists also urged every Democrat they could influence to pressure Tennessee governor Albert Roberts. National party chairman Homer S. Cummings, in a rare long-distance telephone call, reached out to Roberts from the convention. James Cox, the Democrats' presidential nominee, lobbied Roberts as well. As did Wilson, in a telegram most likely written by the first lady, still covering for his physical condition. The message followed her husband's political strategy—that the future viability of all Democrats was at stake. "It would be a real service to the Party and to the Nation if it is possible for you to . . . consider the Suffrage Amendment," the president's wire said. "Allow me to urge this very earnestly."

In addition to the outside pressure, Anita Pollitzer, one of the NWP's key lobbyists, gathered the best legal minds in Tennessee and dispatched them to each legislator to explain away the state constitution concerns. She also helped secure the lawmakers' train reservations to the state capitol and lobbied them while riding together on the railcars.

Meanwhile, as the date for the vote grew closer, Nashville swelled with the most strident believers for and against the suffrage amendment. The opposition was an unofficial coalition of special interests. The corporate ones were worried that women would support labor and drive up prices. The liquor industry, reeling from Prohibition, sought revenge on those who had supported the ban on alcohol, namely, suffragists. Many Christians believed voting would corrupt women morally; and defenders of the South were stuck on race and how giving black women the right to vote could affect society; and there were the states' rights defenders. The Hotel Hermitage, near the capitol, was ground zero. Inside, special interests plied their targets with bourbon, cut backroom deals, and set Machiavellian maneuvers into play.

These nefarious negotiations did not stop, not even on August 10, when Tennessee lawmakers introduced the resolution in the House as well as the Senate. Nor did it stop the next day, when the legislature held a joint hearing in the great assembly hall of the capitol. The room was packed with those for and against, each wearing their own colors: suffragists had yellow jonquils; the antis wore red roses. Finally, it was time to vote. The Senate went first. The clerk called the roll and tallied the results. The amendment passed, 25 to 4, a strong margin that caught the attention of the men in the House. Now all eyes were on them.

There were two representatives whose vote no one was sure of: Banks Turner and Harry Burn. Turner, one of the governor's closest friends, had not said whether he was for or against the amendment. As for Burn, a Republican, he was the youngest member in the legislature, and as popular as he was noncommittal. His constituents in McMinn County, halfway between Knoxville and Chattanooga, did not want suffrage and they did not want a federal amendment. Even the railroad, which had provided his father with work until he died, was opposed. Personally, Burn thought giving women the vote was the right thing to do. Now that his mother was a widow, he believed she should have a voice in government.

At first, Burn had told Pollitzer she could count on him. But a few days before the vote, he told the women, "I cannot pledge myself, but I will do nothing to hurt you."

On the morning of the House vote, on August 18, White and her colleagues Catherine Flanagan and Betty Gram put on their white summer dresses, "Votes for Women" sashes, and prison brooches and walked over to the capitol. Pollitzer pinned a yellow rose in her hat. Inside the capitol, the governor was frazzled. People were pressuring him and he was pressuring people. Turner was sitting in his office, stubbornly refusing to vote for suffrage, when Cox, the Democratic candidate for president, called to check in on the polling.

"Governor, the mothers of America want the League of Nations," Cox said. The subtext was that women hated war, and would vote Democrat to prevent it from happening again.

"I have right here in my office the man who could furnish the necessary vote for ratification," Roberts told him. But only Turner knew what he would do.

At 10:35 a.m., the tired lawmakers began shuffling onto the floor of the House for the vote. The suffragists were there to make one more plea. Senators, lobbyists, and reporters crowded in to watch the proceedings.

As Speaker Seth M. Walker cleared the floor of visitors, Burn arrived wearing a red rose. The women saw him enter and felt betrayed. But they believed they had done everything they possibly could for the cause. Burn sat at his desk, adorned with a spray of yellow flowers that suffragists had placed throughout the chamber. A page brought him a manila envelope. He opened it and read the handwritten note as the debate began.

With each speech, it seemed more lawmakers had switched to no. It was sweltering hot in the chamber and the crowd was growing restless. Women fanned themselves in the galleries, which they had also decorated with yellow satin flags and the tricolor banners. Walker wanted to put an end to the show so he stepped off the rostrum and addressed the chamber.

"The hour has come," Walker shouted. "The battle has been fought and it is won. The measure is defeated."

Cheers, sobs, even a suffragist's horn erupted at the brazen attempt to shut down the proceedings. One lawmaker broke through the din with a motion to table the measure, which would effectively kill it without anyone having to vote for or against the amendment, a brilliant political strategy. The clerk called the roll on the motion to table. Burn voted aye. White, standing at the rail with a paper and pencil to tally the result, was deflated. She listened carefully to the rest of the votes but it was so noisy in the House that it was difficult to say what the result was. The antis believed the vote to table won, 49 to 47. The clerk called it a tie, 48 to 48. The Speaker stormed up and down the aisle, outraged that his plot had not worked. The clerk banged his gavel but it had no effect. He called the sergeant at arms to calm the chamber. On the second vote, it was Turner who flipped, enabling the real vote—on the Susan B. Anthony Amendment—to occur.

Chief Clerk John Green called each man's name alphabetically.

"Burn," Green said.

The heat and stillness were suffocating. Burn felt his jacket pocket, padded with the letter that had just arrived from his mother. In her pencil script, she had told her son she missed him, that he should write her more often, and that it had been raining quite a bit back home. "Hurrah and vote for suffrage and don't keep them in doubt," she added. "I've been waiting to see how you stood but have not seen anything yet. . . . Don't forget to be a good boy. . . . Love, Mama."

Burn took a deep breath and made his mother proud.

"Aye," he said.

Paul was at headquarters, nervously awaiting word from White by rush wire. When the news arrived, she walked out onto the second-floor balcony and looked across Lafayette Park toward the White House. She unfurled a long suffrage flag with a star she had hand-sewn on for each state's ratification, now totaling thirty-six. She hung the flag triumphantly over the rail. Looking down at her compatriots on the sidewalk, she saw women who had sacrificed so much and was grateful to them

After Tennessee ratified the 19th Amendment, Alice Paul unfurled the suffrage banner with thirty-six stars on it, one for each state that approved it.

on behalf of women everywhere. But not everyone she'd hoped would be there at this momentous occasion was. Lucy Burns, the last suffragist to be arrested in America, who'd spent more time than any other NWP protester in jail, was in Brooklyn, having recently moved there to raise her niece after her sister had died in childbirth.

Although Paul was overjoyed that she had changed the course of history, the celebration was brief: she joined her sisters in the struggle downstairs for a toast, posing in front of the banner for the photographer hired to capture the monumental moment, raising a glass of grape juice and smiling. The camera clicked. But Paul knew her work was just beginning.

Epilogue

U.S. Secretary of State Bainbridge Colby completed reading the documents that had been mailed overnight to him from Tennessee. Then he dipped his wooden pen into an inkwell and signed one of the papers, certifying the Susan B. Anthony Amendment. In that quiet moment, at 8 a.m. on August 26, 1920, the freshly installed Colby, cofounder of the Progressive Party, performed a perfunctory duty of his position, which, at least in theory, enfranchised all American women.

Because opponents had been challenging the Tennessee ratification all week, Colby was concerned about further attempts to derail the legislation. But there was one other reason why he rushed to finalize this change to the Constitution: he did not want to serve as a buffer between the two suffrage factions that were arguing over who should attend the signing ceremony. So Colby finalized the law without guests and as soon as possible. He did so cloistered in his own home, on K Street in Washington. There was no fanfare, no photographer, and no suffrage leader present from either the National American Woman Suffrage Association or the National Woman's Party.

Paul had arranged for a motion picture recording and photographer to capture the historic moment and was dejected when she learned the amendment had been signed without her there. She sprinted to the State Department to seek a meeting with Colby and ask whether he would re-enact the signing for the cameras. When Paul arrived, she found Carrie Chapman Catt there, too, also waiting for the secretary of state. Colby agreed to meet with Catt, but he refused to stage a signing and left Paul waiting in the hall for hours, until she decided to leave. These were not the last of the snubs that day for Paul. Later in the evening, Wilson invited Catt to the White House to celebrate, but he, too, excluded Paul.

Despite her personal disappointment about how the day unfolded, the thirty-four-year-old Paul was joyous about the amendment, telling the press that "all women must feel a great sense of triumph and unmeasurable relief at the successful conclusion of a long and exhausting struggle." Although black women were nervous that this victory would be shallow for them, that struggle—beyond even the personal sacrifices and arrests of some 218 women from twenty-six states—served as a model for how to create a movement through protest and grassroots activism for the rest of the century and into the next.

■ ■ ■

While Colby signed the amendment, Woodrow Wilson remained incapacitated at the White House. His wife did not just help care for him physically—she continued to manage the duties of the executive office, bringing documents for him to sign while he was propped up in bed. But without his constant politicking and visibility, many of his regressive policies around freedom of speech and due process atrophied and led to a rebellion. In 1920, suffragists, lawyers, and proponents of peace—including Helen Keller and Jane Addams—founded the American Civil Liberties Union (ACLU) to prevent the government and the police from violating people's constitutional rights. The creation of the ACLU was not the only rebuke to Wilson that year. Congress repealed the Sedition Act in a triumph of the First Amendment. And finally, after eight years of Democratic control in Washington, American voters, including women in every state, elected a Republican president, Warren G. Harding.

Even though Wilson was physically diminished and politically battered at home, he remained a star on the global stage. In 1920, he was awarded the Nobel Peace Prize for drafting the League of Nations Covenant. The award was the capstone of his career. He had hoped to write one more book about government during his last term in office, but he did not complete any page of it beyond the dedication, which was to his wife.

The Wilsons' transition to life outside of elected office in 1921 brought relief for the couple. They settled into a home on S Street, a mile and a half from the White House, where they installed an elevator so he could get around in his wheelchair. His last three years were quiet ones. He died in February of 1924, on an early Sunday morning as church bells pealed. Edith, as always, was there by his side.

■ ■ ■

While Wilson's demise came quickly, Alice Paul had a long life in front of her after the 19th Amendment was ratified. In 1922, as the National Woman's Party reorganized, she earned a law degree from American University (as well as a master's and doctorate in law within that same decade). The next year, Paul envisioned another essential change to the Constitution and drafted the Equal Rights Amendment (ERA). "Equality of rights under the law shall not be denied or abridged by the United States on account of sex," the amendment states. Again, race complicated the matter. Paul asked Mary Church Terrell to encourage African Americans to support the ERA. Terrell, concerned about poll taxes and literacy tests, told Paul she first wanted "to see that no colored women were disbarred from voting on account of their race." Paul explained she would focus on gender, exclusively. Terrell was disappointed, but said she understood. Paul fought for the passage of the ERA for five decades, until Congress finally approved it in 1972. Although the amendment did not receive the necessary three-quarters of the states to ratify it, activists continue to call for its passage. The ERA has been introduced in every session of Congress in the last half century.

In 1929, Alva Belmont provided the funds for the NWP to purchase a permanent headquarters in Washington, a stately brick house on the corner of Constitution Avenue and 2nd Street, where Paul lived in a simple bedroom upstairs. For the next four decades, the District of Columbia officially became her adopted hometown, and she was a fixture. From the front windows, she had an unobstructed view of the Capitol Building. The location served her well. The NWP went on to draft 600 pieces of legislation to improve the rights of women; half of those bills became law. In 2016, President Barack Obama designated the site as the Belmont-Paul Women's Equality National Monument, which operates as a National Park.

In addition to her constant schooling and NWP efforts, Paul still found time to advocate for women's rights globally. In 1938, she founded the World Woman's Party, which lobbied successfully for the inclusion of equality provisions in the United Nations' charter and the establishment of a permanent UN Commission on the Status of Women. The United Nations replaced Wilson's League of Nations, which fell apart when it failed to prevent World War II. Paul also played a significant role in adding protection for women into the Civil Rights Act of 1964. (Of course, the fact that there was a need for such legislation was proof that racism persisted. The federal government did not recognize Native Americans as citizens until 1924, and even then, states did not allow them to vote. The same was true for immigrants of Asian descent, precluded from becoming citizens and voting until 1952. In 1965, Congress passed the Voting Rights Act to address barriers that state and local governments had been using to prevent nonwhites from casting ballots. And yet, voter suppression continues to this day.)

Paul moved from Washington to a tiny cottage in Ridgefield, Connecticut, in 1972, where she lived alone, not too far from her longtime admirer, William Parker—who, after serving during World War I and later writing a book on French finance, also retired in the area. Neither of them married. At the end of Paul's life, as her health began to fail, a nephew moved her into a nursing home about a mile from her family farm in New Jersey. Having relied on the generosity of donors to support her over the course of her entire career, she was now penniless, so poor that the nursing facility asked for donations to buy her clothes. Paul died in 1977. She was ninety-two.

Twenty years after she was laid to rest in the Westfield Friends Burial Ground, in Cinnaminson, New Jersey, the NWP ceased to exist as a lobbying organization and transformed into one with a mission to educate the public about the women's rights movement. As for Paul, although she never sought attention for herself and lived for decades in relative obscurity, her legacy has taken on renewed importance. Paul's likeness has been recommended to be on a redesigned $10 bill in 2020, marking the centennial of the amendment. And August 26 is now #WomensEqualityDay, complete with a trending hashtag. That was the idea, Paul would have said: carry the banner, always.

Acknowledgments

I am grateful to many friends, family members, colleagues, and professionals who supported me over the years as I wrote this book. My parents, Jack and Gloria Cassidy, as always, were there with a hot meal, enthusiastic babysitting, and encouraging words. I love you both so much. My husband and fellow writer, Anthony Flint, ensured our hectic family life—with careers, three boys, and a dog—continued to function happily, all while being willing to talk through research and writing like the nonfiction expert he is. Your love and help mean everything to me. To our sons, Hunter, George, and Harrison, I'm grateful for all the joy you bring and the opportunity to raise a new generation grounded in the ideal of equality for all of humanity. A special thanks to Gail Cummins, the sister/daughter, third arm, and additional brain I always wanted, who makes it all possible. I am also fortunate to have a magnificent work family at InkHouse, a kind, creative, magical place that Beth Monaghan has created. To my agent, Richard Abate, and his team at 3Arts, including Rachel Kim, your wisdom and hard work to give Alice Paul the stage she deserves is enormously appreciated. Stuart Horwitz, a genius on structure and pacing, offered edits in the most constructive way possible; thanks for making me think more and for making me laugh. My editor, Dawn Davis of 37Ink/Atria, understood what this story meant from the very beginning, asked wise questions, and brought a steady hand to finish this book. Chelcee Johns of 37Ink saw to every detail. Additional appreciation goes to Ceceile Kay Richter and the dedicated and helpful staffs at Harvard's Schlesinger Library, the Belmont-Paul Women's Equality National Monument, the Library of Congress, the Alice Paul Institute, the Woodrow Wilson Presidential Library and Museum, the University of Virginia Press, the Boston Athenaeum, the Boston Public Library, Stony Brook University Library, and Rutgers University Alexander Library.

And finally, I offer deep gratitude to all the women, especially Alice Paul, who have worked so hard for equality, and for all of those still committed to the cause.

Notes

CHAPTER ONE: A QUAKER FROM NEW JERSEY

1 *The fur coat*: Alice Paul to Tacie Paul, October 7, 1907, Alice Paul Papers, 1785–1985, box 2, folder #27, Schlesinger Library, Radcliffe Institute, Harvard University, Cambridge, Mass.

2 *Her plain clothes were so threadbare*: Ibid.

2 *As Quakers, the Pauls believed*: Zahniser and Fry, 420.

2 *She was the first and only*: Alice Paul to Tacie Paul, October 7, 1907, Alice Paul Papers, 1785–1985, box 2, folder #27, Schlesinger Library, Radcliffe Institute, Harvard University, Cambridge, Mass.

5 *The men, standing on their seats*: This scene was recreated from news coverage in "Forced Eating Like Vivisection," the *Logansport Daily Reporter*, January 27, 1910.

5 *In fact, Paul's mother*: Zahniser and Fry, 425.

6 *Someone had released*: "Students Night Out," *Pall Mall Gazette*, November 21, 1907; "To Protect Mr. Asquith," *Shipley Times and Express*, November 22, 1907; "Mr. Haldene's Questioners," *Manchester Courier and Lancashire General Advertiser*, November 21, 1907; "Woman Suffrage Meeting Disturbed," *Cheltenham Chronicle*, November 23, 1907; "Petition to Mr. Haldene," *Sheffield Daily Telegraph*, November 21, 1907; "Angry Suffragists," *Dundee Evening Telegraph*, November 21, 1907; "Howled Down," *Dundee Courier*, November, 21, 1907; "Extraordinary Scenes," *Belfast News-Letter*, November 21, 1907; "The Police Called In," *Lancashire Evening Post*, November 21, 1907; "Exchange of Blows," *Nottingham Evening Post*, November 21, 1907; "Pandemonium," *Belfast Telegraph*, November 21, 1907; "Suffragette Repar-

tee," *Sheffield Evening Telegraph*, November 21, 1907.

6 *Paul climbed back on her bicycle*: Alice Paul to Tacie Paul, October 7, 1907; Alice Paul to Tacie Paul, n.d., box 2, folder #31, Alice Paul Papers 1785–1985, Schlesinger Library, Radcliffe Institute, Harvard University, Cambridge, Mass.

6 *Later, at Swarthmore College*: Fry, 17.

6 *She had also helped to form a labor union*: Fry, 17–25.

7 *She was a formidable taskmaster*: Zahniser and Fry, 51.

9 *"This magnificent demonstration"*: "The Suffragist March," *Belfast News-Letter*, June 15, 1908.

9 *"The speeches made in"*: The Fawcett Society blog. https://www.fawcettsociety .org.uk/Blog/millicent-fawcett-royal-albert-hall.

10 *Some hung from their windows*: "Woman Suffrage," *Ludlow Advertiser*, June 27, 1908.

10 *Men, some curious and some hostile*: "Sunday's Great Demonstration, 250,000 People in Hyde Park," *Shipley Times and Express*, June 26, 1908.

10 *"Do you think we're going"*: "Suffrage Sunday," *London Daily News*, June 23, 1908.

11 *"Votes for Women!" the crowd cheered*: "Women's Suffrage Demonstration," *Walsall Advertiser*, June 27, 1908.

11 *But she persevered*: Zahniser and Fry, 84.

11 *"I have joined the 'suffragettes'"*: Alice Paul to Tacie Paul, January 14 and March 17, 1909, Alice Paul Papers, 1785–1985, box 2, folder #29, Schlesinger Library, Radcliffe Institute, Harvard University, Cambridge, Mass.

CHAPTER TWO: PASSWORD: KITCHEN

13 *She opened it right away*: Fry, 47.

13 *When she reached its doors*: Ibid.

14 *When it was Paul's turn to follow suit*: Irwin, 9.

15 *"The only thing you can do I guess"*: Fry, 49.

15 *Such arrests became so commonplace*: Zahniser and Fry, 79.

16 *Mohandas Gandhi*: Ibid.

16 *While fasting is always difficult and dangerous*: Fry, xiii.

16 *"This was something absolutely unheard of"*: Fry, 51.

17 *"When we got there"*: Fry, 54.

18 *"How can you dine here"*: "Two Americans in Guildhall Exploit," *New York*

Times, November 12, 1909; "Charwomen with Tickets," *Votes for Women*, November 19, 1909.

19 *The women leaned through the broken pane*: "Chase Two Ladies Arrested at the Guildhall," *Daily News* (London), November 10, 1909.

19 *"I should like to explain"*: "Suffragettes Sentenced," *New York Times*, November 11, 1909.

20 *When Paul was sentenced to another prison term*: Pankhurst, 459–60.

20 *Friends and family asked the American Embassy*: "Forced Eating Like Vivisection," *Logansport Daily Reporter*, January 27, 1910.

20 *In prison, Paul lay shivering on her bed*: "Miss Paul Describes Feeding By Force," *New York Times*, December 10, 1909.

20 *Each time the ordeal ended*: "Suffragette Tells of Forcible Feeding," *New York Times*, February 18, 1910; Alice Paul to Captain C. M. Gonne, January 5, 1910, Alice Paul Papers, Series II, MC 399, folder #222, Schlesinger Library, Radcliffe Institute, Harvard University, Cambridge, Mass.

21 *"You've grown so much!"*: "Real Live Militant Suffragette Visiting Now in This Country," *Oakland Tribune*, February 2, 1910.

21 *Several reporters interrupted the reunion*: Tacie Paul correspondence, n.d., Alice Paul Papers, Series II, MC 399, folder #222, Schlesinger Library, Radcliffe Institute, Harvard University, Cambridge, Mass.

21 *"There is nothing about Miss Paul's appearance"*: "Real Live Militant Suffragette Visiting Now in This Country," *Oakland Tribune*, February 2, 1910.

22 *The following September*: Alice Paul, "The Legal Position of Women in Pennsylvania," thesis, University of Pennsylvania, Alice Paul Institute, box 2: Education, 1901–07, folder #71.

22 *"As I believe I forecasted"*: William Parker to Alice Paul, September 15, 1912, Alice Paul Papers, Series II, MC 399, box 3, folder #38, Schlesinger Library, Radcliffe Institute, Harvard University, Cambridge, Mass.

CHAPTER THREE: A SOUTHERN BOY

24 *With one million residents*: "Results from the 1860 Census," Civil War Home Page, http://www.civil-war.net/pages/1860_census.html.

25 *"I am sure that you will bear with me"*: Joseph R. Wilson, "Mutual Relation of Masters and Slaves as Taught in the Bible," sermon, First Presbyterian Church, Augusta, Georgia, January 6, 1861, http://docsouth.unc.edu/imls/wilson/wilson.html.

27 *The War Between the States*: "Boyhood Home of Woodrow Wilson," Explore Southern History, http://www.exploresouthernhistory.com/augustawilson.html.

28 *The 14th Amendment also specifically excluded*: The text reads: "But when the right to vote at any election for the choice of electors for President and Vice President of the United States, Representatives in Congress, the Executive and Judicial officers of a State, or the members of the Legislature thereof, is denied to any of the male inhabitants of such State, being twenty-one years of age, and citizens of the United States, or in any way abridged, except for participation in rebellion, or other crime, the basis of representation therein shall be reduced in the proportion which the number of such male citizens shall bear to the whole number of male citizens twenty-one years of age in such State."

29 *"Universal suffrage is at the foundation"*: Berg, 72.

CHAPTER FOUR: FROM PRINCETON TO PUBLIC OFFICE

30 *After graduating from Princeton*: Woodrow Wilson to Ellen Louise Axson, in Link, vol. 3, 389.

30 *"Barring the chilled"*: Southard, 130.

30 *His 1885 doctoral dissertation*: Woodrow Wilson, "Congressional Government: A Study in American Politics" (thesis, Johns Hopkins University, 1896), https://archive.org/stream/congressionalgov00wilsa#page/n11/mode/2up.

31 *"Do you think there is much reputation"*: Berg, 99.

31 *"The question of higher education"*: Cooper, *Woodrow Wilson: A Biography*, 54.

32 *"As compared with the privilege"*: Berg, 101.

32 *"I do feel a very real regret"*: Berg, 10.

32 *"All discussion of the question"*: Gilman and Rhoads, 8.

32 *For one section of the book*: Wilson, *The State*, 321.

33 *Another, the daughter*: Berg, 104.

33 *"I'm tired of carrying female Fellows"*: Berg, 104.

33 *On the final full page*: Wilson, *The State*, 667.

34 *"But the voting population"*: Wilson, *Division and Reunion*, 241.

34 *"The growth of wealth"*: Ibid., 299.

34 *On a brisk October day in 1902*: "Hints from Squints: A Day at Princeton," *Michigan School Moderator* 23, no. 6 (November 20, 1902).

34 *Draped in his academic robe*: John Milton Cooper Jr., "Woodrow Wilson," *Princeton Alumni Weekly* 3 (November 1, 1902).

35 *The procession concluded*: "Woodrow Wilson Installed at Princeton," *New York Times*, October 26, 1902.

35 *"I have studied the history of America"*: Associated Press, "Princeton's Day; Woodrow Wilson Inaugurated as Thirteenth President," *Lowell Sun*, October 27, 1902.

35 *"It is altogether inadvisable"*: Cooper, *Reconsidering Woodrow Wilson, 107*.

36 *By one measure*: "The Tutorial System in College," *Educational Review* (December 1906), Seeley G. Mudd Manuscript Library, AC117, box 63, folder 11, https://findingaids.princeton.edu/AC117/c00297.pdf.

37 *The stress of this defeat*: Berg, 167.

38 *Wilson retreated from the eating club*: Andrew West to the Graduate School Committee, May 13, 1907, Office of the President, 1905–1910, Princeton University Archives, MUDD Reading Room, box 63, folder #1, https://findingaids.princeton.edu/repositories/univarchives.

38 *"The nation is aroused"*: "Princeton," *New York Times*, February 3, 1910.

39 *They told him the role*: Berg, 191.

40 *With these stunning populist wins*: Berg, 233.

40 *"Monopoly, private control, the authority"*: Berg, 217.

40 *He was so concerned*: Wilson, *A History of the American People: Reunion and Nationalization*, 212.

CHAPTER FIVE: THE SUFFRAGE PROCESSION

43 *Tune every harp*: The song's male-focused lyrics were neutralized after women finally were admitted to Princeton in 1969.

44 *Here's to you, Woodrow Wilson*: "Great Send Off for Dr. Wilson," *Fort Wayne Daily News*, March 3, 1913.

45 *In Washington, the morning*: National Weather Service: https://www.weather.gov/lwx/events_Inauguration.

45 *The two women had joined*: The National American Woman Suffrage Association was created in 1890 by the merger of the two major rival women's rights organizations—the National Woman Suffrage Associate and the American Woman Suffrage Association.

46 *"Miss Burns is in appearance"*: Stevens, 175.

47 *On the morning of the procession*: "Avenue for Pageant," *Washington Post*, January 10, 1913.

47 *"It will have no direct bearing on suffrage itself"*: Anna Howard Shaw to Alice

Paul, January 22, 1913, National Women's Party Papers, box 3, Library of Congress; Zahniser and Fry, 141–42.

48 *The smell of coffee and hot dogs*: "Wilson Arrives in Washington," *La Crosse Tribune*, March 3, 1913.

48 *As Paul neared the starting point*: "Wilson Takes Office Today as 21st President," *New York Times*, March 4, 1913.

49 *Paul had specifically invited black women*: Mary Beard to Alice Paul, January 1913, National Women's Party Papers, box 299, Library of Congress.

50 *"I am a Northern woman"*: Alice Paul to Alice Stone Blackwell, January 15, 1913, National Women's Party Papers, box 299, Library of Congress.

50 *Milholland was thrilled*: Inez Milholland to Lucy Burns, February 7, 1913, National Women's Party Papers, box 155, Library of Congress.

51 *The first section of the parade*: Irwin, 29.

53 *Women of color also mixed*: Zahniser and Fry, 149.

54 *Earlier in the day*: "Illinois Women Feature Parade," *Chicago Tribune*, March 4, 1913.

55 *"If the Illinois women do not take a stand"*: Ibid.

55 *When word spread*: "I was arrested of course," *American Heritage*, February 1974, vol. 25, issue 2.

CHAPTER SIX: WHERE ARE ALL THE PEOPLE?

59 *The cars took a roundabout route*: "Wilson Evades Vast Crowd," *New York Times*, March 4, 1913.

59 *"Where are all the people?"*: Stevens, 21.

60 *"I was never so proud in my life"*: "Woman's Beauty, Grace, and Art Bewilder the Capital," *Washington Post*, March 4, 1913.

61 *The next morning, on Inauguration Day*: "Hoodlums vs. Gentlewomen," *Chicago Tribune*, March 5, 1913; "Women Battle Hostile Mobs in Suffrage Parade," *New-York Tribune*, March 4, 1913.

62 *Ellen felt unwell*: Berg, 274.

62 *"There can be no equality"*: The American Presidency Project, http://www.presidency.ucsb.edu/ws/index.php?pid=25831.

62 *While he spoke on topics that appealed to the masses*: Sidney R. Bland, "New Life in an Old Movement: Alice Paul and the Great Suffrage Parade of 1913 in Washington, D.C.," Records of the Columbia Historical Society, Washington, D.C., Vol. 71/72, the 48th separately bound book, 671.

CHAPTER SEVEN: IN THE OVAL OFFICE

63 *In fact, in his first days as president*: Berg, 291.

64 *"Don't be nervous"*: Irwin, 33–35.

65 *She said she wanted to speak for the women of the South*: "Too Busy for Women," *Washington Post*, March 18, 1913; "Will Hear of 'Cause,'" *Washington Post*, March 17, 1913.

65 *"But Mr. President, do you not understand"*: Stevens, 22–23.

66 *"I can't promise that I can comply"*: "Suffragists See Wilson," *New York Times*, March 18, 1913.

66 *He also explained that as someone from the South*: Fry, 91.

67 *With time running out*: Shanna Stevenson, "The Role of Washington State in the 19th Amendment," Washington History, http://www.washingtonhistory .org/files/library/TheRoleofWashingtonStateinthe19thAmendment.pdf.

69 *As the suffragists arrived at the foot of Capitol Hill*: "Impressive March of Suffrage," *New York Times*, April 8, 1913.

70 *The next day, Wilson woke to newspaper coverage*: Berg, 160 and 176.

72 *"Mr. Speaker, Mr. [Senate] President"*: Woodrow Wilson, "Address to a Joint Session of Congress on Tariff Reform," April 8, 1913. Made accessible online by Gerhard Peters and John T. Woolley, The American Presidency Project, http://www.presidency.ucsb.edu/ws/?pid=65368.

73 *When he was done ten minutes later*: "Congress Cheers Greet Wilson," *New York Times*, April 9, 1913; Day, 141–42.

73 *Paul and Burns went to Shaw's home*: Irwin, 270.

74 *"We couldn't possibly take up the amendment"*: "Suffragists Tell Henry House Treatment Is Unfair," *Washington Post*, July 11, 1913.

CHAPTER EIGHT: THE SIEGE OF THE SENATE

75 *In Boston, in mid-July of 1913*: "Over 4,000 Names Now on Suffrage Petition," *Boston Post*, July 26, 1913.

75 *Then they moved on to Providence*: "Suffragist Auto Brigade Starts Tour of New England," *Boston Post*, July 17, 1913.

76 *The success of the campaign*: "Antis Fear Attack," *Washington Post*, July 28, 1913.

77 *The next morning, the weather cleared*: "Invasion by Fair Sex," *Washington Post*, July 31, 1913.

77 *Police Chief Sylvester met them*: "Suffragists Demand 'Votes for Women,'" *Newport Daily News*, July 31, 1913.

78 *shutting down the automobiles*: "Suffragist Army Invades Senate," *Berkeley Daily Gazette* [Evening], July 31, 1913; "A Besieging of the Senate," *Mansfield News* [Ohio], July 31, 1913.

78 *For nearly an hour, women representing their states*: "'Votes for Women' Demand on Senate," *Muscatine Journal* [Iowa], July 31, 1913.

79 *She asked Rheta Childe Dorr*: Zahniser and Fry, 173.

80 *"As it's impossible"*: Gillmore, 41.

81 *"I am pleased, indeed"*: Ibid.

81 *Burns, in particular, drew Shaw's outrage*: "Miss Burns Awaits Arrest for Writing on Capitol Walks," *Brooklyn Eagle*, November 18, 1913.

81 *"You may think we are"*: Zahniser and Fry, 175.

CHAPTER NINE: A HOUSE DIVIDED

84 *The absence of these legendary*: "Milady Is Angry," *Washington Post*, December 2, 1913.

85 *"Victory is at hand"*: "Suffragists Urged to Worry Congress," *New York Times*, December 2, 1913.

85 *As the audience applauded again*: "Miss Burns Awaits Arrest for Writing on Capital Walks," *Brooklyn Daily Eagle*, November 18, 1913.

85 *The audience was spellbound*: Stevens, 175.

85 *"Rarely in the history of the country"*: Irwin, 42.

86 *"These are all matters of vital domestic concern"*: Wilson's speech, December 2, 1913, http://www.presidency.ucsb.edu/ws/index.php?pid=29554.

87 *At an evening session later in the day*: "Suffragists Rap Wilson for Silence," *New York Times*, December 4, 1913; "Suffrage Congress Would See Wilson," Ibid.

87 *The following afternoon, their anger*: "Suffragists Rap Wilson for Silence," *New York Times*, December 4, 1913; "Suffrage Congress Would See Wilson," Ibid.

88 *On Thursday, having watched Shaw*: "Dr. Anna Shaw Still Leader," *New York Times*, December 5, 1913.

88 *By Friday, the last day of the convention*: National American Woman Suffrage Association. *Forty-fifth Annual Report of the National American Woman Suffrage Association*, NAWSA Convention, Washington, D.C., November 29–December 5, 1913 (New York: The Association, 1913), https://babel.hathitrust.org/cgi/pt?id=hvd.rslfe2;view=1up;seq=5.

89 *A suffragist from Boston*: "Suffragists Camp on Wilson's Trail," *New York Times*, December 6, 1913.

89 *As the delegates cheered for Paul*: Catt and Shuler, 504.

90 *As she studied*: Zahniser and Fry, 176.

90 *When the applause for Paul faded*: Zahniser and Fry, 180.

90 *As Catt and Shaw exchanged meaningful glances*: Fry, 97.

90 *Some of the women began whispering*: Fry, 97.

91 *Shaw issued the final word*: Zahniser and Fry, 181.

91 *Paul was blindsided by this public rebuke*: Fry, 97.

91 *On Monday morning, Paul rallied*: "March at Noon Today," *New York Times*, December 8, 1913.

91 *Now that the president was feeling better*: Fry, 102.

91 *Wilson sauntered in*: Stevens, 27.

91 *"I am merely the spokesman of my party"*: Ibid., 27.

92 *"Mr. President, if you cannot speak for us"*: Ibid., 27.

92 *"Well," Paul said*: Fry, 101–3.

93 *The Bristow-Mondell Amendment*: Fry, 103–6.

93 *Paul, Burns, and two*: Fry, 104–5.

94 *Paul sat up in her bed*: Zahniser and Fry, 199.

CHAPTER TEN: DARK DAYS

96 *Just one month*: Kathleen L. Wolgemuth, "Woodrow Wilson and Federal Segregation." *Journal of Negro History* 44, no. 2 (1959): 158–73; Berg, 305–12.

97 *Among those arguing against segregation*: Kathleen L. Wolgemuth, "Woodrow Wilson and Federal Segregation." *Journal of Negro History* 44, no. 2 (1959): 158–73; Berg, 305–12.

98 *As guests took their seats*: "Commander-in-Chief is merged in husband, father, and citizen," *Washington Post*, May 8, 1914; Berg, 328–30.

101 *The women were arriving at Marble House*: "Marble House Is Conference Place," *Trenton Evening Times*, August 29, 1914; "To Fight Against Democrats," *Newport Daily News*, August 31, 1914; "Plan Suffrage Work," *Washington Post*, August 29, 1914.

102 *But first, Paul and Lucy Burns*: "Marble House Is Conference Place," *Trenton Evening Times*, August 29, 1914; "To Fight Against Democrats," *Newport Daily News*, August 31, 1914.

103 *One of these waverers was Katharine Hepburn*: This was the mother of the ac-

tress of the same name; the elder Hepburn was cofounder of the organization that eventually become Planned Parenthood; Fry, 122–23.

103 *"Please don't reveal this"*: Irwin, 75. Quote recreated from paraphrased report.

104 *Paul had created a blacklist*: Kraditor, 231–34; Flexnor, 277.

104 *"Now the time has come"*: Irwin, 76.

105 *In mid-September*: Irwin, 80.

105 *In Denver, the daughter*: Irwin, 80–81.

106 *It was exhausting and exhilarating*: Zahniser and Fry, 229.

106 *The results of the midterms*: Berg, 339.

106 *Out of concern for his health*: Starling, 40.

107 *Wilson was a terrible golfer*: Starling, 34–35; Berg, 303.

107 *"My heart is in a whirl"*: Day, 174.

107 *Given his mind-set*: Berg, 346.

108 *"I am sorry to hear that"*: "Wilson vs. Trotter," *(Cleveland) Gazette*, November 21, 1914.

108 *As one Cleveland newspaper*: "Wilson vs. Trotter," *(Cleveland) Gazette*, November 21, 1914.

109 *As word trickled out*: Berg, 347–49.

109 *Although Wilson tried to backpedal*: Edith Wilson, 38.

110 *On May 4, less than two months*: Edith Wilson, 60–67.

CHAPTER ELEVEN: SUBMARINE WARFARE

112 *The* Lusitania *was six days*: Larson, 240.

113 *As he battled with the decision before him*: Starling, 46; Day, 190–93.

113 *Wilson was still hoping Galt*: Edith Wilson, 63–67.

115 *In addition to the booth*: Adams and Keene, 106.

116 *To heighten suspense*: "From San Francisco," *The Suffragist*, October 9, 1915; Field account, October 14, 1915.

117 *More shocking news*: Zahniser and Fry, 228.

119 *December 18 was no ordinary day*: Edith Wilson, 83.

119 *After the exchange of vows*: Edith Wilson, 86–88.

CHAPTER TWELVE: THE ADVANCING ARMY

121 "We must see to it": Woodrow Wilson, "Address to the Seventh Annual

Dinner of the Railway Business Association," New York City, January 27, 1916, http://www.presidency.ucsb.edu/ws/?pid=117299; " 'Prepare' President Wilson Pleads," *New York Times*, January 28, 1916.

122 *While Wilson's public statements*: Link, *Wilson*, vol. 4, 131.

124 *One man who gave a speech*: Zahniser and Fry, 240–42.

125 *After the final luncheon*: Irwin, 162.

126 *"We want suffrage to come"*: Zahniser and Fry, 246–47.

126 *Never idle, Paul believed*: Lumsden, 120–30.

127 *"She would come away"*: Irwin, 188–89.

127 *Milholland understood the power*: Zahniser, 251.

128 *On Election Day, November 7*: Berg, 413–16.

130 *On December 5, six women*: Irwin, 190.

131 *The Capitol Building's Statuary Hall*: Irwin, 21–26.

132 *Younger, like most of the women*: Irwin, 187–91.

133 *Mabel Vernon led the suffragists:* Irwin, 192–94.

136 *They listened as Blatch*: "Memorial Resolutions," *The Suffragist*, January 17, 1917; Congressional Union for Woman Suffrage Executive Committee minutes, January 5, 1917, Reel 38, National Woman's Party Papers, Library of Congress; Irwin, 95; "Suffragists Will Picket the White House," *New York Times*, January 10, 1917.

CHAPTER THIRTEEN: THE SILENT SENTINELS

137 *By 1917, Alice Paul's plan*: "Wilson Runs Gauntlet of 'Suff' Guards," *Washington Times*, January 10, 1917.

137 *"Gee, whiz. How about eating?"*: Ibid.

138 *They arrived outside 1600 Pennsylvania*: " 'Picket' the White House," *Washington Post*, January 10, 1917.

139 *An elderly man paused*: Irwin, 214.

139 *Visiting the White House from Oklahoma*: "Picket Line of 3,000," *Washington Post*, January 11, 1917.

140 *White House officials were unsure*: Ibid.

140 *The news of this ongoing protest*: "Charge Suffragists Menace Wilson's Life," *New York Times*, January 17, 1917.

140 *Even close allies were upset*: Zahniser and Fry, 257.

141 *On the second day of the pickets*: Irwin, 216.

141 *Even the Wilsons seemed to feel sorry*: Edith Wilson, 125.

141 *Well beyond that second day of protests*: "Suffragists Wait at the White House for Action," *The Suffragist*, January 17, 1917; Irwin, 204–5.

142 *A group of old Confederates*: Ibid.

CHAPTER FOURTEEN: FIGHTING FOR DEMOCRACY

144 *Outside, the Silent Sentinels continued*: Edith Wilson, 128–29.

145 *The next day, the news was as grim*: Berg, 425; Hull conversation recreated from same page in Berg based on paraphrased reporting.

145 *"Whereas, the problems involved"*: Irwin, 207.

146 *The rainy weather in early March*: Wilson, 130; Starling, 83–85.

146 *With the formalities complete*: Edith Wilson, 130.

146 *Across town, it began to pour again*: "Giant Deputation to President on Eve of Inauguration," *The Suffragist*, February 17, 1917.

148 *Just then, the eastern gate opened*: "Rain Soaked, 500 Suffragists Parade Four Times Around the White House," *Washington Post*, March 5, 1917; "On the picket line," *The Suffragist*, March 8, 1917.

150 *On April 2, Washington hummed*: Flexnor, 293; Zahniser and Fry, 262–63.

150 *"Glad to see you're back"*: Irwin, 219.

151 *Inside the House chamber*: Edith Wilson, 132–32.

151 *"Our objective is to vindicate"*: Day, 243–47.

151 *"Its peace must be planted"*: Ibid.

152 *When Wilson was done*: Berg, 438.

152 *When he composed himself*: Day, 248.

153 *She was, in more ways than one*: "Debate Lasted 16 ½ Hours," *New York Times*, April 6, 1917.

153 *It was Good Friday*: Berg, 439–40.

CHAPTER FIFTEEN: THE RUSSIANS

154 *The train rolled to a clanging*: "Greeting to Russians," *Washington Post*, June 20, 1917; "Washington Cheers Russian Mission," *New York Times*, June 20, 1917.

155 *In the five weeks it had taken*: *Woodrow Wilson: A Biography*; Cooper, 417.

157 *The Russians, arriving by motorcade*: Irwin, 215.

157 *Another man, a local builder*: "Flaunt Fresh Banner," *Washington Post*, June 21, 1917.

157 *But the men, so agitated*: Irwin, 215.

158 *Another man was so proud*: Woodrow Wilson, executive case file 89 (Suffrage), 191704-191706, series 4, reel 210, Woodrow Wilson Papers, Manuscript Division, Library of Congress.

159 *Meanwhile, police picked up*: Edith Wilson, 138.

159 *The threats of arrest did not scare Paul*: "Crowd Destroys Suffrage Banner," *New York Times*, June 21, 1917.

159 *Sure enough, within twenty-four hours*: "Enraged Mob in Front of White House," *Washington Times*, June 20, 1917.

159 *No one bothered these women*: "Flaunt Fresh Banner," *Washington Post*, June 21, 1917.

160 *Citizens telegrammed the White House*: Woodrow Wilson, executive case file 89 (Suffrage), 191704-191706, series 4, reel 210, Woodrow Wilson Papers, Manuscript Division, Library of Congress.

160 *Publicly, members of Congress*: "Crowd Destroys Suffrage Banner," *New York Times*, June 21, 1917; Irwin, 216.

161 *back at headquarters*: Irwin, 210; "Crowds Again Rend Suffrage Banners," *New York Times*, June 22, 1917; "Brave Third Day Riot," *Washington Post*, June 22, 1917.

163 *The next morning, on June 22*: Irwin, 211.

163 *"My God, man, you can't arrest that"*: Zahniser and Fry, 268.

165 *Parker had been living in Washington*: Zahniser and Fry, 258.

165 *"To Miss Alice Paul"*: Woodrow Wilson, executive office case file 89 (Suffrage), 191704-191706, series 4, reel 210, Woodrow Wilson Papers, Manuscript Division, Library of Congress.

165 *The press printed the letter*: "Woman Arrests Suffrage Pickets," *New York Times*, June 23, 1917; "'Move Along Pickets,'" *Washington Post*, June 23, 1917.

166 *Police cleared the steps just in time*: Irwin, 220–21; "Bars Cells to Pickets," *Washington Post*, June 24, 1917; "Stirs House to Cheers," *Washington Post*, June 24, 1917.

167 *The next morning, Cameron House*: "New Pickets on Duty," *Washington Post*, June 25, 1917.

167 *The following day, police*: Irwin, 220; "Arrest 12 Pickets," *Washington Post*, June 26, 1917.

168 *By morning, nine suffragists*: Irwin, 220; "Take 9 More 'Suffs,'" *Washington Post*, June 27, 1917.

169 *The judge, Alexander Mullowney*: Irwin, 221; "Suffragettes in Jail," *Washington Post*, June 28, 1917.

169   *In order to seek maximum exposure*: "Suffragettes in jail," *Washington Post*, June 28, 1917.

CHAPTER SIXTEEN: THE BASTILLE DAY PROTEST

170   *The war had cast a shadow*: "Solemn Fourth for the City," *Washington Post*, July 4, 1917; "Militants in Riot," *Washington Post*, July 5, 1917.

170   *Just before 1 p.m.*: "Militants Argue Case," *Washington Post*, July 6, 1917.

171   *The court hearing was a farce*: "Militants Go to Jail," *Washington Post*, July 7, 1917.

171   *The suffragists seemed almost titillated*: Alice Paul to Woodrow Wilson, case file 89 (Suffrage), series 4, reel 210, Woodrow Wilson Papers, Manuscript Division, Library of Congress, p. 59543.

172   *King ran a series of tests*: Hazel Hunkins to Anna Constable, July 9, 1917; Hazel Hunkins to Mary Beard, July 11, 1917; Anna Martin to Alice Paul, July 11, 1917; Cora Smith King to Alice Paul, July 25, 2015; Lucy Burns to Elizabeth Kent, July 26, 1917; Cora Smith King to Alice Paul, July 13, 1917; July 13 minutes, reels 45, 46, and 114, National Woman's Party Papers I.

173   *"I am very sorry to hear"*: William Parker to Alice Paul, mid-July 1917, reel 46, National Woman's Party Papers I.

174   *Missing from the sentinels that day*: Terrell, 316.

174   *Those who did participate*: Woodrow Wilson's appointment book, 1917, reel 3, Woodrow Wilson Papers, Manuscript Division, Library of Congress.

174   *All sixteen women*: "Suffragists Take 60-Day Sentence," *New York Times*, July 18, 1917.

175   *On Monday, Judge Mullowney*: Zahniser and Fry, 265, 271; Fry, 223.

175   *"Silence in the courtroom"*: Stevens, 43.

175   *"This is what we are doing"*: Stevens, 44.

176   *Malone and Hopkins were stunned*: "Suffragists Take 60-Day Sentence," *New York Times*, July 18, 1917.

CHAPTER SEVENTEEN: BEHIND BARS

179   *At dawn, the suffragists*: "Suffragists Take 60-Day Sentence," *New York Times*, July 18, 1917.

179   *"Why, I held a purple, white and gold banner"*: Stevens, 48.

181   *Hopkins gave a curt bow*: Arthur Brisbane to Woodrow Wilson, case file 89,

Woodrow Wilson Papers, reel 210, p. 59601, Manuscript Division, Library of Congress.

181 *The next day, golfing*: Edith Wilson, 138.

181 *"Ladies, there is a rumor"*: "Militants Freed at Wilson's Word," *New York Times*, July 20, 1917; Stevens, 72.

183 *"We're obliged to the President"*: "Pickets Obliged to Wilson," *New-York Tribune*, July 21, 1917.

184 *The morning after her pardon*: Irwin, 228.

185 *"There is a great deal"*: Joseph Tumulty to Woodrow Wilson, July 21, 1917, Woodrow Wilson Papers, series 4, reel 210, Manuscript Division, Library of Congress, p. 59602; Woodrow Wilson to Joseph Tumulty, July 21, 1917, Woodrow Wilson Papers, series 4, reel 210, Manuscript Division, Library of Congress, p. 59603.

186 *"To Envoy Root"*: Fry, 343.

187 *As people tried to flee*: "Washington Crowd Eggs Suffragettes," *New York Times*, August 15, 1917.

188 *A few days later, on August 15*: Irwin, 236–39.

188 *Meanwhile, in Maine*: "Maine Rejects Suffrage, 2 to 1," *New York Times*, September 11, 1917.

188 *The pickets had another unexpected effect*: Catt, 298.

CHAPTER EIGHTEEN: THE HUNGER STRIKES

191 *On October 20*: "Police Arrest Four Pickets," *Washington Herald*, October 21, 1917.

192 *It was a speedy trial*: Irwin, 249.

192 *As Paul was led out of the courtroom*: "Miss Alice Paul Arrested Again," *Washington Post*, October 21, 1917.

192 *"I am being imprisoned"*: "Alice Paul Gets 7 Months in Jail," *New-York Tribune*, October 23, 1917.

193 *The next day, as the guards swept dust*: "Rats in Procession March Around Cells," *Boston Globe*, November 4, 1917.

194 *When word spread outside the prison*: "Militant Sings at Jail Gates," *Washington Post*, November 6, 1917; Stevens, 84–85.

194 *Paul and Winslow, lying*: "Miss Alice Paul on Hunger Strike," *New York Times*, November 7, 1917.

194 *The following day*: "New York Women Urge Treating Jailed Pickets as Political Prisoners," *Washington Post*, November 9, 1917.

195 *The National American Woman Suffrage Association's*: "6 Noted Suffs Fail to Win Wilson Over," *The Sun*, November 10, 1917.

195 *"You will be forcibly fed"*: Irwin, 284.

197 *Although news reports quoted*: "Suffs End Prison Fast of 72 Hours," *The Sun*, November 9, 1917; Stevens, 84.

198 *"I thought when I put this up"*: "Miss Paul Removed to Prison Hospital," *New York Times*, November 19, 1917.

198 *The pickets most recently arrested*: "Back to Jail for 24 Suffrage Pickets," *Boston Globe*, November 25, 1917; "Accuse Jailers of Suffragists," *New York Times*, November 17, 1917.

198 *"You shut up!" Whittaker shouted*: "Jail Is Calm and Peaceful Again," *Washington Post*, November 28, 1917.

200 *Although Wilson's political appointees*: A. P. Blauvelt to Joseph Tumulty, November 17, 1917, Woodrow Wilson, executive office case file 89 (Suffrage), series 4, reel 210, Woodrow Wilson Papers, Manuscript Division, Library of Congress, p. 59389.

201 *Tammany Hall operatives*: Calvin Tomkins to Joseph Tumulty, November 12, 1917, Woodrow Wilson, executive office case file 89 (Suffrage), series 4, reel 210, Woodrow Wilson Papers, Manuscript Division, Library of Congress, p. 59815.

201 *"I think your present reply"*: Woodrow Wilson to Joseph Tumulty, Woodrow Wilson, executive office case file 89 (Suffrage), series 4, reel 210, Woodrow Wilson Papers, Manuscript Division, Library of Congress, p. 59383.

CHAPTER NINETEEN: THE WATCH FIRES OF FREEDOM

202 *"What we demand"*: Journal of the House of Representatives of the United States, Vol. 65, Issue 2, Jan. 8, 1918, 88.

202 *Wilson was concerned*: Woodrow Wilson, "Fourteen Point Plan," transcript, January 8, 1918, Washington, D.C., http://avalon.law.yale.edu/20th_century/wilson14.asp.

203 *The next day, Wilson absorbed*: Publicity Department of the Woman's Bureau, January 9, 1918, in Link, *The Papers of Woodrow Wilson Digital Edition*, 80.

203 *The House was scheduled to vote*: Woodrow Wilson, statement on suffrage, January 9, 1918, in Link, *The Papers of Woodrow Wilson Digital Edition*, 545.

204 *"The President," Raker told them*: "Give Vote to Women," *Washington Post*, January 10, 1918.

204 *An amendment needs a two-thirds majority*: "Constitutional Amendment Process," Federal Register, National Archives, https://www.archives.gov/federal-register/constitution.

204 *The following day, suffragists darted*: "Suffrage Amendment Passed By One-Vote Margin," *Washington Herald*, January 11, 1918; "President's Plea for Suffrage Amendment," *Washington Times*, January 10, 1918.

205 *As the debate wore on*: Zahniser and Fry, 301.

205 *Mann was welcomed*: Kops, 104.

206 *The scene at NAWSA was joyful*: Helen Gardener to Joseph Tumulty, January 10, 1918, in Link, *The Papers of Woodrow Wilson Digital Edition*, 565.

206 *With the House vote behind them*: Sidney R. Bland, "Never Quite as Committed as We'd Like," 19.

207 *Beulah Amidon, Lillian Ascough*: Irwin, 361.

207 *The Senate campaign began*: Irwin, 342.

208 *As winter melted into spring*: Joseph Tumulty to Governor, March 12, 1918; Woodrow Wilson to Minnie Fisher Cunningham, March 26, 1918, in Link, *The Papers of Woodrow Wilson Digital Edition*, 144, 608.

208 *"In the matter of woman suffrage"*: John C. W. Beckham to Woodrow Wilson, May 9, 1918, in Link, *The Papers of Woodrow Wilson Digital Edition*, 580.

208 *Wilson received a similar response*: Benjamin R. Tillman to Woodrow Wilson, May 10, 1918, in Link, *The Papers of Woodrow Wilson Digital Edition*, 597.

209 *"Mrs. Catt, Mrs. Gardener"*: Joseph Tumulty to Woodrow Wilson, May 7, 1918, in Link, *The Papers of Woodrow Wilson Digital Edition*, 547.

209 *Catt, who had worked as an activist*: Carrie Chapman Catt to Joseph Tumulty, June 8, 1918, in Link, *The Papers of Woodrow Wilson Digital Edition*, 271.

210 *The Wilson administration . . . created*: George F. Will, "What World War I Unleashed in America," *Washington Post*, April 7, 2017.

210 *On that day, at half past noon*: Irwin, 355–56.

212 *The protests persisted*: Irwin, 368.

212 *Those who were still drinking water*: Irwin, 360.

213 *As the women assembled*: Irwin, 363–65.

215 *The last day of the month*: Irwin, 370; "Wilson Makes Suffrage Appeal," *New York Times*, October 1, 1918.

215 *After the speech*: Woodrow Wilson to Carrie Chapman Catt, September 30, 1918, in Link, *Papers of Woodrow Wilson Digital Edition*, 161.

215 *But his effort, just as suffragists*: Irwin, 371.
216 *In Europe, a war of attrition raged*: Edith Wilson, 170.
216 *"Autocracy is dead"*: Berg, 513.

CHAPTER TWENTY: THE AMENDMENT

218 *The president and the first lady:* Edith Wilson, 170.
218 *Edith enjoyed the smooth sail*: Edith Wilson, 172–73.
219 *Wilson had only scheduled three weeks*: Edith Wilson, 206.
219 *Next was Italy*: Starling, 124.
220 *While Lewis stood over the flames*: Irwin, 391–93.
221 *In all, four suffragists*: Irwin, 396.
223 *"That is necessarily a domestic question"*: Irwin, 398.
223 *"Why does not the president"*: "Suffragists Burn Wilson in Effigy," *New York Times*, February 10, 1919.
224 *Police moved in and arrested White*: Irwin, 402–3.
224 *"I come from the South"*: "Speech by Senator Pollock in the Senate Debate on Suffrage," *The Suffragist* 7, no. 1 (February 15, 1919), 12.
225 *On February 15*: "The Prison Special," *The Suffragist* 7, no. 1 (February 15, 1919), 5.
225 *As the women rolled south*: Day, 320.
225 *When Wilson's ship arrived*: Irwin, 408; "Reminding the President When He Landed in Boston," *The Suffragist* 7, no. 1 (February 22, 1919), 6.
226 *Wilson wrapped up the formalities*: Edith Wilson, 242.
226 *Next, Wilson met with Senator Andrieus Jones*: Irwin, 411.
226 *Outraged that he would leave*: Irwin, 412.
227 *Assisted by soldiers and sailors*: Stevens, 147.
228 *The president reassembled the group*: Edith Wilson, 272.
229 *"Will you permit me"*: Irwin, 428.
229 *The day after Wilson sent his telegram*: Irwin, 429.
230 *"La séance est lévee"*: Berg, 600–601; Edith Wilson, 269–71.
231 *The following day, the Wilsons boarded*: Edith Wilson, 271.

CHAPTER TWENTY-ONE: THE VOTE

233 *In California, he received his most*: Berg, 634.
233 *When they returned to the train*: Berg, 635.

233 *At 11:30 p.m., the president knocked*: Edith Wilson, 284–85.

234 *"I have no feeling in that hand"*: Edith Wilson, 288.

235 *His absence from politics*: Edith Wilson, 297.

239 *There were two representatives*: Elaine Weiss, 305.

239 *At first, Burn had told Pollitzer*: Elaine Weiss, 298.

241 *In her pencil script*: Febb Burn to Harry Burn, undated but postmarked August 17, 1920, Harry T. Burn Papers, C. M. McClung Historical Collection, Knox County Public Library.

241 *Paul was at headquarters*: Bland, "Never Quite as Committed as We'd Like," 14.

EPILOGUE

243 *Because opponents had been challenging*: "Colby Proclaims Woman Suffrage," *New York Times*, August 27, 1920; Patri O'Gan, "Traveling for Suffrage Part 1: Two Women, a Cat, a Car and a Mission," The Smithsonian, March 5, 2014, http://americanhistory.si.edu/blog/2014/03/traveling-for-suffrage-part-1-two-women-a-cat-a-car-and-a-mission.html.

244 *Despite her personal disappointment*: "Colby Proclaims Woman Suffrage," *New York Times*, August 27, 1920.

244 *That struggle—beyond even*: Kraditor, 295.

244 *Even though Wilson was physically*: Edith Wilson, 308–10.

245 *The Wilsons' transition*: Edith Wilson, 359–60.

245 *She asked Mary Church Terrell*: NWP letter to Walter White, September 2 [1924], reel 15, Mary Church Terrell Papers, Library of Congress.

Bibliography

Adams, Katherine H., and Michael L. Keene. *Alice Paul and the American Suffrage Campaign*. Champaign, Ill.: University of Illinois Press, 2010.

Adiche, Chimamanda Ngozi. *We Should All Be Feminists*. New York: Anchor Books, 2012.

Alice Paul Papers, 1785–1985, Schlesinger Library, Radcliffe Institute, Harvard University, Cambridge, Mass.

Bland, Sidney R. "Never Quite as Committed as We'd Like: The Suffrage Militancy of Lucy Burns." *Journal of Long Island History* 17, no. 2 (Summer/Fall 1981): 19.

———. "New Life in an Old Movement: Alice Paul and the Great Suffrage Parade of 1913 in Washington, D.C." *Records of the Columbia Historical Society*, vol. 71/72. Washington, D.C., 1971/1972, 657–78.

———. "The Suffrage Militancy of Lucy Burns." *Journal of Long Island History* 17, no. 2 (Summer/Fall 1981): 11.

Berg, A. Scott. *Wilson*. New York: G. P. Putnam's Sons, 2013.

Catt, Carrie Chapman, and Nettie Rogers Shuler. *Woman Suffrage and Politics: The Inner Story of the Suffrage Movement*. Seattle: University of Washington Press, 1969.

Cooper, John Milton, Jr. *Reconsidering Woodrow Wilson: Progressivism, Internationalism, War, and Peace*, Woodrow Wilson Center Press Series. Baltimore, Md.: Johns Hopkins University Press, 2008.

———. *Woodrow Wilson: A Biography*. New York: Vintage Books, 2009.

Davis, Angela Y. *Women, Race and Class*. New York: Vintage Books, 1983.

Day, Donald. *Woodrow Wilson's Own Story*. Boston: Little, Brown, and Co., 1952.

Flexner, Eleanor. *Century of Struggle: The Woman's Rights Movement in the United States*. Cambridge, Mass.: Harvard University Press, 1975.

Fry, Amelia R. "Conversations with Alice Paul: Woman Suffrage and the Equal Rights Amendment." Transcript of an oral history conducted 1972–73, Oral History Center of the Bancroft Library, University of California, Berkeley.

Fulford, Roger. *Votes for Women*. London: Faber and Faber, 1956.

Gillmore, Inez Haynes. *The Story of the Woman's Party*. New York: Harcourt, Brace and Co., 1921.

Gilman, Daniel Coit, and James Evans Rhoads. *Addresses at the Inauguration of Bryn Mawr College*: Bryn Mawr, Penn.: 1885.

Graham, Sara Hunter. *Woman Suffrage and the New Democracy*. New Haven: Yale University Press, 1996.

Hunt, Helen LaKelly. *And the Spirit Moved Them: The Lost Radical History of America's First Feminists*. New York: Feminist Press, 2017.

Irwin, Inez Haynes. *The Story of Alice Paul and the National Woman's Party*. Fairfax, Va.: Denlinger Publishers, 1964.

Kops, Deborah. *Alice Paul and the Fight for Women's Rights*. Honesdale, Penn.: Calkins Creek, 2017.

Kraditor, Aileen S. *The Idea of the Woman Suffrage Movement, 1890–1920*. New York: Columbia University Press, 1965.

Larson, Erik. *Dead Wake: The Last Crossing of the Lusitania*. New York: Broadway Books, 2015.

Link, Arthur S. *The Papers of Woodrow Wilson Digital Edition*. Charlottesville: University of Virginia Press, Rotunda, 2017. Originally published in *The Papers of Woodrow Wilson, 1966–1994*. Princeton, N.J.: Princeton University Press, 2017.

———. *Wilson: Confusion and Crises, 1915–1916*, vol. 4. Princeton, N.J.: Princeton University Press, 1964.

Lumsden, Linda J. *Inez: The Life and Times of Inez Milholland*. Bloomington: Indiana University Press, 2004.

National American Woman Suffrage Association, The. *Victory: How Women Won It; 1840–1940: A Centennial Edition*. New York: H. W. Wilson, 1940.

O'Toole, Patricia. *The Moralist: Woodrow Wilson and the World He Made*. New York: Simon & Schuster, 2018.

Pankhurst, Sylvia. *The Suffragette: The History of the Women's Militant Suffrage Movement*. Mineola, N.Y.: Dover Publications, 2015. Unabridged republication of the original 1911 version.

Southard, Belinda A. Stillion. Militant Citizenship: Rhetorical Strategies of the National Woman's Party, 1913–1920. College Station, Tex.: Texas A&M University Press, 2011.

Starling, Col. Edward W. *Starling of the White House*. New York: Simon & Schuster, 1946.

Stevens, Doris. *Jailed for Freedom*. New York: Boni and Liveright Publishers, 1920.

Terborg-Penn, Rosalyn. *African American Women in the Struggle for the Vote, 1850–1920*. Bloomington: Indiana University Press, 1998.

Terrell, Mary Church. *A Colored Woman in a White World*. Washington, D.C.: Randsell Publishers, 1940.

Timberlake, James H. *Prohibition and the Progressive Movement, 1900–1920*. Cambridge, Mass.: Harvard University Press, 1963.

United States Constitution, The.

Von Drehle, David. *Triangle: The Fire That Changed America*. New York: Grove Press, 2003.

Weiss, Elaine. *The Woman's Hour: The Great Fight to Win the Vote*. New York: Viking, 2018.

Weiss, Nancy J. "The Negro and the New Freedom: Fighting Wilsonian Segregation." *Political Science Quarterly* (March 1969): 66.

Wilson, Edith Bolling. *My Memoir*. New York: Bobbs-Merrill, 1938.

Wilson, Woodrow. *Division and Reunion, 1829–1889*. New York: Longman, Greens & Co., 1898.

———. *The State: Elements of Historical and Practical Politics*. New York: D. C. Heath & Co., 1918. Woodrow Wilson Papers, Manuscript Division, Library of Congress.

Zahniser, J. D., and Amelia Fry. *Alice Paul: Claiming Power*. Oxford, U.K.: Oxford University Press, 2014.

Illustration Credits

CHAPTER ONE

1. Courtesy of the Library of Congress.

CHAPTER TWO

2. Courtesy of the Library of Congress.

CHAPTER FOUR

3. "Princeton Class Alligators," 1879, WWPL1219, Woodrow Wilson Presidential Library Photo Collection, Woodrow Wilson Presidential Library and Museum, Staunton, Virginia.

CHAPTER FIVE

4. Courtesy of the Library of Congress.
5. Courtesy of the Library of Congress.
6. Courtesy of the Library of Congress.
7. Courtesy of the Library of Congress.
8. Courtesy of the Library of Congress.
9. Courtesy of the Library of Congress.

CHAPTER SIX

10. Courtesy of the Library of Congress.
11. Courtesy of the Library of Congress.
12. Courtesy of the Library of Congress.

CHAPTER SEVEN

13. Courtesy of the Library of Congress.
14. Courtesy of the Library of Congress.
15. Courtesy of the Library of Congress.

CHAPTER EIGHT

16. Courtesy of the Library of Congress.
17. Courtesy of the Library of Congress.
18. Courtesy of the Library of Congress.

CHAPTER TEN

19. Photo by Tina Cassidy.

CHAPTER ELEVEN

20. Courtesy of the Library of Congress.
21. Courtesy of the Library of Congress.

CHAPTER TWELVE

22. Courtesy of the Belmont-Paul Women's Equality National Monument.
23. Courtesy of the Library of Congress.

CHAPTER THIRTEEN

24. Courtesy of the Library of Congress.

CHAPTER EIGHTEEN

25. Courtesy of the Library of Congress.
26. Courtesy of the Library of Congress.

CHAPTER NINETEEN

27. Photo by Tina Cassidy.
28. Courtesy of the Library of Congress.

CHAPTER TWENTY

29. Courtesy of the Library of Congress.

CHAPTER TWENTY-ONE

30. Courtesy of the Library of Congress.

Index

Page numbers of photographs appear in italics.

About the Author

Tina Cassidy is the author of two other books about women and culture: *Birth: The Surprising History of How We Are Born*, and *Jackie After O: One Remarkable Year When Jacqueline Kennedy Onassis Defied Expectations and Rediscovered Her Dreams*. A former journalist who spent most of her career at *The Boston Globe* covering business, fashion, and politics, Cassidy is also the executive vice president and chief content officer at InkHouse, a public relations and digital marketing agency. When not writing, she volunteers for female candidates, promotes the passage of the Equal Rights Amendment, and serves on the board of the New England Center for Investigative Reporting. Cassidy lives in the Boston area with her husband, the author Anthony Flint, their three sons, and a Norfolk terrier named Dusty.